NARRATING LOVE AND VIOLENCE

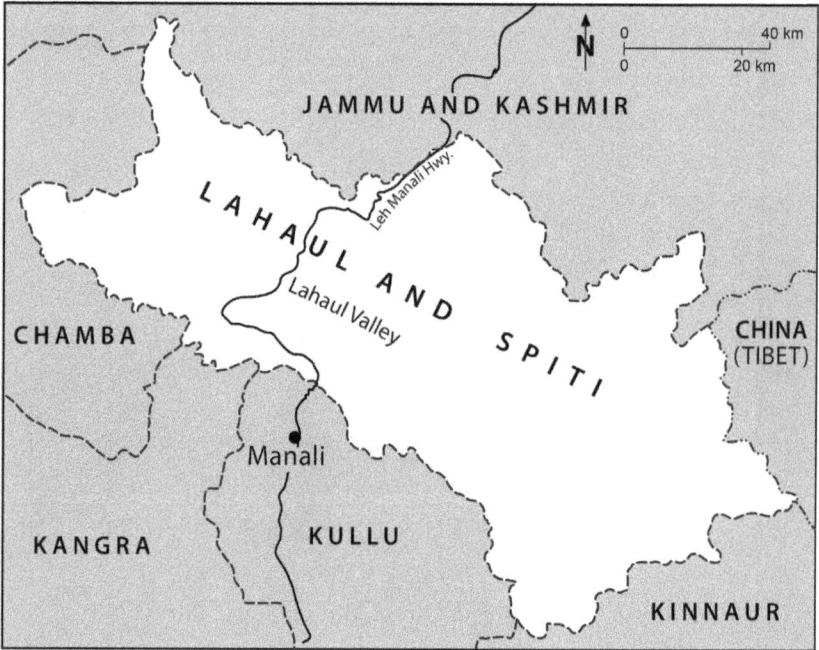

Map of Himachal Pradesh

NARRATING LOVE AND VIOLENCE

Women Contesting Caste,
Tribe, and State in Lahaul, India

HIMIKA BHATTACHARYA

RUTGERS UNIVERSITY PRESS
New Brunswick, Camden, and Newark, New Jersey, and London

Library of Congress Cataloging-in-Publication Data
Names: Bhattacharya, Himika, 1975– author.
Title: Narrating love and violence : women contesting caste, tribe, and state in Lahaul,
India / Himika Bhattacharya.
Description: New Brunswick : Rutgers University Press, [2017] | Includes
bibliographical references and index.
Identifiers: LCCN 2016050296| ISBN 9780813589541 (hardcover : alk. paper) |
ISBN 9780813589534 (pbk. : alk. paper) | ISBN 9780813589558 (e-book (epub)) |
ISBN 9780813589565 (e-book (mobi)) | ISBN 9780813589572 (e-book (web pdf))
Subjects: LCSH: Dalit women—India—Lahaul—Social conditions. |
Women—India—Lahaul—Social conditions. | Women—Violence
against—India—Lahaul. | Lahaul (India)—Social conditions.
Classification: LCC HQ1745.L34 B43 2017 | DDC 305.40954—dc23
LC record available at https://lccn.loc.gov/2016050296

A British Cataloging-in-Publication record for this book is available from the British
Library.

Visit our website: http://rutgersuniversitypress.org/
Manufactured in the United States of America

This book is dedicated to Kavita.

CONTENTS

NARRATING LOVE AND VIOLENCE

PROLOGUE

From Fieldwork to Lifework

The kernel of this book took shape in 2011, but its journey began quite by accident, several years before then, when I worked at CAPART,[1] a government agency in Delhi. I was asked by my supervisor to cover for a co-worker who had suddenly canceled a work trip to Lahaul.[2] With little planning, I left for this week-long trip as her replacement. I had no inkling then, that it would be months before I would return to the Kangra or Delhi offices, nor that I would spend the next two and a half years in the Lahaul valley. My task for that week was to monitor and evaluate the Ministry of Rural Development's rural marketing fair in the valley. The fair was not what I expected. Having made the trip from the much lower Himalayan region of Kangra, past the drive through very high mountains, to the stalls in the district headquarters of Keylong, I beheld a new side of the organization that I was employed by. I had a list of the participants whose stalls were funded from the Delhi office, and I was to evaluate the project. Yet all the stalls I saw were owned and run, not by Lahauli women, but by middlemen from Shimla, Manali, and the surrounding towns. It began with that moment of dissonance. Somewhere between reporting the discrepancies in the fair, raising funds from CAPART to organize workshops that were geared to support Lahauli women, and facilitating a trip for a group of women the Delhi office decided to support, I began working as an organizer with a small *mahila mandal* (women's group). This decision to work with the women's group took shape during a journey with twenty-five

Lahauli women. It happened thus: CAPART had offered a grant to a group of women from different parts of Lahaul to visit women's organizations across (rural) north India. They would travel for two weeks in the month of October, right after the harvest season and the Dussehra festival.[3] The idea was for the Lahaul group to share and learn organizing strategies from women leaders and organizers who had been campaigning and working on (women's) issues that were relevant in their communities across the country. We were assigned a chartered bus, with a driver and his assistant, to travel across the country and meet the collectives we had identified, and had contacted.

In the weeks prior to the trip, Lata, a young Lahauli woman began working with me to plan the trip, in place of her mother, Ane Dolma, who worked for the district headquarters and had been originally assigned the task of co-planning this event with me. Thus, through a series of accidents, Lata and I began traveling together to different parts of the valley to convince the families of the women who were active in their village's *mahila mandals*, to consent to their participation in this trip. The process of proposal writing, planning and persuading the families that the trip would be safe for the women, brought us very close and filled us with an excitement about the future. The sheer adventure of travel brought its own share of thrills as well, especially as several of the women and girls had never crossed the borders of the valley. All in all, the excitement on the bus was palpable as we left Keylong, the district headquarters.

A few hours later, we reached the Rohtang Pass, locally known as the "top," the highest pass in the mountains along the Manali–Leh highway separating Lahaul from the Kullu valley. The highway remains non-motorable through the extreme winter snowfall for nearly six months of the year. During these months, the Lahaul valley is almost completely cut off from the rest of the state.

We drove past road signs full of innuendos (such as, "I want you darling, but not so fast"/ "Go easy on my curves"). We laughed and lamented the outrageousness of the gender and sexual politics of the ITBP (Indo-Tibet Border Police) officers who had plastered these quips all along the highway. The group grew louder as we literally went over the top. For many of the women in the bus, crossing over to the other side of the "top" meant leaving behind the restrictions imposed by family and community in a tight-knit and sparsely populated area like Lahaul. It symbolized access to another world and brought forth excitement, while simultaneously carrying the fear and anxiety of spending several days away from family, in a densely populated, non-tribal, and unfamiliar terrain. Thus, the journey brought laughter and excitement, but also angst for home, and the trepidation of crossing boundaries, literally and metaphorically.

Our first stay was in Tehri Garhwal, with the women of the Sangh (the Collective), formed by the local chapter of *Mahila Samakhya*, a highly successful national-level organization that focused on women's empowerment through education across India. The Sangh women talked about how antiviolence work, mainly issues pertaining to domestic violence and rape, gradually became the key focus of their organizing efforts. This work included providing collective support to women across different caste and class groups in navigating the gender politics undergirding their survival in the high mountains. Creating and participating in the Sangh had transformed their lives, despite the reality that larger structural shifts had been very slow.

The Sangh members shared their organizational trajectory—from an initial impetus to create a space where they could share their experiences with other women, to the formation of a collective across villages, with women who were facing similar issues. They narrated the forging of a collective praxis in solidarity with others in their community despite their individual differences, such as caste, class, and disability. At the initial meetings between the two groups, the group from Lahaul talked mostly of the burden of hard physical labor that fell almost entirely on the women in their community. Two days into the sharing came the first testimony of an experience of "marriage by abduction,"[4] as a form of violence in Lahaul where the threat of social dishonor was used to make individual women "consent" to marriage with their abductors. Savitri (who later became one of the participants in a collaborative research document co-written by the women's group and me) broke the silence the group was maintaining on the subject of violence and marriage by abduction in their community. She spoke on behalf of a number of women she had known with similar experiences, and told us the story of how she had been forced into marrying a man who had abducted her. When she stopped speaking, it was as though a dam had broken. Seventeen of the twenty-five women present eventually spoke of similar experiences, especially with regard to marriage by abduction. Only three women had given their consent and then been married through the system of *mangni biyah*.[5]

After Savitri's testimony, the group talked through much of the nights in Garhwal, in the October chill with a small fire in the Sangha office where we were staying. That trip remains among the most meaningful and energizing times of my life, in and beyond the "field." It was the moment that defined for me that my fieldwork—whether then as an organizer, or subsequently as an ethnographer returning "home"—was inseparable from my life's work, what I now refer to as "lifework."[6] Eventually, the group returned to Lahaul with plans to organize a larger collective in the near future. Around this time, discussions with my office in Delhi (CAPART) began to get increasingly strained and difficult. I decided to stay on in the valley and continue working with the women, who were now organizing with renewed zeal. I moved into a small house in Jispa,[7] a small village located in one of the upper regions of Lahaul, nestled in a wide valley between several high mountain peaks, next to the river Chandrabhaga, and one of the coldest areas within Lahaul. It was my first winter there. The women began discussing the possibility of a central women's collective working throughout the valley, which would adopt marriage by abduction as its first campaign, before the harsh winter set in.

We began working together in earnest, toward these modest goals—of organizing against marriage by abduction, to end the practice as it existed in its current form. The campaign against marriage by abduction and the work of the women's collective was no pure political process, if such a thing is ever possible. It was in fact, precisely the strategy of *negotiation*[8]—between articulating an oppositional anti-violence politic and appealing to a sensibility about justice among different members the community—that resulted in several successful conversations between the group and several village elders, local governing groups and even the Dalai Lama, who raised this issue as a social concern in a public speech. At some point along this journey, I decided to pursue a graduate degree. It turned out that the highest financial aid I was offered was from a school in the rural midwest in the United States. And that was how my geographical location for the next few years was determined.

Given the nature of my work as an organizer in the valley, and the kinds of issues I was working on with the collective, by the time I was due to leave, I had built lasting relationships with many people, including Lata, Savitri, Achi Yangmo, Parvati, Angmo, Sonam, Dechen, Palmo, and Kavita. Although communication across continents and in harsh climatic conditions has been difficult, I have remained in contact and continued to work with several of the women from my early days in the valley. My decision to pursue a research project, which entailed "fieldwork" in Lahaul such that I could continue working there, led me to this book. The steps leading to it were shaped by a range of relationships based on care, trust, and solidarity with several Dalit[9] and Adivasi[10] women in Lahaul.

Yet, after the initial research project was complete, when I decided to continue working within U.S. academia, I struggled with my own position, as a non-tribal, non-Dalit,[11] caste-privileged woman, now located in the global north, writing this book in English, a language many of the women do not speak or read. The representational dilemmas I was working through should not be interpreted as a methodological exercise in reflexivity. In following several feminists who have written about the inseparability of theory/method (Chowdhury 2011; Swarr and Nagar 2010), I too approach ethnography as a dialogic process, and this academic writing that has stemmed from it, as co-performance and collaboration (Denzin 2000; Madison 2005). Thus, my struggle arose from the messiness of such dialogue—in embracing the uneven terrain of solidarity across difference for what it is. As a woman of color feminist in the United States, navigating multiple borders, living out of spectral homes, rummaging through the daily workings of empire, inhabiting the transnational,[12] my own experiences in conjunction with the stories the women tell here, lead me to situating this book—my life/work and field/work—in the *borderlands*. Writing within and from a *third space*, my concerns shifted from *whether* to write the book to *how* to do so. I chose the negotiations and translations within *this* act of solidarity, by navigating the dangers of representing intimate histories of violence while also believing in the power of *remembering intentionally*.[13] In repeatedly co-performing *marginality* "as a site of radical possibility, a space of resistance" (hooks 1989, 208), my interlocutors and I, the ethnographer, with my "eye" to bear witness (Johnson 2011) seek to enter that space as co-performers "where we move in solidarity" (hooks 1989, 209).

Between the years 2010 and 2011, I returned to Lahaul for a year.[14] This period allowed me to work through the ethical and representational concerns I had about the book. The turning point came when I met with my fellow interlocutors, the women whose life histories are at the center of this book. Walking, talking, and listening with my interlocutors helped me understand how and why the book was not only possible, but something

I wanted—physically, emotionally, intellectually, and politically. Thinking through questions of translation, intimacy, language, and power with the women who had shared their stories with me, and all those who appear in these pages, carved the path for a fissured, but deeply grounded solidarity to emerge. One such conversation bears mention here.

Achi Yangmo, known in the valley for her wit and humor, took me into her home during my first visit to Jispa. True to character (as I was soon to find out), she announced that she would decide how I was going to spend my time in the valley. This early interaction set the tone for the rest of our relationship over the years. At some point during the initial years, she stated clearly that, no matter what, I was to spend at least two nights in her house every time I entered the Lahaul valley. Over several years, we have both talked about our lives and our struggles with each other. In bits and pieces she shared her history with me, of being a landless, single mother, who found her husband murdered under a tree and went on to raise three children by herself. I told her about my own past and my hopes and fears for the future. She talked to my worried mother on the phone, assuring her that I would be all right through the winter months in Lahaul or while working with the *mandal* in the early years. Any time a local person (usually men) would crack "jokes" about my own impending abduction in Lahaul, Achi (Yangmo) would provide a long detailed discussion on how such jokes were violent threats, undermined the experiences of Lahauli women, and rendered me vulnerable too. I trusted her despite our disagreements and often sought her counsel. It followed naturally that upon my return in 2011, I mentioned some of the ethical dilemmas I was working through to her. After listening to me patiently, she suddenly left the room and returned with a toothpick, which she stuck between her teeth. Talking through an open mouth, she kept making a sound that went "*phu-phu-phu,*" and began laughing loudly while "speaking" thus. Taken aback by this amusing gesture, I asked her what she was doing. In response, she said:

> Oye, Himika, you sound all *angrezi* with this stuff . . . all phu-phu-phu. You too are not making any sense. You are worrying whether writing a book about our Lahaul is ethical or not, but why are you wasting your time worrying? Only some people in life walk with us. If you have walked with any of us, then write it *bejhijhak* (with abandon). You have known so many of us for so long. You have so much education. You speak English. You are not tribal. And

here you are worrying, not doing the work. Stop this phu-phu-phu and start
the interviews for the book. Then bring me a copy!

By naming my privileges, my emotions, and my relationships of solidarity in the same breath, Achi had responded with a critique that began
on the other end of the continuum of moral-ethical-political-positioning
where I had been stuck, with my ruminations of the precariousness of my
location in the project—a focus that was indeed rich in privilege. Further,
her teasing comment about how I was acting *angrezi* (translating to "English," a reference to "foreigner" in this context), with the knowledge that
it would rile me, and uttering the incomprehensible "phu-phu-phu" deliberately, should not be read (or romanticized) as a gesture that frees me of
any ethical responsibilities or as some kind of permission granted to me to
attempt writing this book. Nor does it reduce the relevance of the politics of
location. Rather, it complicates the meaning of solidarity across difference/s
by stretching the notions of accountability that I held so dear, that I failed to
see the very differentials of power I was attempting to question. Her directive calls upon us to understand solidarity relationally.

Achi articulates *a* mode of differential belonging. The clarity of her directive, even as she rejects what she jokingly calls my newly acquired foreign-
ness, is situated in a model of solidarity that is woven through practices of
intimacy, including grief, privilege/access, and marginality, and which provides a point of departure for my own politics of location through a *theory in
the flesh* (Moraga and Anzaldúa 1981).

This book is based on the research I conducted in 2011. Most importantly, by returning to think through the ethics of writing any kind of book
that was connected to Lahaul, I had found the kernel of this project—my
co-interlocutors' stories. It was during their storytelling when I came to
understand that the women were narrating through love. It was my return
to Lahaul in 2010 and 2011, and my conversations with several of the people
whose lives appear in the following pages, that persuaded me to write this
book. It is thus one of several steps in my field and my life's work thus far. In
writing about the affective intricacies of everyday life, the salience of friendship and love in coalition work, while also representing counter-memories
of intimate violence, I have chosen a representational style that also inhabits
an in-between space, a practice that is a deployment of Sandoval's *differential consciousness*. In adopting a *tactical subjectivity*, where women of color

feminists often navigate multiple discursive spaces, shifting between tactics in order to re-center power, I shift between a storytelling approach *and* academic writing conventions, while always privileging the former. I do this rather than opting for only one or the other, in order to deliberately position the lives/relationships/narratives that appear throughout this book, as the women's performance of theory.

In writing this book, I have often struggled with Virginia Dominguez's question, about "how to incorporate and acknowledge love in one's intellectual life, indeed in one's writing, and how to incorporate and acknowledge love in one's politics" (2000, 368). This has been particularly challenging, as representation is always oozing with power. I am clear that I write this book not to provide anyone—academic or otherwise—with an understanding of Lahaulis as a community. I am writing it to expose the social structures and mechanisms that officially justify the violence of caste; to offer the women's stories as knowledge not just about Lahaul, or about Dalit and Adivasi communities in general, but about caste, tribe, and state in India. In following several Third World and U.S. women of color writers and feminists who, in Chela Sandoval's (2000, 135) words, "understand 'love' as a hermeneutic . . . a set of practices that can access and guide our theoretical and political 'movidas'—revolutionary maneuvers toward decolonized being," this book is a labor of love. I follow Dr. B.R. Ambedkar, who in the preface to *Ranade, Gandhi and Jinnah* (1943, 3), wrote,

> No one can hope to make any effective mark upon his time and bring the aid that is worth bringing to great principles and struggling causes if he is not strong in his love and his hatred. I hate injustice, tyranny, pompousness and humbug, and my hatred embraces all those who are guilty of them. I want to tell my critics that I regard my feelings of hatred as a real force. They are only the reflex of the love I bear for the causes I believe in.

For this book to be a labor of love it must also expose injustice. To this end I can only hope that it will make some contribution in understanding the potential of such a love, demonstrate some of the political maneuvers through which the Dalit and Adivasi women of Lahaul re-craft seemingly mundane moments into powerful acts of resistance, and most importantly, articulate any amount of the knowledge/s that emerged through this co-performance of solidarity.

1 ⩿ CROSSING THE TOP

While the foundation for much of my research was laid during my early work as a community organizer in the valley, this book is grounded in a second research project based in this region. Upon completion of the first,[1] I returned to the valley for fieldwork spread out in phases between 2010 and 2011. The return to the valley over this time led me to this book, which has at its heart the (oral and textual) life histories of thirty women from Lahaul ranging in age from twenty-five to eighty-five years, across different caste and class striations. The stories in this book focus on violence: as experienced, understood and defined by the women, in conversation with me over the course of multiple oral life history interviews.

Though the overarching topic of this work is the women's experiences of violence, the lives they narrated included much more. Indeed, they spoke at length about a range of experiences beyond violence. They covered a wide range of topics, which illuminate multiple identities—such as gender, caste, tribe, and class—and their intersections. These are the very intersections (caste/tribe/gender/class), that when situated within the broader sociopolitical context of India have marginalized and disenfranchised members of Dalit, Adivasi, and Bahujan communities nationally.

Even as they shared their experiences of violence, the women chronicled their lives through the mundane. They told stories of local festivals; harvest celebrations; harsh winters; mountains and rivers; cash crops (potatoes and peas); traditional crops (*kuth*); the village *Yak*; the contemporary version of indoor heating systems once modified by the Moravian missionaries; the never-ending supply of *namkeen chai* (salt tea) in their homes; jokes

about army officers and the border roads organization; the rapidly changing glacial action in the mountains; seating arrangements in their homes,
the variety of *bethkus* (seats); the *gompas* (monasteries); their reverence (or
not) for the *lamas* (monks); their relationship to land; the *top* (Rohtang
Pass); the calm of the winter months spent weaving and knitting; and all
kinds of goods and things that constitute the texture of daily life in Lahaul.
It was through these details that they narrated both, individual enactments
and everyday processes of violence at the intersection of caste, tribe, and
gender. In doing so, the women chose love as a genre of storytelling. Love
repeatedly emerged as the mode through which the women narrated their
experiences.

The stories of the women in this book then reveal larger questions of
identity formation and power relations as they play out within the context of the northwestern Himalayan border region of Lahaul. Thus, my
goal in this book is diverse: to demonstrate the performance of theory by
women marginalized by gender, caste, and tribe; to call into question the
conflation of caste and tribe within governmental, academic, and popular
writing; to demonstrate how state discourses about violence and sexuality
serve as proxy for caste/tribe politics; to trace love as a politic signaling
epistemological shifts, and to fill a void in the available literature about
this region by prioritizing the narratives of women on the margins of caste
and tribe.

The organic manner in which the research topic itself emerged during
my return to the valley in 2011, the theoretical and political critiques the
women offered in the conceptualizing of the project, as well as the possibilities and failures of the work I was attempting to continue as a caste-
privileged academic researcher with a faculty position in the United States,
all led me toward a methodology that had at its heart the women's stories. I
thus chose (oral and textual) life histories within a critical performance ethnography framework as my method. As narrators of their own lives, these
women critique, resist, and at times even affirm a range of power relations
constructed at the intersection of caste, tribe, gender, and state.

The *first* aim of this book is to center the women's narratives as a *source
of knowledge*. To this end, I situate the women's oral narratives within a
long history of Dalit and Third World women of color feminist theorizing that examines the intersection of gender and caste/race hierarchies
through storytelling, autobiography, poetry, and layered writing genres, as

exemplified in the works of Baby Kamble (1986); Bama (1994); Urmila Pawar (2008); Urmila Pawar and Meenakshi Moon (2008); Cherrie Moraga and Gloria Anzaldúa (1981); Zora Neale Hurston (1928); June Jordan (1974); Chela Sandoval (2000), and Trinh T. Minh-Ha (1989), to name a few. Building on these traditions, this book offers ways of approaching love as a mode of narration through the lives of women on the margins of caste and tribe.

The *second* central goal of this book is to draw attention to, and trace the complexities of statist classification systems of caste and tribe in India which borrow directly from colonial and colonizing knowledges, notions of religion, caste, and tribal identities. These classification systems create the terms for both epistemic and embodied violence upon communities that lie at their intersections, such as Lahaul. To this end, I draw upon the oral and textual life histories of Lahauli Dalit women, who in narrating their lives, theorize and challenge the exclusion of their experiences from state and community discourses of "protection" from caste atrocities. In this way the women's stories disrupt and expand current understandings of tribe and caste in India.

Rather than engage in a nostalgic and/or romanticized notion of women on the margins (of caste and tribe) narrating either love as resistance (as "exceptionally resilient") or experiencing violence only as victimhood, this book centers life histories of Dalit and non-Dalit women from the Adivasi community of Lahaul. I build upon Sharmila Rege's (2013; 2006) call (for non-Dalit feminists in particular) to recognize, acknowledge, and begin from Ambedkar's feminist intersectional legacy by framing the book within and through these different (and often differing) genealogies. Through Moraga and Anzaldúa's "theory in the flesh" which accounts for the body as knowledge situated within and against relations of domination; Rege's re-articulation of "testimonio" as Dalit women's collective counter critique of Brahmanism from a gendered lens; and Pawar's "memoir" that fuses storytelling with politics in its articulation of a Dalit feminist theory, I understand these oral and textual histories as a performance of theory by the women. Thus, it is *not* my goal to generate an understanding of the tribe, or the region—rather, by deconstructing dominant narratives of caste and tribe, and by centering the women's life histories, it is my hope to challenge the colonialist ideologies behind knowledge production practices in general, and to expose the specific knowledges and mechanisms that officially justify the violence and exclusionary practices that shape and inform the women's experiences.

Therefore this book is situated within an intersectional and de-colonial framework that is rooted in an Ambedkarite and Dalit feminist legacy (Bama, Urmila Pawar, Baby Kamble, Meenakshi Moon), while also engaging with U.S. women of color and transnational feminisms (in the tradition of Cherrie Moraga, Gloria Anzaldúa, Jacqui Alexander, Kimberle Crenshaw, and Chandra T. Mohanty). I draw upon these diverse genealogies to situate this project within their convergences and alliances in creating space for a multiplicity of narratives and voices from, and in solidarity with marginalized communities to push against hegemonic constructions of knowledge about the world. While the transnational nature and impact of Dalit politics is often considered to be a recent phenomenon, there is a long tradition of alliance-building and solidarity work between Dalit emancipatory and feminist politics and U.S. women of color politics (particularly with black feminist politics). While some of these earliest alliances have their roots in the scholarship of Dr. B.R. Ambedkar, and subsequently in the alliances between Dalit Panther and Black Panther movements,[2] over the last three decades through the formation of what Shailja Paik (2014) calls "margin to margin solidarities" the shared histories and political overlaps between Dalit feminisms and U.S. women of color feminisms have been discussed by several activists and intellectuals in both locations. In particular, the theory of intersectionality considered a key epistemological intervention of U.S. women of color theorizing, is another major point of theoretical overlap between these different contexts. In this book I thread through the powerful genealogies of Dalit intellectuals (including the foundational work of Dr. B.R. Ambedkar) who have been theorizing intersectionality and caste-patriarchies for more than a century. Sharmila Rege in her 1998 article "Dalit Women Talk Differently" provides a detailed discussion of the political and intellectual overlaps between U.S. women of color transnational feminist and Dalit feminist genealogies. In this essay Rege (1998) does both—offer the terms and possibilities of solidarity work and alliance-building between feminists across contexts, and also presents a scathing critique of Indian feminist activism[3] and intellectual work (what Rege calls "mainstream Indian feminism") which continued to marginalize and ignore the lived realities and concerns of women from Dalit, Adivasi, and Bahujan communities. Savitribai Phule in the 1850s as an active member of the Ambedkarite-Phule movement in Maharashtra was among the first Dalit activists to write about the dual marginalization of Dalit women on account of caste and gender. The first oral history documenting Dalit women's participation within the Dalit emancipatory movement, was published in 1989 by Urmila Pawar and Meenakshi Moon, and was translated into English and published again in 2008. Baby Kamble (1986) and Sharmila Rege (1998) have both written extensively about the tensions between brahmanical feminism and Dalit feminism.

Through these and other feminist writings, the category "Indian feminism" has been challenged as being proxy for Brahmanical feminism. Mainstream Indian feminists have also been challenged for decades for their insistence on demanding provisions for custodial rape, but not adequately pushing for caste-based rape as atrocity in the anti-rape campaigns of the late 1970s and 1980s following the custodial rape of an Adivasi girl Mathura from Maharashtra.[4] Several Dalit Studies and Dalit feminist intellectuals including Shailja Paik (2009, 2014), Mary Xalxo (2012a), Lata P.M. (2015), and Gopal Guru (2007; 2012), among others, have provided eloquent critiques of particular genealogies within mainstream Indian feminism where theorizations of caste and gender as analytical categories have continued to invisibilize the everyday workings of systemic injustice faced by Dalit and Adivasi women.

Thus, my reason for weaving these frameworks together is not to suggest a symbiotic and perfectly mutually aligned relationship across these feminist theories and frameworks. Instead, weaving both frameworks (as already linked) in this book is appropriate not only on account of the longer tradition that it follows, but because it also offers ways to remain attentive to the broader political genealogies that the women in this book address.

Within such a framework that emphasizes the daily realities of women whose lives have been shaped through such intersecting systems of oppression, the stories that the women tell in this book produce complex meanings, *beyond* love, and *beyond* violence, which disrupt the common approach to violence within a "victim–agent" framework. Further, when recounting how they reject and resist the shame and dishonor associated with violence, or in how they understand marriage, family, and community; or in how they experience the mundane details of their lives, the women in this book deliberate upon love as something they *know*. There are few, if any, books where women from communities marginalized by caste and tribe speak so freely about love and violence.

While the state's rhetoric around caste and tribe neatly separates them, in much of the (often well-meaning) literature on the oppression and atrocities against members of such marginalized communities, "caste" and "tribe" are used interchangeably, as tools of analysis, without attention to historical specificities, distinctions, and indeed *intersections* between the two. Yet both these definitional trajectories also construct and enable violence, its representation, and the redressal mechanisms available through state intervention.[5]

Through careful attention to the historical[6] distinctions and intersections between caste as a system of domination, and tribe as a community rather than an anthropological unit (Xaxa, 2008), I argue against the common intellectual practices of either conflating the two, or of neatly cleaving[7] them[8] across contexts. The tendency to lump the two together is common in a lot of scholarly and popular writing on caste, particularly when discussing violence and atrocity against both, members of oppressed castes (including Dalits) and those from Adivasi communities. Here I am not referring to the reliance on a broader Dalit framework of oppression as articulated by several Dalit feminists, the Dalit Panthers, and many leaders of the Dalit emancipatory movement in India. Under this framework, "Dalit" not only refers to those historically placed outside the varna system and labeled "untouchables" (*ati shudra*), but also includes other historically oppressed social groups such as communities placed at the lowest end of the four *varnas* in the caste order and *Adivasis* (members of indigenous communities). However, when the terms caste and tribe are simply used interchangeably they pose several risks, including that of continuing exclusionary discursive practices. Further, the trend in Indian Sociology to frame "tribe" through caste has been critiqued heavily by Virginius Xaxa, particularly in his 1999 essay "Tribes as Indigenous People of India" as not only carrying on legacies of differentiation between colonial subjects which rely on racist ideological positioning of Hindu origins within an Indo-Aryan framework, but also as a refusal to understand community beyond the paradigm of Brahmanical patriarchy.[9]

My attempt in paying such close attention to the distinctions and intersections between caste and tribe is not in order to uphold any kind of anthropological and governmental categorization of tribe as "static"/"primitive," nor is it to argue for any nationalist[10] project of the Hinduization of Adivasi[11] communities across India. And it is certainly not with the intent of arguing against the recognition of constitutional status (and the benefits/reservations that accrue from such categorizations) for those Adivasi communities, which are entrenched in caste heirarchies, such as Lahaul. Rather, it is to go beyond understanding caste and tribe as analytical/anthropological/constitutional categories (whether static or fluid) and to emphasize their material and discursive "lifeworlds"[12] as narrated by my interlocutors. This distinction between caste and tribe and indeed the intersection of the two are key to understanding the fabric of daily life in the valley.

The relationship between tribe and caste repeatedly emerged directly and indirectly in the stories that were narrated by both, the Dalit-Adivasi and Adivasi non-Dalit women in this book. And indeed, the relevance of caste hierarchies in Lahaul was the key focus of several of the stories narrated by the Dalit-Adivasi women and the leaders of the Janajatiya Dalit Sangh. Yet, the salience of caste society in this community is often overlooked in discussions about the region. If at all the presence of caste *within* tribe does appear in the literature available about this region, it is presented by way of descriptive details about the workings of the carryover of the *varna* system into the tribe, rather than by examining their intersection to analyze caste as a system of domination. The first mention of caste hierarchies in the region appears among the earliest written documents about the region by colonialists such as A.F.P. Harcourt in his 1871 book *The Himalayan Districts of Koloo, Lahoul and Spiti.*

My emphasis on and engagement with this distinction also demonstrates the daily performance of theory by my co-interlocutors whose lives have routinely been written out of history, and who, if and when represented, have always been the object of theorizing. My initial work in the valley had begun in the Stod region, and it was in this upper valley that I based myself during my fieldwork. What really stood out for me was how clearly lines were drawn across all the valleys, irrespective of terrain, climatic conditions, and religious influences, in the articulation of caste, tribe, and gender politics. While extreme climatic conditions in the winter could result in a Dalit person seeking refuge in the home/hearth of a privileged-caste Lahauli, purity and pollution rules were strictly enforced. For example, Achi Yangmo of village Gemur, in the Stod valley, a privileged-caste member of the tribe, lives right by the bus stop on the highway, and has on many

occasions offered shelter to members of both, Dalit and non-Dalit communities during inclement weather. In order to be able to continue to do this,
and host whoever needs shelter, she has set aside specific utensils, bethku
(local seat), and shawls, meant only for her Dalit guests. In interviewing Achi Yangmo, and several other non-Dalit members of the tribe, what
emerges is the complicated terrain of marginality in Lahaul. While considered "privileged-caste" members most non-Dalit Lahaulis (with the exception of the princely families) are also socially located at the intersection of
multiple margins, within and beyond the region. The enormity of the class
gap between the members of the ruling and landed class (Thakurs, also
known as the *samant*) of Lahaul and all other caste groups is stark. In the
Stod valley up until my last visit to Lahaul (in 2012), when any male member of the Khangsar Thakur family, who is a direct descendant of the *wazir*[13]
of Lahaul visits the family castle in Khangsar, people of the village do not
walk in front of them. As per the Atrocities Act of India and its most recent
amendment in 2014, such social rules can not only no longer be enforced,
they are also directly punishable. Yet, the inapplicability of the PoA Act[14]
in a fifth schedule area such as Lahaul and the remoteness of the region,
which prevents a lot of people from leaving the valley, normalizes the social
performance of caste beyond its ritualistic and customary performance at
the Khangsar fort—once the site of militarized power. The reverence and
deference provided to members of the Khangsar Thakur family by other
Lahaulis, particularly those of the non-Thakur families, is ironically also
reinforced by PESA.[15] Another hierarchy that is reinforced by the current
rendition of PESA connects to both class and gender, across caste groups
in Lahaul, and allows for the continuation of the custom of women not
inheriting land, despite the erosion of polyandry and joint systems of marriage in the region, which have historically provided protective measures for
women.

DEFINING VIOLENCE

The focus of the oral and textual narratives here is on the experiences of
violence in the lives of Lahauli women at the intersection of caste, tribe,
and gender, as understood and articulated by them. The focus of much of
my previous work in the region emphasized different forms of violence,

particularly marriage by abduction, domestic violence, and rape, all of which constituted a broad category of what is considered "violence against women" (VAW), and often also labeled "gender violence." Without conflating gendered violence with such nomenclatures of VAW as gender violence, I would like to clarify that in this book the women offer storied meanings of different *forms* of gendered and caste-tribe violence as experienced by them. Thus, I use the term "violence" to refer to both, specific acts of violence discussed by the women, and the enactments of a series of complex tensions which lead to *processes* that conduct violence, beyond singular acts of violence. Broadly then, I understand violence as a discursive and material process, repeatedly enacted in the lives of the women, through a nexus of overlapping systems of domination. More specifically, this book is a storied exploration of different *forms* and *processes* of intimate and structural violence as narrated by the women of Lahaul.

LOVE AS NARRATION

As mentioned earlier in this chapter, when narrating their experiences of violence, the women also talked about many different aspects of their lives. In doing so, they storied their lives through ideas of "love." Thus, while violence is the central focus of the book, love is the mode of narration that the women adopt in telling their stories and narrating their lives. Love appears in the narratives as a form of storytelling, a broader construct through which women talk about various aspects of life, particularly identity and power relations, often becoming synonymous with struggle and producing counter-discourse, and often signaling epistemological shifts, rather than visceral feeling. Even when talking of love in the context of romantic relationships, the women *rarely discuss it as a feeling.* When using the Hindi word commonly used to refer to love as feeling (*pyar*), whether romantic or otherwise, a number of my co-interlocutors wove through their stories references to love as a *doing*, as something that had to be *done* and *made*. Repeated references to their life stories as *prem kahani* (love story) appeared during our conversations. Often self-deprecating jokes were cracked about the *prem kahani*, especially if someone had inadvertently begun narrating their romantic history, thus stretching the idea of the love story to refer to their life-story. In this spirit then, I do not approach love in this book within the intellectual terrain of affect and the viscerality of feeling. I approach love as a mode of narration in these life histories.

METHOD

My research has been conducted as a co-performative and dialogic exchange. Over the last several years, my relationship to the region has evolved and undergone many shifts. Things that I had considered simple when I started working in the area, have become much more complicated over the years. My experiences in the region over time have also shaped how I approached this particular project there. As a caste and class-privileged researcher invested in exposing and working toward the eradication of the violent nexus of Brahmanical patriarchy, tribe, and state, my work had to be collaborative and in dialogue with the communities that my research is situated in. "Solidarity"—as an idea and practice, in spite of its wide-ranging assumptions and meanings, is what I understand to be at the heart of my work. The manner in which I have approached this work/research over the years signals *who* I am: *what* it is I care about in this work and *how* it has transformed and grown through my interactions with these communities is the process I understand and define as solidarity. In this way, how I think about my overall research—the subject at hand and the methodology I have adopted in the work—*is* my feminist political praxis.

Therefore, rather than approach this research as the original work of the researcher-as-expert, I consider it as one that traverses and affirms the interplay and interdependence[16] of "theory in the flesh" (Moraga and Anzaldúa 1981) and "specialized knowledges" (Madison 1998) via dialogic co-performance. Since this research is one among different acts of solidarity work I have been engaged in over the years, it is crucial that I remain accountable to the stories they have trusted me with and honor the relationships we have shared. Moreover, Lahaul has a long tradition of oral (and art-based) storytelling, which, as it travels across generations, historicizes and carries forward ancestral knowledge of medicine, theology, and culture. And finally, as discussed at the start of this chapter, there is a long legacy of oral narrations and autobiographical storytelling by Dalit feminists and liberationists to counter and resist hegemonic inscriptions of both, caste and gender. Thus oral life histories within the framework of ethnography as dialogic co-performance seemed the most appropriate methodological choice in this context.

Additionally, these decisions were also motivated by the manner in which this research began, when I returned to the valley in 2010 and 2011. After completing the first collaboratively written project, and after my decision to accept a tenure track position in the United States, I returned to the region in order to have conversations with the women of the collective who I had worked with in the past. I undertook this trip in 2010 to understand whether I should write about the work of the collective. I wanted to explore the possibility of working on a book based on the collaborative work that formed the crux of my earlier work, which was also my first academic (doctoral) research. In particular, I wanted to explore if there was an ethical and politically constructive way in which this could be done. As is often the case with fieldwork, the topics I had planned to focus on evolved into other kinds of conversations very swiftly. This was also impacted by the fact that this project had emerged from my earlier work and involved many women and men in the region whom I had known for several years and, during this period, their lives had undergone radical changes. Over the initial shorter trip (2010), what came up repeatedly in conversations with the women was an interest in a book about *their* Lahaul. By this I mean that several of the women who were previously active in the mahila mandal seemed less interested in a book or research that told the story of the formation and work of the collective—and indeed this was my interest. My initial plan was to focus on the prior work of the women's collective—including its most successful anti-violence campaign—against the practice of marriage by abduction, the complexities of solidarity work within the valley, and the gradual disintegration of the collective despite a continuing interest among several members in working on a range of different forms of "violence against women." Instead, in the conversations we had, a number of the women were more interested in seeing a book about Lahaul that was written through their experiences, focusing on their understandings of violence—a book where they would tell the story of their ("my") Lahaul, something that most women in this book articulated as a "doing of love."[17]

Based on these conversations I opted for oral and textual life histories within a critical performance ethnography framework as my primary method. By textual, I am referring to the life histories (two of which are included in the main text of the book) where the women in question are no longer around to tell their stories. These textual life histories have emerged by combining parts of police records as well as media reports and interviews with the women's family members, neighbors, and other members of the community who were familiar with the events and, police representatives. Although logistically it was not easy to include these life (and death) histories, I felt it was crucial to include at least two of these women's stories, to center their experiences of violence, because this allowed me to reflect on the structures and institutions being discussed by the women who were there to tell me their stories. The logistics of putting together these life histories were fraught for a number of reasons: travel over long distances in difficult climatic conditions; disruptions in collecting police records (especially those pertaining to violence) from police stations and courts in small towns; constant resistance and failure of various governmental staff to locate files; pressures of holding on to an academic position on the other side of the world; and sheer ravages of time, dust, and memory resulted in restricting access to many other records that I had sought.

I returned in 2011 to further figure out the details of the project and to do the bulk of the research. During this period, I conducted in-depth multiple and dialogic interviews with over thirty Lahauli women, five Lahauli men, and five state representatives who worked in some or the other capacity in the district offices and belonged to different parts of the Lahaul valley. Of the thirty women, eighteen identified as Dalit-Adivasi; three of the five men also identified as Dalit-Adivasi, and only one state representative was Lahauli, while the rest, who were from other parts of the state, did not discuss their caste location. When I first returned I also began conversations with several women who I was already familiar with from before. I had remained in contact with them over time, when possible, given the treachery of time zones, problems with phone connections and mail delivery through winter months. Most of them were previously active in the women's collective and during the course of my fieldwork several of the women self-selected into the book. It bears mention that four people— Kavita Devi (who moved from vill. Jispa to Kullu); Achi Yangzin (vill. Jispa); Shri Lal Chand Dhissa (Janajatiya Dalit Sangh, Kullu), and Shri Chhering Dorje (who splits his time between vill. Ghusker and Kullu)— actively spoke to people about this project, even when I was in the States, between my trips in 2010 and 2011, without me ever asking.

FIGURE 1.1. Bhaga river, Stod Valley

In the end, I decided to stop at thirty oral narratives. This was because I needed to be mindful of the focus on women's experiences of violence. It followed then that I only interviewed women who had interacted with me and known me in some capacity during the course of the last several years. Moreover I wanted to speak with the women several times, rather than over one or two recorded meetings. On numerous occasions we returned to topics and memories that had come up during earlier conversations, carrying over in unexpected ways into other moments. Each story then, was shared over several meetings and interviews. This meant that I split my time in different parts of the valley based on where my co-interlocutors lived. Given the physical spread of the valley (discussed below in the section titled "Locating Lahaul") and the climatic conditions, my movements in the region were also often restricted.

These were not traditional, unidirectional interviews between researcher and narrator. Instead, they were dialogic, co-performative acts of storytelling. Such an understanding of the interview as dialogue, E. Patrick Johnson points out, directs us to "the co-performative witnessing inherent in critical ethnography that disavows a static representation of the other or the self, as both journey on a collaboration toward making meaning of the social

and cultural world around them" (Johnson 2008, 10). Rather than looking for *the* truth, co-performative storytelling produces *a* version of events
and "truths," through a series of events shared between the interlocutors
(Johnson 2008). This re-articulation of ethnography as co-performance is
premised on the epistemological approach that "we cannot study experience directly. We study it through and in its performative representations"
(Denzin 2009).

I build upon the scholarship of Soyini Madison, E. Patrick Johnson, and
Norman Denzin among others, who demonstrate that the researcher and
narrators are not only co-interlocutors, performing for one another, they
are also actors connected to one another through their presence, in bodily,
intellectual, emotional, and relational ways. In Soyini Madison's (2006, 323)
words, "co-performance is a doing with deep attention to and with others."
Sharing and constructing the space between the researcher and the narrator
with care, attention, and love, leads us to co-performance. That space, even
as it spills over with feelings, words, utterances, gestures, expressions, tears,
identities, privileges, injuries, and all the things that shape our lives, is also
the space that holds us together as co-performers to bear witness, affirm
and legitimize the testimonies being shared. Because telling, sharing, and
dialoguing over histories of intimate violence opens the wounds collected
in our hearts and changes the contours of our mind and pushes the spirit
beyond its limits, these moments of sharing–listening–sharing were never
static. Even when we understand violence as a process and locate it within
larger structures of oppression, to narrate a story of violence requires the
courage to be vulnerable and honest towards self and other in that moment.
Because memories inhabit the fragrance of the earth we walk on, carve their
paths through our flesh and live in pores and crevices of our bodies we never
knew of before, storying them through co-performance opens the grounds
for their acknowledgment, recognition, and affirmation. Many such
"interviews"—whether about a story of violence or concerning the little
memories that make and re-make our lives—would end in a mixture of tears
and laughs. Many were recorded officially on a digital recorder and they
appear throughout the book, but without the sounds of the river, the wind,
sometimes vehicles and often animals—all part of the co-performative
encounter. Yet others were recorded through journaling before bed or on a
bus. Still others could only be engraved in my own memory, held within my

senses; those unruly words, defining moments, and unexpected touches, which I never could string into sentences. Loss—across physical, geographical, social, emotional, and political divides—is therefore a big part of this process.

These losses are also exacerbated by what is lost through layers of linguistic translation. Most of the conversations I had with the women were in Hindi, interspersed with Stod (a dialect spoken in the Stod valley in particular). Each valley within Lahaul speaks a distinct dialect, though there are overlaps, since most are rooted in Tibetan. Because of concerns over confidentiality and preserving the privacy of the women and the difficulty of locating a fellow translator, I did all of the translations myself. I had help from several people who were familiar with the dialect, and I had collected several grammar and phrase books written by Tobdan. Additionally, for conversations and interviews that I was formally recording, I made detailed notes whenever possible on finer nuances of words and expressions spoken in Stod right after completing the interview. Chhering Dorje, a well-known scholar of Orthodox Bon and Tibetan Buddhism, especially as practiced in Tibet, Chang Thang, and Lahaul was another source of both, historical and linguistic knowledge. During my trip in 2011, he unreservedly opened his home to me and volunteered multiple interviews about the region and upon my return to the States, he expressed nothing but delight at each phone call for clarifications.

Multiple translations and transcriptions later, I was overwhelmed by the task that lay ahead. Weaving through translated stories and memories, looking for a meaningful and ethical representational strategy, and straddling the multiple audiences this book seeks to reach, there was one thing in the project that never failed me—the power that the women demonstrated in these political acts of storytelling.

It follows then that I understand oral history as a method that narrates identity and difference as complex, fluid, relational, and political. When we narrate our experiences we tell stories about ourselves, articulate our understanding of identity. When we commit to telling the stories, irrespective of the truth-telling imperative of the testimony (Felman 1992), we engage in a political act (Pawar 2008). Thus, I argue that in the narratives of these particular women, telling their stories of violence becomes an exercise in re-telling selves, moving through their *whole* lives, beyond the violence that they discuss. Similarly, love emerges repeatedly through a range of iterations as a politic that works against and often also within the structural processes of violence constituted through caste, tribe, and gender.

Using oral history and critical performance ethnography as a combinational framework for decolonizing feminist practice, as illustrated in the works of Soyini Madison (2005), Norman Denzin (2002; 2008) and E. Patrick Johnson (2011b), I have made methodological and representational decisions which center the theoretical interventions performed by the Lahauli women with whom I engage in a dialogic and co-performative storytelling. By choosing what Walter Mignolo (2012) has termed an "enactive and border epistemology" I have actively chosen to depart from "hegemonic epistemologies with an emphasis on denotation and truth" (Mignolo 2012, 26) and locate this work within the domain of "performance and transformation" which demonstrate the contentions and struggle for power in the making and un-making of knowledge. In this vein my own feminist praxis has been deeply inspired by these connections with the women in the project and I have always been motivated by a political commitment to work with them.

Yet in more ways than one, in spite of situating this work within a praxis of accountability to the communities I am connected to, I also benefit as an individual (academic) from the production of this book. I remain the academically acknowledged author even as this co-performative storytelling traverses the space which, as in Guru and Sarukkai's (2012) discussion on experience and theory, emerges as the distance between the *felt* and *ethical* possibilities of theory making. While the book recognizes and upholds the *ownership* of the stories to the women, this co-performance is also *a* collaborative step, between the women and me (Nagar 2006; Chowdhury 2011). It is also a product of the structural violence of caste-society, that even though I draw upon Ambedkar's intersectional critique of Brahminism and capitalism, my own subject position (as both caste and class privileged) is embedded in the very structures I seek to disrupt and challenge.

Thus, I approach this book as an act of solidarity, rather than an act of theory, challenging and challenged by the risks of that "enduring moral stamina" (Guru 2012) that such a project presents. Nevertheless, it simultaneously pushes against the dangers imminent in separating (and hierarchizing) theory and experience, knower and known, and body and discourse. To this end, I take my cue from the scholarship of Sharmila Rege (2013;

2006; 2005), Richa Nagar (2014; 2006), and Kalpana Kannabiran (2015a; 2015b; 2014), who have all navigated and carved new paths and demonstrated possibilities of writing in solidarity with communities across difference in the context of the caste–gender–class nexus in India.

Because a co-performative *doing* of storytelling across difference requires that I meet "vulnerability with vulnerability and honesty with honesty" (Carillo Rowe 2008), it also requires that I put my story on the line (Johnson 2011a). That is, situate myself relationally with the women and challenge my own subject position every step of the way (Nagar 2014). My attempt at doing this is not with the idea of reifying essentialist understandings of caste by focusing on my trajectory as "upper" caste or to engage in what often gets touted as "navel-gazing." I have indeed heard the directive in many academic circles asking for a declaration of caste status on what Dalit intellectuals (Guru 2012; 2007; Xalxo 2012b) have often considered essentialist terms in order to invoke the salience of caste hierarchies in working across difference or to "reduce" (as if it were an added ingredient) the presence of the researcher in the narrative. While some of the caution is well-intended, such declarations serve little else than to continue the assumptive meanings of caste limited by a privilege-based model, irrespective of the heterogeneity and complexities of caste hierarchies, which constitute community and individual trajectories, including those of the researcher. And contradictorily, the emphasis on removing the self from the process or in not situating one's story while remaining the recognized academic author of a text invariably undercuts its own stated goal as it continues to place members of the so-called twice-born *varnas* as the producers of academic analyses without situating their self/selves within larger structures of domination (Paik 2014; Rege 2013; Guru and Sarukkai 2012). By not putting my own story on the line, while indeed doing so with, and claiming the theorizing of, the oral, textual, literary, and cultural narrative of the other, I risk the reification of the structures they challenge yet this is a balancing act that is charged on both sides. Therefore I should also clarify that this is not an attempt at claiming any "right" path to research, write, and work against caste, especially as a member of a community which remains entrenched in a historical trajectory that reeks of the violence that *is* caste. Nor is it to say that in attempting to work ethically with activist, intellectual, and solidarity-based communities despite (and because of) difference, there are no failures[18] or moments when I have been pulled up short by my privileges through the very workings of the systemic domination that I wish to challenge. But this *is* to say that if I require myself to build the moral stamina needed to work ethically in such a context, it is not enough that I want to affirm the women's histories through dialogic co-performance, or that I am motivated by the project of representing these oral narratives as knowledge, against the grain of hegemonic theorizations. It is imperative that I also share my story and demonstrate accountability and solidarity with what and who I write about, in my choice of ontological and epistemological frameworks, methodology, representational strategies, citations, as well as continuing relationships and work in the valley. My praxis of accountability as a researcher/co-performer often emerges from the women's narratives, appearing in both, fragmented and continuous threads throughout this research. In writing *their* everyday stories (of violence), I show how my own messy trajectory as collaborator, friend, feminist, and ethnographic co-interlocutor is thrown into relief.

The critical performance ethnographic framework I have adopted in this book is relevant not only to the subject at hand and the materials that I represent, but also in terms of how this work contributes to the production of knowledge[19] within the United States and Indian academia. To this end, my citational practices re-emphasize and visibilize "histories and communities of struggle" (Davis 2005). I primarily draw upon Dalit and Adivasi scholarship that cannot be neatly ensconced within the disciplinary boundaries of ethnographic research in Anthropology and Himalayan Studies. Doing otherwise would defeat the very point of the book, because indeed Dalit and Adivasi scholars (akin to black and women/queer of color writing in the United States) have been systematically denied the position of the "scholar."[20] I also center (and reference) the scholarship of tribal (Adivasi) scholars such as Xaxa (1999a, 1999b, 2005, 2008); Dhissa (2011); Dorje (personal communication, 2011); Xalxo (2012a, 2012b); and Bora (2010). I have deliberately and carefully chosen to cite scholars whose work is often not located within the boundaries of conventional disciplines. Indeed it is the very violence of caste that this book draws attention to, which also forms the basis for such a zealous guarding of disciplinary boundaries.

It thus follows that I am *not* a theorist of Dalit and Adivasi lifeworlds in India. I do not approach the women's life histories as data that I can analyze in order to produce knowledge about the Western Himalayas and Lahaul. In this book, I am less invested in producing my interpretations of events or to theorize or historicize them. Instead, I am focused on co-performatively understanding the meanings enmeshed in these committed (and political) acts of storytelling. I am interested in continuing to look for ways to build the moral stamina needed to collectively speak truth to power and to continue to learn and strengthen feminist solidarity praxis across difference, in order to be an effective ally to Dalit emancipatory movements. In this book then, I am interested in bearing witness to the women's life histories. And in this process, I am guided by a directive from one of my co-interlocutors, Palmo, who sums it up very clearly for me "if you are going to write my story, don't add sugar to it. Remember, we Lahaulis like our tea salty."

LOCATING LAHAUL

The Lahaul valley[21] is situated in the northwestern Himalayan region, in the northernmost part of the state of Himachal Pradesh. While administratively Lahaul is a part of the district Lahaul-Spiti, geographically, socially, and culturally the two regions remain distinct. The Lahaul valley shares one border with Tibet and another border with Ladakh, which is in Jammu and Kashmir. The valley is located at an elevation of around 11,000 feet on average and is flanked by two high motorable passes—the Baralach La pass on its border with Ladakh, at 16,200 feet and the Rohtang Pass at 13,000 feet, which connects it to the Kullu region of Himachal Pradesh. The highway between these two passes becomes unmotorable due to heavy snowfall through the winter months and usually renders the region inaccessible between November and May of each year.

A third pass, Kunzam La separates Lahaul from Spiti and it too remains unmotorable during the winter thus pretty much cutting off the Lahaul valley during this time. Koksar is the mountain fork from where there are two different routes leading to each region. The mountains in the valley range from an elevation of 18,000 feet to 21,000 feet and the lowest point of the river Chenab (also known as Chandrabhaga, starting in the Baralach La mountain) that branches into Chandra and Bhaga, is at 9,000 feet. As mentioned above, the official district itself encompasses two regions of Lahaul and Spiti and they remain cut off from each other during the winter months. This book is based in the Lahaul valley, which itself is further divided into four valleys whose contours are defined by the river Chenab.

FIGURE 1.2. Snow Removal, Baralacha La

Briefly, the general distribution and nomenclature of the valleys is as follows: The first valley is Yunan, and is uncultivated and mostly uninhabited. It is also at the highest elevation. The second is Bhaga, or Punan in Tibetan, the upper part of this region is called the Stod valley (in Tibetan), and has the strongest Tibetan Buddhist influence. This third valley is known as the Chandra or Ranglo, in Tibetan. This valley has the joint stream of the Chandrabhaga river and is called Pattan, or Manchat in Tibetan, literally meaning "lower region." It has the strongest influence of Hinduism in Lahaul and is most demonstrative of the workings of Brahmanical patriarchy, through rigid operation of the *Jajmani*[22] system, strict endogamy rules and multiple caste striations. I discuss the social hierarchies in greater detail in chapter three.

According to the district census[23] people of the Lahaul valley practice both, Hinduism and Tibetan Buddhism. In talking to several village elders across the valley, I found different theories about the origins of the tribe, range of religious influences and its entrenchment in caste-Hindu society while simultaneously practicing a form of (Tibetan) Buddhism. This reflects a seeming contradiction considering the long history of Dalits in the

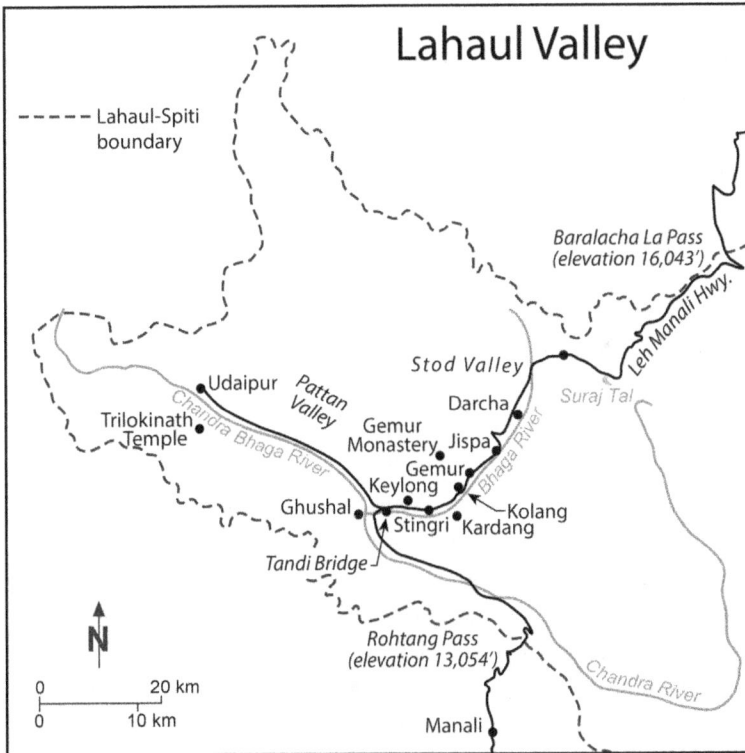

MAP 1.1. Map of Lahaul. *Source:* Joseph Stoll, SU Map Shop, mapshop@maxwell
.syr.edu

Hindu society across India converting to Buddhism in order to reject caste, as, for example, B.R. Ambedkar, one India's foremost leaders, had done.[24] That said, there is a general consensus that most people in Lahaul identify as both, Buddhist and Hindu—with Buddhism having the strongest influence in the Stod Valley and Hinduism having stronger presence in the lower region of the Pattan/Swangla Valley.

Broadly speaking, rituals, practices, and festivals relevant to both religions are followed, and very often children are named as per Hindu as well as Buddhist traditions. For example, a woman may have both names—Shakuntala (Hindu) and Tashi Yangzom (Buddhist). The most significant deity that the entire valley worships is Raja Ghepan, considered to be goddess Parvati's father, who has a temple dedicated solely to him.[25] While Raja Ghepan is an indigenous deity, folklore has it that the Hindu deities

Shiva and Parvati were wedded in Lahaul. There is a historic Shiva temple in the Udaipur region of the Mayadh valley, which, like Stod, has a strong Buddhist influence. The entire valley is also equally entrenched in Tibetan Buddhist religious and socio-cultural practices. There are chhortens[26] marking off most villages, new and ancient monasteries with long links to Zanskar, Tibet and Ladakh, Men-Tsee-Khang centers,[27] and traditional Amchis[28] all over Lahaul, particularly in Stod and Mayadh.

Almost every deity, every high mountain pass and every spirit that constitute the region's cultural, geographical, and religious imaginary, is connected to both, Hindu and Buddhist, traditions. For example, the Rohtang pass, which sits between the Kullu and Lahaul valleys, and is the highest motorable pass on one side of the valley, holds a central place in the Lahauli cultural imaginary *and* material reality—as it is *the* dividing line between the higher Himalayas and the plains, thus determining a wide range of things like external influence in the valley, healthcare and access to food during the harsh winter months, so on and so forth. The local term for the Rohtang pass, "top," is now part of the vernacular of the region. There are several stories about the origins of the top. First, the words "Ro" and "Tung" literally translate to "corpse" and "stack" in Tibetan. It is widely believed that in 1869 a group of 70 men from Kullu attempted to cross the Rohtang on foot, and never made it to Lahaul. All of them are said to have died at the pass and thus it came to be named "Rohtang." Indeed, as someone who has crossed the Rohtang on foot during the winter, even if only on two occasions, the death of a large group of climbers despite all the radically reduced glacial action over the centuries seems just as likely as all the other stories. Routinely even now, year after year, the Rohtang claims lives every winter. It continues to define Lahauli life in a multitude of ways.

Another story states that the Tibetan king Gyapo Gyasar was going through Lahaul and wanted to go over to the other side, to see Kullu. Because the mountains between Kullu and Lahaul valleys were continuous, he attempted to cut into the mountain and create a pass with his sword. After he made the first dent in the mountain, the goddess Gurnam Gyamo stopped him, because she was worried that making a deeper dent would result in a lower pass thus allowing too many people of the plains entry into the valley, thus bringing too much Hindu influence. A third story accords credit to the Hindu deity Shiva for the creation of the pass.

FIGURE 1.3. Snow Removal, Rohtang

The range of simultaneous influence (and presence) of Hindu and Buddhist practices, legends, rituals, and beliefs also extends to origin stories of the entire community of Lahaul. According to some of the elders (women and men) I interviewed, such as Lal Chand Dhissa, Chering Dorje, Tashi Yangzom, and Tobdan—who are all revered on account of their knowledge of what other locals often referred to as the "'history, sociology and geography" of the valley—different theories about the origin of the people exist across the valleys. Broadly, among the people mentioned above, there was consensus that historically this region has been influenced by three and not two religions. Buddhism, according to them was already enmeshed with Orthodox Bon, which is claimed to be the indigenous religion of the region. According to this theory, Lahaul now has a mixed religion—Buddhism enmeshed with Orthodox Bon, followed by the new (Tibetan) Buddhism merged with Hinduism. However, because there is so little information about Orthodox Bon, and very few people know about the religion, its overall influences in the Lahaul valley are mostly identified as a combination of Hindu–Buddhist religion and culture. There are however different approaches to thinking about the influence of Hindu society among them, especially in the framing of caste. I address this in depth in chapter three.

While there is a significant body of anthropological research conducted in the nearby region of Ladakh, especially within Himalayan Studies (Aggarwal 2004; Aggarwal and Bhan 2009; Middleton 2013; Smith 2013; Van Beek 2000), very little scholarship has focused on the Lahaul valley. Ladakh occupies a central place in Border and Himalayan studies also on account of literally constituting a marginal and yet key position within India's most contested border zone in recent decades, that of the state of Jammu and Kashmir, located on the Indo-Pak border (Aggarwal and Bhan 2009). This scholarship has also discussed how borders are not fixed; how the border itself lives through an embodiment of political discourses and spatial memories in spaces that are (physically) distant from state-defined national borders (Smith 2013).

What is striking about the Lahaul valley is that despite constituting a physically defined border zone, it exists within this fluid sensibility. This is to say that Lahaul despite its physical location, lies somewhere between the militarized and most definitive border, on the one hand, and a more liminal undefined border on the other. This liminality is produced through and continues to keep Lahaul as an almost forgotten region (in its everyday significance as far as the Indian state's articulations of threats to national security and inter/national contestations over territories are concerned). Always non-threatening, the Lahaulis have historically never demanded autonomy, and take much pride in their relationship with the state as a geopolitically significant border region.

Because the Indo-Pak border and the Kashmir conflict maintain a spectral presence in Lahaul, primarily through the militarized maintenance and provision of strategic and motorable roads for army supplies to Kargil, the valley continues to receive attention and support (most often through infrastructural support and a general principle of non-interference) from the state in ways that several other tribal communities along India's borders do not. Further, the valley is also considered a strategic location on account of the Indo-Tibet border (officially called the Sino-Indian border). In 2013, the state government of Himachal Pradesh requested the central government of India for a security boost for the entire district of Lahaul-Spiti.

This request followed India's recent (2012–2013) accusations against China of violating its airspace.[29] On account of these alleged aerial incursions, the region was soon placed on high alert. Additionally, the Himachal government appealed to the central government that the area also be considered a grade "A" border state for the Modernization of Police Forces (MPF) funding support, which would substantially enhance central funding allocations to the state under the Border Area Development Programmes. This assignment of grade "A" border state already occurred for neighboring Ladakh and Northeastern Himalayan states, which too are on the Sino-Indian border.

The Lahaul valley is strategically located in this "high alert" region, because it has the longest seasonally non-motorable region on this border. A 9-km tunnel (called the Rohtang Tunnel) is under construction to make the valley (and the main strategic highway running through it) motorable throughout the year. The construction of the tunnel and the state's appeal for greater militarization in the area are reasons for deep concern given the gendered and, often, violent consequences of such actions in neighboring border regions.

On average, most people with whom I discussed the tunnel construction[30] (including several women in this project) were deeply invested in the successful completion of the Rohtang tunnel, despite its obvious ecological and cultural intrusions. For the women, affinity toward the construction of the tunnel was articulated through a discussion of the material possibilities of escaping the exceptional isolation of the winter months. During the long harsh winters, men often migrate to the lower districts of the state, such as Kullu, looking for work mostly within the tourism industry. The women stay back, looking after the animals, weaving, and mostly surviving on dried/stored food from the summer months. In several conversations, women discussed how they imagine the construction of the tunnel might offer new possibilities through the winter, including fresh food, proximity to other members of their families, healthcare and access to hospitals outside the valley. Yet they also spoke at length of the risks it poses—advent of uncontrolled tourism, impact on children, increased surveillance of what constitutes their "own" time through the winter, and the possibility of increased violence. It is important to mention that not a single Lahauli I spoke to ever doubted that the construction of the tunnel was entirely to support the army and had little to do with the often touted logic (presented by the government) of "tribal welfare."

As was repeatedly articulated to me, especially by local men (both Dalit and non-Dalit members of the community), this support for the tunnel is not only on account of the benefits to the community during the harsh winter months, but is also viewed as an extension of the tribe's important role in securing the borders of the nation-state. This positioning of their community as not only willing[31] and proud to serve the larger national interests of the country as needed by the Indian state, while also maintaining the tribe's distinctiveness often sets the stage for a collusion of otherwise unequally located patriarchies—those of state and tribe. Such self-positioning of the tribe as a whole, unified, and often self-loving community, in relation to the caste-Hindu communities of the plains often obscures the very existence of caste hierarchy within tribe. The rigidity and hierarchical relationship across caste groupings as they exist in non-tribal communities of Hindu-society in the plains (such as in UP, Rajasthan, and MP) should not be comparable to or conflated with caste striations *within* tribe. Such a reading would be dangerous on two counts. First, the tribe in itself is already located in the margins of caste-society and there is a long history of disenfranchisement of Adivasi communities across the country. Second, this would also continue the invisibilization of the added layer of injury that those Lahaulis who identify as Adivasi *and* Dalit experience. Put simply, being Dalit within the Adivasi community of Lahaul doesn't preclude the participation of Lahauli Dalits in the self-positioning of the community as a whole when placed in relation to the non-tribal caste-Hindu imaginary of the nation-state. Nor does it preclude the participation of Lahauli Dalits within self-preservatory and internally hierarchized workings of Adivasi patriarchy. In fact, these are the identities and self-contradictory locations that the women in this book routinely discuss, challenge, and often also affirm.

Broadly speaking, the literature about Lahaul can be divided into three categories. First, which is most popular, is the travelogue and memoir style writing about the region. This genre provides a lot of information about the mountains, their beauty, and the remoteness of the region and its people. This approach toward the region was presented fairly recently, when in the preface to the second edition of his much acclaimed memoir *Himalayan Wonderland: Travels in Lahaul and Spiti* Manohar Singh Gill (2010) calls upon India's public servants to choose (as he clearly did, in choosing Lahaul), "adventurous" and "challenging" postings in "remote parts of the country with varying landscape" over and above "urban flesh pots" and the "World Bank." On occasion Gill refers to the valley as his "kingdom," on account of having held the highest administrative position in the valley, that of the District Commissioner (DC). In his and other similar accounts, which depict the region as "heaven" for travelers and adventure seekers, local histories and struggles are invisibilized and the people of Lahaul are cast through the landscape of the mountains as "unique and remote" and "stark and exotic," much like the Himachal Tourism brochure—inviting the reader to experience the joys of an unabashed consumption of the region and its communities.

A second body of literature consists of the descriptive and numerical data made available through government records and census reports. A third and burgeoning body of work consists of anthropological and sociological studies conducted in the region. These have their earliest roots in the documents and manuscripts written by the German Moravian Missionaries (who lived in the region from the late 1800s until about the 1930s) and colonial anthropologists and researchers, including A.F.P Harcourt (1871). Over the last fifty years several scholars have written about the region including Lahauli scholars such as Lal Chand Dhissa, C. Dorje, and Tobdan. While the work of C. Dorje and Tobdan (who have also collaborated on a number of projects) focuses primarily on cultural, linguistic, and religious practices and histories of the valley, Lal Chand Dhissa's is the only writing which documents and analyzes caste as a system of domination in the region.

To my knowledge, there is no work on the region which tells the story of the valley from the perspectives of its women. *Narrating Love and Violence* fills this void by positioning tribal women's life histories as central to the production of knowledge about gendered violence in Lahaul and indeed India. Further, by paying attention to the workings of caste within tribal society, I have stepped away from homogenizing tendencies that place all Dalit and Adivasi women's experiences within one monolithic category. Rather, building upon Ambedkar's (1936; 1990) critique of caste and sexuality, my book teases out the relationship between caste, tribe, and gender to highlight that they are relevant not *only* for Dalit and Adivasi women.[32] Through such an anti-caste lens, I add to a rich body of existing Dalit feminist scholarship (Bama 2005; Rege 2004, 2013; Irudayam et al. 2011;

Kannabiran and Kannabiran 2002; Paik 2009; Rao 2009). I have adopted a decolonizing framework, which challenges the feminist theorizing of violence that often ignores the salience of caste in India, conflates caste and tribe, and centers Eurocentric feminist representations of violence against women in the Global South (Mohanty 2003; Alexander and Mohanty 1997).

Over the last few decades, a rich body of feminist research and writing on gendered violence in South Asia in general has illustrated the ways in which women's bodies become sites of contestation for patriarchal power at the intersection of the (postcolonial) state, caste, and community. While such scholarship has strengthened this book's scaffolding of meanings of violence as a process, the lived experiences of Lahauli women is the central criterion of meaning for me. In this book I have chosen to represent and demonstrate the performance of theory by women whose lives have been written out of history. Further, the bulk of the literature mentioned above doesn't address caste and tribe from the perspectives of ordinary women who live on these margins, which is the central focus of this book.

I build upon Sharmila Rege's reclaiming of Ambedkar's legacy as intersectional and feminist, as well as the Dalit feminist legacy of Bama, Pawar, Moon, and Kamble who, much like U.S. women of color feminists (Moraga, Anzaldúa, bell hooks, Audre Lorde, and others) reclaim theory from its ivory and savarna towers, in positing oral narratives, testimony, autobiographies, and poetry *as* knowledge. Finally, it is also my own embodied experiences in the co-performance of this ethnography (often mis/understood as the solo author in the academy) that lead me to place the sociality of caste within these multiple genealogical formations of knowledge making.

In this spirit, I have chosen a representational style that stays as close to storytelling mode as possible. Throughout the book I have adopted a layered writing style that weaves daily details with epiphanic revelations as storied by the women. I string together narrative and analytic writing styles. Ideally, I would like to tell a whole, complete story in each chapter. But this isn't how storytelling works: even when we succeed in "structuring" our stories, we may not be able to contain them (Chawla 2014). The unruliness of everyday life, the fleshiness of discourse, the pain of loss and the changing contours of identities invariably spill over. Thus, throughout the book I adopt a combinational writing strategy.

Each time I present any part of a life-story for the first time, I introduce the woman who tells the story in a brief paragraph following parts of the story itself. In most of the chapters the stories are presented as dialogues, in which my interjections, questions, or simply the co-performance between us, as researcher and narrator, is woven into the storytelling. I have changed names of people, sometimes places and created composites from different parts of several stories. In the third chapter, while sticking to the same as far as names of places and people, I present four oral histories in first-person narrative form. Such a first-person mode of storytelling has been used in several life history projects, oral histories, and performance ethnographies, including those by Lorde (1982), Butalia (2000), Rose (2004), Madison (2006), Pawar and Moon (2008), and Johnson (2011b). This is done not in order to preserve any (false) sense of the narrator's voice or to excise my own voice from the text. Indeed, these first-person life and love stories are large chunks of what was narrated by the women over the course of several conversations; but these are presented without the noticeable interruptions, questions, and/or audible utterances from me, which are integrated through the other chapters. While the text in this chapter appears not to have my active presence, and indeed through many of these conversations I didn't necessarily always utter audible words, my body, movements, gestures, expressions, and my attention were all an integral part of the dialogic process, affirming and co-performing these stories. In order to avoid repetition, I have chosen four of the stories that do not appear in other chapters as story-excerpts. In order to contextualize these other story-excerpts, which appear in small and big waves throughout the book, I have introduced each woman at the start of the excerpt in a brief summary paragraph to the reader. The one story which is part-textual has the supplementary documents (the first information report from the police record) included as an appendix. In this way, throughout the book I have presented a layered and mixed genre of storytelling. In particular, by opting for four of the most representative narratives as stand-alone tales written in first-person style, the third chapter takes the reader to the heart of the book—the women's life histories.

Narrating Love and Violence comprises six chapters (including this first chapter), a prologue, and an epilogue. I open the book with a prologue, an autobiographical narrative about my early work as an organizer with the women's collective in the Stod valley of Lahaul. It is a glimpse into that period of my life, which became the basis for my interest and commitment to documenting women's life histories in Lahaul. It also lays the foundation for the discussion of ethnographer-interlocutor shifts that emerge throughout the book.

The second chapter borrows its title "Shades of Wildness," from Ajay Skaria's 1997 article and delves into the intricacies of caste and tribe in Lahaul. It opens with a background on the workings of caste and tribe in Lahaul, the range of constitutional, anthropological, and political nomenclature in India, and locates the intersection of caste and tribe within a broader national context. This is followed by the stories of two women, Kavita and Pema.

Chapter three is titled "Storied Lives." To enhance the communicative power of the life histories and to demonstrate that the women in narrating their lives generate knowledge about this region with the full force and power of their own reflexivity, this chapter has three first-person narratives with no formal introduction from me. The women whose love-stories are included here are Keerthi, Parvati, and Yangzin. The first, Keerthi identifies as a tribal Dalit woman who has been very active in the work of the women's collective in the past. She tells the story of her sister's rape and discusses specifics of caste society and challenges popular origin-stories about the tribe in general. Parvati, who is tribal Dalit, tells the story of both her marriages. Yangzin has tribal privileged-caste Thakur family history and she offers a glimpse into the gendered complexities of government categorizations of scheduled tribes like Lahaul, despite her caste-privilege.

The fourth chapter is titled "Narrating Love" and opens with a brief discussion of love as a politic and traces the ways in which women discuss love as an epistemological shift. It offers a brief discussion of joint marriage, termed polyandry in anthropological and state literature, and then presents three stories that demonstrate the ways in which women use love in their narrations. One of the stories, which is focused entirely on joint marriage, is also juxtaposed with an interview with a state representative to illustrate the ways in which state discourses on love actually serve as proxy for caste and tribe.

Chapter five, "Magic Tricks," is where I elaborate upon the self-definition and self-positioning of the Lahaula tribe. This leads to an important contribution of the book—its discussion of the relationship between tribe and the state in Lahaul, and in the Northwestern Himalayas in general. I discuss the collusions that exist between these competing patriarchies, especially those of state and tribe in the context of gendered violence.

In chapter six, titled "Remembering for Love," I analyze different relationships of remembering and I place them in conversation with one another. I illustrate the relevance of feminist counter-memory in remembering violence through women's own narratives, against the grain of public and official memory. I return to Kavita's memory and my own memory. Here, I also discuss the idea of remembering for love (Alexander 2005), an ethical love, which several women in my project articulate through a politics of hope and transformation, often cited as their reason for wanting to tell these stories.

In the epilogue I return to a story from my early work in Lahaul, which takes a different turn at the moment when I was back in Lahaul for research on this book. This story offers an entry into a discussion of failure as an important step in feminist research that traverses huge social divides.

2 ⚹ SHADES OF WILDNESS

In July 2013, a leading English-language Indian newspaper published a black-and-white photograph of a lone Northwestern Himalayan woman wearing a *cholu* in the middle of a large field with thunderous clouds looming overhead (see Appendix). The caption read: "'Gone with the Wind': Women's Land Rights in Kinnaur, Lahaul and Spiti are denied to them." *The Hindu* newspaper photo from the article, "My Land, My Right," had the accompanying subtitle: "Women's organizations in Himachal Pradesh rally for property rights in customary laws." Similar to the image and the text that use exoticizing tropes of remoteness to illustrate the distance between laws governed by custom-tribe and the postcolonial state, the reporter juxtaposes the "stark beauty of the mountains" with the "unjustified and discriminatory tribal law" to call for an end to the so-called age-old, primitive, and unfair tribal laws that tie women to land ownership and move toward modernity by championing popular notions of women's rights.

Next, the article's call for gender equity can be read through race. *Gone with the Wind* (Cukor and Fleming 1939), for example, is a media representation of the U.S. Confederacy (Berlant 2012) that erases racial violence in the American South. Similarly, the reporter masks the racial othering of the tribe even while reproducing it by emphasizing women's right to property. It is as if Scarlett's fight for the colonial plantation Tara has been metaphorically mapped onto the lone woman in the field who represents all tribal women fighting for the land they toil and love. Adapting the narrative style from the film, the reporter not only romanticizes the region and re-inscribes the tribe as static, but also expresses outrage toward (pre-British) customary law and points to the need for state intervention to save tribal women from tribal men[1] like the United States' states had to do, in order to end the "peculiar institution" of racial slavery in the South. What is the relationship between colonial discourses and state and media representations of Lahaul? How do the discourses in the postcolonial context participate in the complete erasure of multiple (gendered) marginalities within the region?

Building on Ajay Skaria (1997), Soma Chaudhuri (2013) has illustrated how colonial constructs of tribe as "wild," "savage," and "primitive" in South Asia need to be understood as "shades of wildness," and that for the colonial masters, the privileged castes were also part of the larger "savage community" that was in need of rescue and civilization, but placed higher than the "primitive" tribes within the racial hierarchy. Through the article, the photograph, and its title, the reporter reifies the construction of tribe as a racial other, located at the bottom of this racial hierarchy—the other who is always, already seen as uncivilized and backward compared to the non-tribal and privileged caste communities of the plains within the postcolonial context.

One of several interrelated discursive tropes found in the representation of Adivasis[2] in India, here too, the women are represented as both *agents* reaching out to the modern protectionist state for their rights and as *victims* of a primitive regressive custom enforced by "tribal" men. At this intersection of woman as agent and victim, is where a broad set of popular, scholarly, and state discourses come together to shape how we see and understand women from tribal communities such as Lahaul, and where I locate this chapter.

POLITICS OF CASTE AND TRIBE

In Lahaul, the community's ethnic identity as tribe is crucial to the maintenance of caste hierarchy *within* tribe. Rules of purity and pollution,[3] new-old versions of untouchability, are strictly enforced and with impunity in Lahaul where the PoA Act of 1989 and the Civil Rights Act of 1955 are not applicable. The physical border, the Rohtang, often defines this self-positioning of the tribe as distinct from the rest of the state. Keerthi, a

Dalit woman from the Patan valley (whose story appears in chapter three), best summed this up when we were talking about marriage practices and the problems women face in general and the discussion shifted to caste in Lahaul. "Of course people don't admit it. We Lahaulis love to say we are tribal, and Buddhist. We are also Hindu. And there are castes here. For the outside world, on the other side of the top, we must appear as 'Lahauli' and no more and no less. But inside the valley, well, many won't even let us eat from the same utensils."

Chhering Dorje, a privileged-caste member and a highly regarded scholar of and from Lahaul, also articulates this stratification of the tribe by caste. He ended a long discussion with me by laughingly stating, "Lahaulis, except the Dalit-Lahaulis don't like to acknowledge that we have castes even in the upper valley, but the discrimination against STs in Himachal and upper Himalayas is nothing compared to the discrimination against SCs in the plains." He gave me an example of this hierarchical relationship between tribe and caste, "For example, betaji, even as an Adivasi, I said to the Chief Election Commissioner when Nehru was PM—'Sir, I may be a ST, but I am from the same caste as Jawaharlal Nehru.'"

Privileged-caste status, within the otherwise marginalized community of tribe, can ostensibly allow for a proximity that narrows the distance between Adivasi and non-Adivasi (Hindu–Buddhist) societies nationally, while maintaining the (violent) exclusion of Dalits within the tribe. The dual existence of Hindu and (Tibetan) Buddhist religions in the region further sets the stage for such possibilities. Despite the consistent interest in understanding and analyzing caste and tribe from a range of perspectives in Indian Sociology and South Asian Studies, there has been little attention paid to the production of caste marginality at their intersection. Ravina Aggarwal's (2004) ethnography of border performance in neighboring Ladakh includes a rare analysis of the workings of caste hierarchies in everyday life among the tribal communities in that area. She discusses the shift from caste to tribe, and the continuation of practices of purity and pollution within tribe and also points to the paucity of literature on these topics. Similarly, in the oral histories of the women and the interviews and conversations with men and state officials, caste logics repeatedly emerged as a key mode of social organization in Lahaul. Within Lahaul the oppressed castes (Dalits) are doubly marginalized. First, by being members of a hill tribe who are repeatedly produced as the racial other by the non-tribal caste-Hindu communities of the plains in the national imaginary (Bora 2010). And second, by belonging to the most oppressed caste category as positioned nationally, but also within the parameters of the tribe.

How does caste as a system of domination appear in all its ugly avatars across communities? What kinds of vulnerabilities and modes of resistance does this produce? How do scholars, activists, and community members use the vocabulary of caste and tribe, and which (discursive and material) practices do we wish to change and how? What is the relationship between the unjust exclusion of Keerthi who asks for her space experiences ("... make room for me"), and the struggle for constitutional recognition as articulated by the leaders of the Tribal Dalit movement in the section below and throughout?

The experiences shared by my interlocutors map the shifting contours of the sociality of caste, tribe, and state—emphasizing the resultant marginalities, the injustices, and the multi-layered social, cultural, and constitutional struggles that emerge. For example, the entire population of Lahaul falls under the governmental categorization of "Scheduled Tribe" (ST) as defined by Article 366 of the Indian Constitution. The Lahauli community positions itself simultaneously as historically disadvantaged and marginalized because of its tribal status, while maintaining a strict caste order internally. Unlike several Adivasi communities in the Eastern and Western Himalayan regions, Lahaulis received recognition as a Scheduled Tribe and the affirmative action benefits that accrue from such a designation, in the earliest assignments of tribes by the postcolonial state in India. This modern constitutional nomenclature (ST) is rooted in colonial classification of tribes (labeled "hill tribes" and "criminal tribes") as primitive social groups who needed social benefits, along with Dalits ("untouchables" in colonial and Brahmanical usage) and has been highly problematized by scholars in the field of Adivasi Studies.[4] They were considered "depressed classes" of Indian society and placed within the broad category of "Scheduled."[5] The constitutional distinction of "Scheduled Tribe" was introduced by the postcolonial state and neatly separated tribe from caste. A large number of oppressed castes (Dalits) were labeled "Scheduled Caste" (SC). These constitutional definitions were considered India's equivalent of affirmative action policies, usually known as "reservations," and continue to generate violent contestations from large numbers of privileged caste-Hindus.

The usage of these governmental labels when referring to tribes (and oppressed castes) is thus highly discriminatory and problematic, yet often these were the only terms state officials I have interviewed over the years ever used when referring to the Lahaula community. In Lahaul, as in the case of the northeastern belt of India, the English word/term "tribe," also an anthropological category (rooted in colonial definitions and often considered problematic) remains the chosen self-descriptor used by most local people. This is particularly the active choice among members of the tribal Dalit community who wish to distinguish between tribe as anthropological category and Scheduled Tribe as constitutional category. These preferences and distinctions exist over and above the use of the term Adivasi, which translates to "original dwellers" and is often the politicized term used by many to replace the anthropological nomenclature of "tribe," thus signaling the autonomous existence of these communities prior to colonial intervention.

As I understand this usage of "tribe" among several of my interlocutors, the term creates room for an understanding of tribe as community, rather than only as a problem of nomenclature or analytical category that is rooted in a discourse of citizenship and state. Through such a usage, the community that lives at the intersection of tribe (as a marker of difference) and caste (as a system of domination), i.e. the Adivasi Dalit, seeks legibility and recognition as equal (but oppressed) citizens from the state and the community. Thus it necessitates a reading of the anti-caste, Dalit liberatory discourse of rights, citizenship, and nomenclature as equally rooted in community. A quote from Keerthi, who in another interview, summed up the discourse when she said: "Whether they say I am a tribal Dalit or Dalit or tribal, I have a question: I want my space and share. This is my struggle."

Throughout the book I opt for the usage of "tribe," "tribal," and "Adivasi," as they were used by my interlocutors, opting for the usage of Adivasi particularly when discussing state, community, and politicized discourses of indigenous heterogeneity in general. The terms of the constitutional category of ST were defined in Article 342 of the Indian Constitution, which includes characteristics pertaining to "primitiveness," "geographical isolation," "shyness of contact," "distinctive culture, language and religion," and "backwardness." These markers of difference that are literally a continuation of colonial constructs of tribes as primitive, static, and in need of modern intervention for survival continue the colonialist rhetoric of the Constitution (Ambedkar 1990).

Ambedkar at all points in his intellectual and political life argued against the very existence of a caste society and eventually in resignation converted to Buddhism in order to reject caste society. In his groundbreaking essay Castes in India (1916), he dismantled the racist ideologies underpinning colonial intellectual practices that continually understood caste as race through the Indo-Aryan theory of Hindu society. Most importantly, he articulated an intersectional model of understanding caste as a system of domination (not only a set of social hierarchies) that was constituted through class (hereditary control of profession as determined by birth), gender (control of women through violence), and sexuality (enforcement of endogamy).

Instead of caste reform (as espoused eventually successfully[6] by Gandhi), Ambedkar sought a departure from key Hindu texts (the religious justification of a caste society) as the only solution to ending caste, class, and gender oppression in India. His vision of modernity did not exclude Adivasis from this radical intersectional paradigm of a society free of Brahmanical patriarchy and colonial rule. He squarely held Brahmanical patriarchy responsible for the marginalization of not only oppressed-caste communities, but also Adivasis across India (BAWS, Vol. 5), by continually excluding them both from every benefit available to privileged-caste communities of Hindu society.

In The Injustices of the Constitution, Lal Chand Dhissa (2011), the president of the Janjatiya Dalit Sangh (JDS)—a grassroots Adivasi-Dalit organization in Lahaul and Kullu, Himachal—uses "tribal-Dalit" when discussing his community's struggle for constitutional recognition, but Adivasi when discussing the community in general. He is the leader of the Janajatiya Dalit Sangh, an organization fighting for the constitutional recognition of his constituency, and discusses precisely this fallout of the clear separation between caste and tribe in the Indian Constitution as the reason for the oppression of those who embody the intersection of Dalit and Adivasi identities. In 2004,[7] the state government granted dual (SC and ST) status to some Dalit communities in the region. According to the JDS, of the roughly

14 percent of Dalits, the state recognized only 7 percent as both SC and ST. There are an equal or greater number of Dalits who are still struggling to gain this dual status.

The granting of dual status is far from ideal, however, as articulated by the members of the JDS and several of the women whose narratives I documented. In 2013, the JDS has put forth a petition to the (national) High Level Committee on Scheduled Tribes requesting special status as "Scheduled Tribal Dalits," instead of dual status. From the numbers mentioned above, this dual status is clearly not even being offered to all members of the Dalit tribal community. Further, while dual status grants some benefits to the Dalits of the tribe, it still does not recognize Dalits as the most oppressed members of tribal communities when they are stratified by caste.

Further, the granting of dual status, rather than an intersectional status does not address the problem of zero representation in local governance, nor does it recognize or protect the particular vulnerabilities produced by the intersection of belonging to two marginal identities—Dalit and Adivasi. This intersection seems especially relevant as a constitutional category when the challenges that are posed by the tendency to either conflate or neatly separate caste and tribe (mentioned previously in this chapter) are considered. Three such challenges are briefly explored in the following examples. These examples are based on interviews with people across the valley.

The first challenge includes the exclusionary (and often violent[8]) responses to people's struggle for inclusion into the constitutional categories of SC and ST across India. Laxmi Orang, a young Adivasi girl from Assam was brutally assaulted while participating in a student demonstration seeking ST status for her community. Not only was this case yet another illustration of how discrimination against and disenfranchisement of Adivasis are upheld through the enactment of particular modes of sexual violence, it demonstrated the impunity with which such violence is conducted and then literally obliterated from public memory, despite (and indeed because of) the circulation of the video of this assault across the country. Pashupati Prasad Mahato (2000: 36), discusses at length yet another form of violence, through processes of cultural silencing, what he has termed "Nirbakization." Another example of exclusion was narrated by Mr. Lal Chand Dhissa of JDS during an interview I conducted with him. The case refers to two Adivasi

Dalit communities—Beda and Gara—who are members of the tribes of Lahaul and its neighbors (Ladakh and Kinnaur), and ethnically fall within the broader scheduled area, and are thus considered part of the "Scheduled Tribes." They were, however, seeking dual recognition as "Scheduled Caste" on account of the community's Dalit-caste identity. Yet, instead of recognizing the Dalit status of the Beda and Gara communities, the state responded (Scheduled Tribes Order, 2004) by granting them status as independent Scheduled Tribes (a pointless designation since their communities already had ST status). By denying Dalits the benefits currently available (and possible future protections) that could only apply to these groups through the granting of "Scheduled Caste" status, the state used the rhetoric of "development of tribal areas" to mask caste discrimination through a constitutional caveat.

A second challenge includes the application of benefits of the reservation system for members of these communities. Because the entire tribe falls within a scheduled area and is viewed as a marginalized community needing benefits, reservations, and development, all members of the tribe are considered equally disadvantaged, including those members of the privileged caste who have last names that clearly denote their caste status, such as the Thakurs. While the Thakurs and other privileged-castes own the largest amount of land in the valley, the reservation policy meant to benefit the entire tribe has excluded Dalits. Privileged castes (including the historical ruling class caste of Thakurs) are also the ones who have the highest representation in high and mid-level government jobs, political parties, state assemblies, and local self-governance units, such as the Panchayats, who were granted greater autonomy after the passing of PESA (The Panchayat [Extension to scheduled areas] Act, 1996) that included tribal areas[9] of Himachal Pradesh.

As articulated by Keerthi in her comments about the politics of caste-based purity and pollution practices in Lahaul, a third and key challenge posed concerns discrimination on the basis of caste, and the (in)applicability of legal protections, such as the The Civil Rights Act of 1955 (banning untouchability) and The Scheduled Castes and Scheduled Tribes (Prevention of Atrocities) Act, (also known as the PoA Act) of 1989. Once again, because the entire Adivasi community is considered equally marginalized, and similar in status to the Dalits of non-Adivasi caste society, the PoA Act is not applicable in scheduled areas. Thus, under the current version of the Act, only a non-Adivasi may be accused of discrimination against an Adivasi by definition.

For instance, Kavita, who identifies as both Adivasi and Dalit (her story appears later in this chapter and again in chapter four), was unable to file a case under the PoA Act despite being raped by a privileged caste member of the tribe. Even though the act covers rape as caste violence, a case could not be registered because the Act does not consider the intersection of this smallest social and constitutional minority—that of the Tribal Dalit. Similarly, the Himachal Tribune (Sandhu 2007) reported the violence against a young Dalit man of the Kinnaura tribe in the neighboring region of Kinnaur. Through methods that are chillingly reserved for, and enacted in numerous instances of caste violence in different parts of India, this Dalit person was stripped, hung from a pole, beaten, and sexually abused over the course of a night as punishment by a group of privileged-caste members for entering the village temple premises. The banning of untouchability and the subsequent constitutional amendment through the PoA Act are meant to provide protection for Dalits against such caste atrocity/violence by caste-Hindus. Yet, under the current legal and (constitutional) framework of protection/ rights, no action against the aggressors under the category of Caste Atrocity was possible.

In a national environment where despite the applicability of the Atrocities Act, a steady increase in gendered violence against Dalits and Adivasis (particularly enacted in the form of sexual assault, stripping, humiliation, mutilation of sexual organs, and rape) has prevailed, the state's continual refusal to recognize the magnitude of the vulnerabilities of Adivasi Dalits equals the granting of constitutional impunity to privileged castes within tribes. In 2014, an amendment to the Atrocities act (Article 17 of the Indian Constitution) was approved by the parliament, and included specific acts that were previously not mentioned in the IPC (Indian Penal Code) as caste violence. The specific acts prohibited included stripping, parading naked, and a range of acts commonly used as tools for maintaining caste hierarchy. The amendment was of no use in the context of Fifth Schedule Areas such as Lahaul. By continuing to ignore the relationship between tribe and caste across different contexts, the state not only refuses to acknowledge the deep entrenchments of caste hierarchies and structural violence in India, it actively participates in these re-enactments of gendered violence in order to maintain a caste society entrenched in Brahmanical (hetero)patriarchy.

By returning to the life histories of two women and one man, the leader of the Dalit Janajatiya Sangh, this chapter attempts to demonstrate the violent nexus of multiple (hetero) patriarchies—those of state, caste, and tribe. Each co-interlocutor's story makes sense of caste hegemony, violence, and honor differently from the commonly available definitions available from the multiple patriarchies (including the state/Brahmanical, Tribal, and Dalit patriarchy). Repeatedly, by engaging with aspects of their *selves* as embodied and relational, the women articulated the viscerality of discourse. While the meanings performed (Conquergood 1991; Madison, 2011) in these narratives may not always be directly oppositional to hegemonic ideas of caste, even when working within such a discursive framework, they nonetheless shift and reshape the contours of the discourse.

KAVITA

Kavita is a Dalit-Adivasi woman from the village Tholong who was in her late thirties by the time of the most recent interviews with her. She lives in Kullu and has had to switch her home base from Lahaul to Kullu-Manali several times over the last twenty years. The last move from Lahaul to Kullu was in order to start her life afresh. Nearly a decade ago, she moved to her parents' home in Tholong in order to escape a violent marriage during a second pregnancy. Eventually she moved back to Kullu, once again to escape her ex-husband who knew she lived with her parents and continued to harass her, and to search for employment and caste-anonymity. Excerpts from our conversations and her story follow a discussion of the events that led up to our conversation that day.

"The Sun in my gut, the Moon in my heart." Kavita had been humming these two lines from a well-known Chinaal folk song about "Sobhnu" over and over, while ironing the children's clothes at the boarding school where she was employed as a helper. She worked in exchange for free schooling for her daughters and a small monthly salary. I was in the adjoining room, listening to the teachers recount a recent case of sexual abuse in the hostel. A resident *lama* (monk) had been accused of assaulting a five-year-old girl in the hostel. Kavita was the first to discover the injuries on the child's body and raise an alarm. She had informed the staff that she no longer wished to sit in through these planning meetings, but would stand witness, in court or in community interventions, to address the case, as and when needed. The teachers, staff, and board members of the school were planning the best course of action, and they had requested my presence in this meeting. Periodically, I heard her voice floating in, "The sun and the moon live in Sobhnu's home . . . Such that even the queen of Beeling was fooled into entering his hut!"

An hour later, Kavita and I were sitting in the fields outside the school premises tugging at the long grass and discussing the details of the case. Unable to get the persistent tune out of my mind, I ask her about the song. She offered me her hand, "Come let's walk to the other side of the river from where we can see Beeling." Beeling is a village in the Stod Valley though in the song the reference is to yet another Beeling. While not visible from where we were standing, the direction the river followed led to Beeling. A little taken aback by her suggestion, I asked how she proposed we would make it along the river without notifying someone in advance to bring the carrier across the ropeway for us. She started laughing and said, "oye if you and I can't just walk along the river, what's this about how the 'innocent' queen all the way from Beeling crossed it to visit Sobhnu, all the while unaware that he was Chinaal (Dalit) because she saw the sun in his house!"

We walked up to a big rock by the river. From there we still could not see Beeling but we were facing in the direction of the village. She continued, "I like this song because I am (like) Sobhnu.[10] I am Dalit too, but like him I too know that I am no less than them." Gesturing in the general direction of the land of the Khangsar Thakurs, she sang again; only this time changing the lyrics: "The sun[11] lives in my gut and the moon in my heart."

The lyrics of the original folk song referred to Sobhnu, a young Chinaal/Dalit man from Lahaul. The song represents Sobhnu as an extraordinary person, while also marking his oppressed (caste) status by referring to the queen's transgressive entry into his hearth as a result of what the queen's family called his deceit. Sobhnu is no ordinary man, for the sun and the moon live in his house. The next line affirms how Sobhnu is indeed remarkable—so much so that even the queen of Beeling was fooled into entering his home.

The lyrics can be interpreted in several ways. One reading interprets the presence of the sun and the moon in his house as evidence against the origins theory of Dalits in Lahaul thereby rejecting the idea that Sobhnu's (caste) status was lower than the queen's (Dhissa, 2011). Lal Chand Dhissa (2011) draws attention to the historical error in the assignment of Dalit status to certain groups in Lahaul. His critique and challenge to the commonly circulating origin stories about tribal Dalits and tribal non-Dalits in Lahaul not only disrupts current understandings of caste and tribe in the region, but allows for a dismantling of the very terms of Brahmanical patriarchy by not only questioning the production of the *avarna* (Dalit) in this context, but also by questioning the production of the Brahmin (as *savarna*). During the course of our conversation, he discussed the politics of caste in land distribution across India and the historical injustice of Brahmanism in rendering Dalits in Lahaul (and elsewhere) landless, finally ending the conversation with, "*mujhe bas mere zameen ka hissa chahiye*" ("I only seek my share of the land"). Thus he connects his earlier argument of questioning the very presence of Brahmanism in Lahaul to the political reality of landlessness of Dalits nationally and situates landlessness within what he calls the "conspiracy of Brahmanism" in generationally dispossessing Dalit communities across the country as landless laborers.

The same lyrics could also be read, from Kavita's re-working of the lyrics, as exemplifying the history of a politics of resistance to the everyday violence of caste in Lahaul. The interpretation of caste rejection through access to the sun (also considered "untouchable") is one among several strategies Kavita practices in her everyday. For example, when she directs her daughters to use the privileged-caste last name "Sharma" because who would know their caste status in Kullu, she asserts another form of this rejection of caste. Like Sobhnu, in this instance she too destabilizes caste by deliberately messing with its most mundane enactment—the politics of caste-identification via last names. By collapsing the distance between Sobhnu and herself, she actively performs an embodied Dalit self as one that is remarkable (the sun and the moon now reside within her body) and oppositional, "no less than" that of the Thakurs of Lahaul.

Both these moments can be read as resistive utterances that lie between James Scott's (1990) "public transcripts" and "hidden transcripts." In this chapter, I do not wish to posit an either/or model of understanding this particular folk song, by discussing Kavita's quotes as a kind of celebratory or pure, "uncontaminated" (Theodossopoulos, 2014) resistance, nor do I present her resistive performance through her everyday life as necessarily oppositional (Scott, 1990). Rather, I am interested in how Kavita maps her life onto Sobhnu and allows for the possibilities of different meanings of caste violence, honor, and resistance to emerge—through her life and experiences—instead of those defined by others around her, such as the school staff, the state officials, and the tribe.

In this space, somewhere in-between the varying readings of this song, I offer Kavita's story. I explore this space "between the transcripts" because it allows resistive meanings to emerge—without necessarily aligning itself with normalized definitions of violence, resistance, and emancipatory politics that are more readily available about caste and gender oppression. Thus in this chapter, I do not discuss the way particular subjectivities are mapped onto Dalit bodies and what resistances to caste/gender violence look like through such readings. Instead I present two narratives to demonstrate how they craft meanings and identities for their tellers' selves and, in doing so, expand existing definitional boundaries—of caste and gender violence as they recast hegemonic notions of honor.

In another interview, while we were sitting by the highway after her work hours, Kavita talked about her experiences at the school.

K: Only women work in this school. There are two men—all the others are women. But all the women are looked upon with suspicion. The suspicion is especially high toward us—the helpers, who work like domestic help at the hostel—as compared to the teachers. Our work hours are daily 7:00 A.M.–11:30 P.M. Wake up in the morning and start getting the kids ready for school—brush their teeth, wash them, and take them for breakfast. Wash their clothes when they go to school.

I began working here in May 2005. I did not get the job the first time I applied. I was refused. The school authorities refused to hire me. I would keep coming over and asking them to give me work, but the person in charge would tell me to go work on the highway construction site as a wage laborer. But I refused. I know he said it because that is what Dalits have to do—the worst jobs. Often women like me have to resort to those jobs, because we do not live with our men. But I was fortunate. My mother knew one of the school committee members, Daler Singh, and she requested him for a personal favor. He spoke to the Lamaji (monk) who manages the school. And he is the reason I got this job. Otherwise they would always send me back.

The people in charge would send me away every time saying they didn't need any more helpers.

But finally when they hired me, they promised to employ me here for as long as the school runs. I have two daughters and my children's education is free, thanks to this job. My older daughter, who is four, studies here.

H: So is this the same Lama who has been accused of child abuse—the one the teachers were meeting about earlier?

K: Yes, it's him. That was why it was so difficult for me to bring up this whole thing. I was in shock when I found the marks on the girl's body. He has always been so helpful to me, and my own daughter is the same age. At first when this child gave me the details, I could not believe it. But I had to do something. I had to do the right thing. So I told the principal and one of the committee members. They were worried about the girl, but also about what the funders might say, about the implications for the monastic order, all of it. Such a scandal it is bound to create. But something has to be done. He must be stopped and also penalized. This is why the school staff is meeting. Next there will be a meeting with the parents, maybe a community meeting—village level. Let's see. But at least for now the monster (Lamaji) is on a leash.

H: It took a lot of courage to stand up against the Lamaji in this place, right? Then why don't you want to be part of the school meetings on this issue?

K: No matter what I do, in this school my opinion doesn't count. Not all of them can admit it even, but they don't think a (Dalit) woman's point of view matters. Even if I did the right thing, they have to decide what the "right thing" is on their own. I already filed a report, made a complaint to the school authorities, then why do they want me to sit in on these meetings? I shall speak if they need me to, when the community meetings happen, or if the police get involved. They don't treat us well here.

H: Us, meaning all the helpers?

K: Whomever they think is lesser. Let me give you an example. One evening around 9:30 P.M., while we were ironing student uniforms after putting the children to bed, one of the teachers said: "One of these nights, after midnight, a man had visited the school. We saw a man in the dining hall." She said this in a manner that suggested that one of us had a late night visitor. We were shocked. I asked, "Who was here? Nobody visited any of us. Also if a man came into the school to visit one of us, why would he go to the dining hall?" Tell me, why would he do that? We told her what we knew. In the morning nobody said anything. But they waited and asked us again when we went upstairs the next night. And this led to an argument.

I asked why would any men come only for us in the hostel? Even you all live here. Anyone could have had a visitor. Why are we being singled out? Why is your honor more important than ours? Is it because we are poor, maybe? Or is it because I am Dalit? Where do we even have time for all this?

I felt terrible because I knew they were suggesting that I was the culprit. Because they know I left my husband they think I must not be a good mother and wife—I do not have honor. But such things can have consequences for people, I told them angrily. If rumors like these spread my husband will think I am getting involved with other men here and his case will become stronger in court. He already says that I have always been like this. It will only reinforce his suspicions and beliefs about me. And tilt the court case in his favor.

But the teachers were not happy at all that I had voiced my opinions so clearly. How could they not think about me—about my past (which they all know about) and my already tarnished reputation? And since then they began maintaining a log. Now they keep track of how much time which one of us is resting or working, throughout the day and evening. Plus, they have also written down details of what happened in our argument, in which it says that I answered back and was rude and harassed the teachers. It is difficult for women like me to survive in this world. This place is an educational institute. It's like a temple. But still . . . And then why should I attend meetings for a case where this poor child was abused? Why do they have to meet so many times anyway? Why can't they just report the Lamaji or publicly shame him right away? You know how hard we work. You know what the winter here is like. You know how cold the water is. Even now, just after summer—it freezes the fingers, when we wash dishes or clothes. Sometimes, of all of them, only the principal treats us with some respect. But none of them—none—ever acknowledge our work. And for me, they have already put me in a box—Dalit—thus, downtrodden I must be. To them, I am wrong in everything I do and say because they think they know me, because they think I don't know my place. They want me to believe that I am not honorable.

H: And you?

K: How shall I say it. . . . mmm I suppose the best way would be to say: I am Sob-hnu. The sun is in my gut and the moon is in my heart. There is no difference between the Khangsar Thakurs and me. But they have the land and the money.

Their daughter/s never face/d what I did every day. They have the government jobs, English accents, land, respect (*samman*)—at least here. But I have the same honor (*izzat*), yet don't receive the respect (samman) for it. I am honorable, no matter.

H: You make a distinction between respect and honor . . . could you talk a little more about that?

K: Well, yes. I understand that usually they go together usually, *samman* and *izzat*. But for me the two are not the same. I don't need the respect of the Thakurs to be honorable. I know I am honorable because I did nothing wrong. I didn't hurt anyone. I didn't force anyone. I didn't steal anything or run away with anybody's money. I am honest. This is why I said, the sun and the moon live inside me—I guess, I must be a step ahead of Sobhnu!

I want to tell my story. I want the world to know it. Especially other girls like me. Anyone else in my shoes would have killed herself—like others I have known. But I don't think it's worth my life—everything that has happened. I want other women to know through my story that there is hope; that they have reason to live; not die. I know you are not writing something that everyone will see, but I want to make a start. And since we were talking about honor, I want to tell you some more about why honor is so important to me. You know, after I was raped, [by the village priest], everyone expected me to die.

H: To die . . . as in physical death?

K: Yes, to commit suicide, like so many others before and after me. In films, in real life, we see it all the time, don't we? But I decided otherwise. Is my honor not honor? How is it that it seems so easy not to think of that—just because I'm from a "low caste" (*neechi jaati*). I am honorable too, because I am not guilty here. I am a woman and I had to be ashamed that a man did this to me. Only because I am a woman. Those men who rape should be ashamed. If he [the priest] can lift his head and walk, then why shouldn't I?

They must have hoped that I would give up and kill myself. That's what the priest wanted. This would have made everyone else's lives easy. But I never even contemplated suicide. I became isolated. I was now different from all the other girls. But still, I didn't want to give up. I thought to myself that if this is what he has done to me, I should also wait and watch the drama of his life unfold. His honor should be questioned, not mine. This is why I liked the campaign the *mahila mandal* did—because that's what we were asking, right? *Kiski Izzat Gayi*? Even if they don't respect me, my honor is intact. Why should I give up after he raped me ... I thought to myself, even on the worst nights, that I *will* stay alive and watch the drama of his life unfold ... his sorrows ... he is sure to be punished for his sins.

And in a later conversation:

K: I *will* raise my daughters differently, safely, that is something I really want and need now. At that time, I didn't know. Even when I met Vikram,[12] I didn't know I would have these two girls. But I really want them to be safe, and to love themselves.

Thus, Kavita re-makes the definition of honor, through a process of meaning-making embedded in her social experience of rape, of caste, and of gender. These *different* meanings that emerge from her own intersectional and complex subjectivity lead to a redefinition of honor that rejects the injustice of dominant caste and gender logics. Such a redefinition then, contrasts its own performance with available definitions of honor that structure femininity such that logics of gendered caste discipline individual women and the (caste) groups that they are part of.

By claiming her (Dalit) self as no less than the Khangsar Thakurs, Kavita rejects the normalized understanding of Lahauli Dalits ("Scheduled Caste") as "lesser" and thus "less" honorable than the warrior and priestly castes of the tribe. Rather, through the redefinition of Dalit (herself) as no different than the Thakurs, she illustrates even more starkly the dispossessed and oppressed status of Dalits within the violent system of domination that is caste. In narrating how she is not allowed entry into the school based solely on her caste until her mother uses her connection with a member of the committee, she battles and rejects the expectation of the non-Dalit tribal head of the school board who advises her to work on the highway construction team as a laborer and not in a school. Even when finally employed at the school, she faces caste and gender discrimination from the teachers who look upon her with suspicion—as already "tarnished"—for being Dalit and for living away from her husband. Further, she resists the violence of erasure, where her opinion does not count, by refusing to participate in school meetings about the incident, while still holding on to her position on the matter. Through this and several other stories, Kavita narrates the everyday injustice of the gendered terrain of caste society through her experiences and rejects the definition of honor within the politics of (gendered) caste as available through state and community discourses of honor. By thus performatively drawing upon a range of meanings of herself (Dalit/honorable) as the source of her resistance, she pushes against the multiple structures that simultaneously enact the (gendered) violence of caste.

In a similar performative maneuver of redefining honor by reclaiming it, another woman I interviewed, Phuntsok, the sister of a woman (Pema) who committed suicide when branded "dishonorable," rejects the dominant logic of caste and gender in restoring honor to her sister's memory.

RETURN TO US, HER LOST HONOR

Following a big argument with her husband one morning, Pema Devi walked out of their home with her son. Her husband followed them and, based on eyewitness accounts of people who crossed them on their path down the mountain, he continually yelled abuses at her, some that specifically meant "tarnished" and "loose." At some point during their walk, he attempted to hold her back physically, but Pema was very upset, said that she could not take his words, nor him hitting her again, and continued to walk away. When they reached the highway, she told her husband that she just wanted to be by herself with their son for some time. According to him, this was the point at which he decided to let her be and go to the local teashop and drink chhang (local brew), while waiting for her.

Per all eyewitness accounts, Pema Devi continued walking by herself, and walked off the bridge with her son tied to the front of her body, right over the confluence of the two rivers at the center of the Ghushal bridge. She tied her scarf to the railing (she was seen doing this by a witness who was walking down the mountain on the other side of the river) and then jumped off the bridge with her son tied to her back. While nobody witnessed the actual jump, the person who saw her tying the scarf stated that one minute she was tying the scarf, and when he looked at the bridge again, the next minute, she was gone. Her body was not found, nor her son's. A few people who had seen her last, and then saw her disappear, raised an alarm. Eventually, when people asked her husband where she was and he couldn't find her, but saw her scarf on the bridge, he realized that she was gone.

FIGURE 2.1. Tandi Bridge

Based on her family's statements, the police registered a case of suicide and one of abetment to suicide against her husband. Pema had visited her aunt a couple of days before her suicide and spoken at length of the violence that she experienced at her husband's and her in-laws' hands. However, when I spoke to the investigating officer, the police were on the verge of taking back the case against the husband, as they believed that her husband was innocent.

When I spoke to the police commissioner, he suggested that he had "heard reports" that the couple had been arguing about the fact that she became pregnant while he was away. However, her family denies this completely, and none of the witnesses who heard the couple fighting said they heard anything about a pregnancy, even when they did hear words being yelled at her that meant disrepute and dishonor, often used only with reference to the "loss" of a woman's chastity. Questioning the "honorability" of her actions because of a possible pregnancy emerged after her death, first to justify her death (an immoral woman has no option but to die) and to establish the man (her husband) as the "victim," rather than the aggressor, thereby freeing him of any responsibility for the violence before her death.

The local newspaper, *Dainik Bhaskar* (*Daily News*) covered the incident and stated that in the middle of the afternoon on that summer day, a woman from village Shumnam jumped off the bridge[13] with her son after tying her scarf to the railing of the bridge. The article also stated that the woman in question was a few months pregnant and that her husband who was a *jawan* (frontline foot soldier) in the army had only just arrived home from his posting last week after several months, thus suggesting that the child she was carrying had been conceived through an extra-marital relationship. This article, though apparently quite inaccurate, sealed the response to her suicide as not only inevitable, but also *necessary*.

The news article infuriated Pema's parents and her sister, who were enraged that her husband, the police, and the news media had relied on the age-old trick of rendering women dishonorable in order to preserve the honor of the men often responsible for their violation and devastation. They vehemently opposed the narrative being produced that Pema was not of "good moral character." Her sister, Phuntsok, fought with the newspaper editor and accused him of printing false news, since she was not even pregnant. The newspaper printed an apology a week later that was printed at the bottom of one of the inside pages where it would not receive much attention.

From Pema's sister and parents, I learned that she was routinely harassed and abused by her husband and his family on a variety of pretexts, including money. I was also told that they argued often over his (false) accusations that she was meeting other men while he was away for his army duty. She was extremely unhappy and, though she had left home on several occasions to return to her parents, she was sent back to her "true home" (since her parents were hoping for their problems to iron out and were also keen to follow societal norms wherein after marriage, every woman "belongs" in her husband's home). Somewhere along the way, Pema unfortunately stopped reaching out for help and ended her own life, along with her child's.

While interviewing Pema's sister, Phuntsok, the local newspaper's reliance on a dominant definition of honor to justify Pema's suicide came up several times. The theme of honor emerged in interviews with others in the family too (Pema's parents and aunt); however, Phuntsok had the strongest critique and redefinition of honor. A brief excerpt of one of my interviews with Phuntsok elucidates her perspective.

H: Did you have to go meet the editors at the *Dainik Bhaskar* several times before they issued their statement of apology?

P: It came as a shock to our entire family, this entirely fabricated story about her getting pregnant while her husband was away. We were grieving, we knew it was their relationship and her husband's abuse that finally led to Pema feeling so trapped she committed suicide. Otherwise she would never have taken such a drastic step. But we never expected that he would stoop so low to save his own skin. You know how valuable a woman's honor is considered to be, but here he was, slinging mud at her. And these irresponsible journalists spreading such rumors, only because it sounds juicy. But there are consequences. What about how my sister will now be remembered? Can they, can he, ever return to us her honor? They cannot, because to do that, to return her as honorable, they would have to return her to us.

In another conversation:

P: In our society, we have this honor talk wrong. The men use it to hide their faults and society continues to dishonor those it wants to keep inferior. But my sister was not dishonorable. In fact, it was the opposite. She was honorable— she fought for so long, tried so hard. She made a terrible decision in the end, and I will always regret not having brought her back home sooner, so that this would not happen. But no, she is not dishonorable. She had no choice, she did her best and then ended her life.

Repeatedly Phuntsok returned to the injustice of her sister's suicide and the narrative of (dis) honor that surrounded it, eventually entirely rejecting prevailing notions of honor as gendered, unjust, and wrongly understood. The return of honor to her sister's name was not a symbolic gesture reifying its violence. For her, the return of honor would also entail the impossible—the undoing of her sister's death. Further, the gesture of asking for a "return of honor" was also the means by which she established her sister as honorable. By shaming the dishonorers (Pema's husband, journalists at *Dainik Bhaskar*, and those entrenched in social ideals of honor) and by exposing the impossibility of a "return," Phuntsok also separated honor from its conventional "coatrack" approach (premised on the sexed body), to one that emphasized the viscerality of discourse and challenged the injustice implicit in the dishonor-ing narrative—that somehow Pema *deserved* to die.

In general, no coverage of any form of violence against women appears in the local media. Pema's case was in the media but not as a story about domestic violence. The article in the local paper supported the idea that she was dishonorable and doubly disparaged Pema by suggesting that she deserved death (since she was a dishonorable woman, and "our" culture upholds ideals of death before dishonor). Thus, even in death she remained dishonored because her "shame" was made public. The public awareness of her supposed dishonor and shame of course would also help her husband, who was now cast as the victim, in court when proving his innocence. By the time I interviewed the police officials, they were already considering dropping the charges against the man.

Pema's case illustrates how media coverage operated from the same ideological framework that guided the practices of the state. Cyclically, by operating from the same framework, the media corroborates the state's narratives. Further, the case reflects on a microcosmic level what happens at the macrocosmic level. Without deciding which account is true, at the very least the official version of the incident is markedly different from the accounts from Pema's family and from available eyewitnesses. Between the public and the private exists a discrepancy, but the intervening agent in the tension between these conflicting narratives is the media. Speaking from a journalistic position, the newspaper claimed "truth," and in doing so, the media undermined what the family might say about the loss of their child/daughter/sister. Pema's family uttered a narrative, officials of the state uttered another, and an intervening ideological discourse—the media—corroborated the narrative of the state. The meanings of honor and dishonor circulated within this intervening space, and it was finally Phuntsok who redefined honor. Similar conflicts and disconnects happen on a larger scale with individuals, the nation, and tribal political rhetoric.

Although the nation and tribal political rhetoric are different entities, they have a common ideology of honor that is based upon identification. As is discussed in greater depth in the following chapter, tribal political rhetoric asserts that their communities are honorable and that their standards of honor are the same as the nation's. Adivasi rhetoric takes great pains to show that Adivasis are not the nation's uncivilized Other. The newspaper in

Pema's case upheld this rhetoric when it assigned her the position of a dishonorable woman who committed suicide when she realized her folly. As with nationalism, a politics of identification is evident in the tribal political rhetoric. The tribal political rhetoric asserts a distinct tribal identity that needs to be restored to its glory. The terms of this restoration, however, privilege the ideology of the nation and the construction of women in ways that support Brahmanical patriarchy.

Pema's case is illustrative of precisely the tension that results from being honorable by upholding the ideology of the nation and by seeking a distinct identity of tribe. Thus the discourse corroborates the narratives of the nation in terms of honor and identity, while individual narratives, such as the narratives of Pema's family, become subordinated. When the nation speaks about tribal identity as though discrimination were non-existent, it obliterates—which literally means to make illegible by writing over letters that are already there—the narratives of individuals within the tribe. Similarly, the local newspaper reported Pema's story without speaking about the conditions of her life that led to her suicide. Instead of telling a story that accounted for her social location and the hierarchies that enabled the violence she experienced in her life, the news article shifted the focus to a discussion of honor thus justifying her suicide.

3 ⇴ STORIED LIVES

KEERTHI

As a child I did not exactly understand what being a Sipi meant, except that our community was different from the other communities, even though we lived in the same village. I heard stories from my grandfather that when he was a child in school in Lahaul, some practices connected to untouchability were changing. For example, people of higher caste would drink water from the hands of Dalits in my grandfather's generation. They could enter the houses of Thakurs and Brahmins in the village. By the time I was growing up, we were sharing food and were even offered the *bethku* in the homes of so-called higher-caste people. Repeatedly I heard my elders say it was not so bad in our Lahaul as in the plains, and after all, we were Lahaulis, all from this side of the Rohtang. And while I can agree that SCs of Lahaul are not as badly off as in other places, because we are still part of a tribal community, why should a little less discrimination be considered a good thing! For a long time I did not know the difference between a Sipi and a Thakur, especially in situations where both had the same amount of land. Let me explain: some Thakur descendants and Sipi families have equal amount of land. So I didn't know the difference in any direct way until I was old enough to understand that our (Sipi) land was always outside the village, not inherited from as far back, because it was gifted by the *Jajman* a couple of generations back. And of course, once I understood the caste rules for marriage, I grasped the difference better.

I went to the local village school and in one of my classes, I had a teacher from Kullu. He took a lot of interest in the students who did well; thus I got much encouragement. When I was home, trying to do my homework often my mother would tell me to just leave all that and learn how to get better at housework and farm work. But I loved going to school and wanted to do well, so I could go to college some day. That teacher from Kullu, he would tell me that I would go to college if I worked hard enough, no matter what anyone else said. I used to dream of college in Kullu or maybe even Shimla while I was finishing high school, until my younger sister who was only twelve years old was raped.

One afternoon, Kungrup, a man who lived in a neighboring village followed her when she was coming back from school and tried seducing her. When she realized what he was trying, she ran. It was right down by the creek. The sound of the water was so strong that none of us heard her screaming for help. In an attempt to escape from this man, my little sister ran into the clearing that was on the other side of the creek, surrounded by big trees into a location, where nobody would even be able to see them. It was terrible. He chased her and finally caught her in that clearing where she was hoping to hide.

She told me later that when he finished with her, he picked her up and made her wash herself with the water from the creek. She was so scared and hurt she was shaking. He carried her back into the path through the mountain and left her midway, so that someone would find her. Our neighbor found her there, crying, shaking. She was a child who had never harmed anything in the world.

It changed all our lives forever. My father filed a case, the mahila mandal women helped him. You were there, you know how the police weren't willing to help out, until the mandal got involved. Would they have done the same if we were not Sipi? There was no justice, really. But yes, there was some relief, some hope when he went to prison for five years. Yet we lived in fear of the day he would return. He promised to marry her. The village elders were keen to get their marriage fixed, even though it would be inter-caste. It was horrible; now where were their marriage rules? Or were they so scared that one of their own might stay in prison that suddenly nobody would mind the inter-caste marriage? Even the police were encouraging this marriage, instead of doing their job. Some in our family felt it was a noble thing he was offering to do, that he did not have to do it, but he was marrying her to save her honor. As though she had any interest in honor, at that age, when facing such injustice. I felt a kind of anger that I have no words for. I carried that anger for years.

It was as though her life, her body and her tears didn't matter in any of these discussions. Only in the mandal meetings was there some space for her needs. She kept silent through it all. After this event, I used to sleep next to her at night, and for a very long time, the only occasions I heard her speak was when she was asleep. She would cry night after night. And when my parents asked what she wanted to do, she would just stay silent. I knew she couldn't speak because she had demons in her body and her mind.

It brought us some consolation that he did go to jail for a few years, that the mahila mandal stood by us and helped my father through every step. This was when I became more involved with the mahila mandal too. People were supportive, but they could not do much as Kungrup, the man who did this is also a member of a ST. By the time he returned to Lahaul from prison, we had moved my sister to Kullu. This was why and how I went to college in Kullu, so that she could stay with me. It was no longer the fulfillment of a dream. It was to get past the nightmare. Even after I finished college she continued to live with me over there. She could not finish school—the thought of returning to that school or any other school created a lot of fear in her. But she began to weave and knit regularly, and started making really good designs for shawls, bethku covers, and socks. She is a very creative person, and weaving provided her solace, so I supported her. While living in Kullu I became much more active with the mahila mandal in Lahaul. I took care of many details for the group on the other side of the top. We had people in Kullu who supported us from the start—non-tribals and some Kinnauris.

Things were much smoother for us in Kullu, because we could just be part of a bigger crowd and people only identified us as Lahauli, not as Sipi so nobody knew our caste. And generally it was also easier to hide her history, which helped her heal. We were of course identifiable as Lahaulis. But in Kullu valley, Lahaulis are well regarded, despite being ST, even though a lot of people are jealous because of the agricultural success of the Lahauli farmers. The way Lahaulis are regarded in Kullu is very different from how people treat other STs in the plains. In Kullu we are generally seen as more prosperous, and as helping the local economy. A lot of families have two homes like us, one in Lahaul and one in Kullu for the winter and we are often considered good looking because of our skin color. Many Lahaulis have government jobs too, in particular those from Thakur families. They are IAS, IPS, and other such high-ranking civil servants. Even from our castes people get government jobs, but not like the special twice-born tribals! Our community members get jobs with district offices as peons, typists, clerks, and such, depending on education and skill level. A few people have qualified for civil exams, but not many. And in general, Lahaulis have a reputation of being hardworking and strong. At least the women do. Our labor shows in our bodies. Lahauli men were very active in the Indo-China war in the 1960s. Other than that our men aren't as hardworking as us! And I think because most Lahaulis including me, often identify as both, Buddhist and Hindu, there is greater respect for us. I think it would be different if Bodh *dharam* wasn't seen as the spine of our society. Then we would be treated worse as STs, even in Kullu I think. But there is this thing—oh, they are Buddhist and they are in a remote region so they are ST.

But then, here is what I don't understand about our Lahaul. If we are Buddhist, why is there caste? Didn't Ambedkar convert to Buddhism because of caste among Hindus? But in Lahaul, even Buddhists did not eat with the Lohars and Sipis. Now they eat together, but still don't inter-marry. Even though inter-religious marriages are allowed, it is an unspoken rule that inter-caste marriages are not accepted. There have been a few cases, but not many. In fact, with inter-religious marriages, i.e. Hindu–Buddhist, no conversion is even expected or needed. Say the wife is Buddhist and the husband is Hindu, each person's last rites and cremation will be conducted as per their respective religion's rituals and rules. Thus I always question where all these different groups of people who call themselves "Lahauli" or "Lahaula" came from. They must not have all moved together else why and how would there be so much diversity within our tribe? I have always been very interested in knowing the origins of things around me—people, regions, words and such. If I had studied beyond my college years, then I would have opted for a post-graduate degree in History. I used to dream about first studying history, then getting a B.Ed. degree and becoming a history teacher. But that's not quite what life had in store for me. Still, I have no problem with the things I do. I have studied many things, learnt a lot and I hope to continue doing so. My main goal is that future generations should definitely not be robbed of the same opportunities; they should not suffer because of this *jati-pratha* (caste system) that has been forced upon us in Lahaul.

Because I studied history in college and this interest never left my heart, I continue to study it—not only through books and exams but from all kinds of teachers like my elders. My grandparents in particular, have taught me a lot about our community.

When I was growing up it was different for my community than the time in which my grandparents and parents were raised.

There are so many stories about where we came from or even where the people of Lahaul have come from. There is the belief that the Swangla (of Pattan valley) are Hindu, and claim they were Shaivaites, consisting mainly of Brahmins and Rajputs, whose ancestors moved to Lahaul from Kashmir. They are supposed to have brought the caste system with them. They also brought the *Kirati* people whose labor and skills they needed in order to survive in a new place. These Kiratis are *lohar*, *sipi* and other so-called low trade castes, i.e. Dalits, like me. But here is the problem with this story: how can they claim that the Swangla people were both Adivasi and Hindu? And say for a moment that was possible, because indeed a lot of Adivasi gods and goddesses were absorbed into the Hindu pantheon of deities, the question of language remains. How is it that the Kiratis speak a language that is much closer to Sanskrit than the Swangla? This is a question that Mr. Lal Chand Dhissa raises too.

My attempts at understanding the origins of us Lahaulis have exposed one thing for sure—that there is no definitive answer, nor is there any rigid historical trajectory that was handed down by the Gods or such. No. Groups of people in the Himalayas—different communities who are called "nomadic tribes"—moved around, like in the rest of our country, and wherever they settled, they decided to continue the enforcement of these hierarchies. Thus caste discrimination is still burning and alive, even when there is no logical explanation as to how caste came to be relevant in this region. But as we like to say here, *hai toe hai na ji* (it is what it is)! What we have is what has been handed down from our ancestors, but a lot of it has also been heavily modified by later generations to suit those who are the *satta* (government) and the *samant* (ruler). Some groups need to control other groups in order to survive, this is just how the world continues, not just in our Lahaul.

It is like how men behave in general too. Unless there is control over women, unless men have the final say, there is too much drama. Here in Lahaul too, for example they say our society and families are structured around women, and our women are highly valued and such. But at the same time, women don't get property as per our customary law; they sit at a lower level *bethku* than men in public and family functions, they get less elaborate *bethkus*, even in the so-called better castes, the list goes on. All of this of course is within caste boundaries. Caste is like a big blanket that covers every other social grouping and it blocks any light from entering the room.

But no matter what anyone claims I am; whether they say I am Adivasi-Dalit or Dalit or Adivasi, I have a question: I want my space and share. This is my struggle.

After I finished college I got a staff job in the district court. For a while I thought I could study more and become a lawyer, but it was more important to have a job at that moment so I studied for a computer certificate instead. I got a job with a trading company in lower Kullu. I got a big salary, more than I had ever thought possible. I also helped my sister sell her shawls to the local shopkeepers who of course sold the same shawl for a much higher price to tourists! But that was only in the beginning. Then, through the mahila mandal in Lahaul the Kinnauri shop owner in Manali became linked to us because of his interest in supporting the group. My sister also got linked with the NGO in Manali and a few individuals who were trying to support single Lahauli women become financially independent. My sister did quite well, selling those shawls. And she met this man who came from Chandigarh to buy shawls for his shop. The Kinnauri shop owner asked us to meet him. It was so unexpected the way things happened—I couldn't be happier for my sister. Even though at first I was very worried, because at first I thought this man from Chandigarh was just using her. You know, these big city men, they just sometimes take advantage of simple village girls, so I didn't trust him. But then he turned out quite alright. They got married and she has a child, and lives in Chandigarh with him. She helps him run his business, and they have a small quarter. I feel like Ghepan took care of her after all; he gave my family the strength and support we needed to not leave her at Kungrup's mercy.

I was happy for my sister, but my own resolve to remain single continued, even though I did not have to worry as much about my sister anymore. Mostly I decided to remain single and unmarried, even though I have had a few lovers, because I did not want to live under a man's control. I felt then, and continue to feel now that I did not need to be married to be with someone. Because then I would have to work on his family's land and also continue with a job if I got a posting in Lahaul. In my case though, something unexpected happened: my brothers gave me a part of the family land. It was my father's promise, so that my sister and I would not be dependent on anyone after his death. Thus, after my sister got married and moved, I eventually returned to Lahaul to take care of my own piece of land. If I got married I would lose that, and would work on someone else's land.

Not only do Lahauli women not inherit any land, as a Sipi (Dalit caste) woman to have land in my name brings me an incredible feeling of freedom. It makes me so happy when I think of that. What my father did when he left equal share of the land for us, that was love. He knew that the land he had inherited from his ancestors was land which our ancestors were never considered the rightful owners of. It was land that at one time belonged to the Jajman and was given to my ancestors for pleasing the Jajman. So really, if you think about it my ancestors knew what it was like to be landless, and thus their love for this land came from their struggle within the unjust *Jajmani* system. This is why my father left my sister and me some land. He must have thought that we may not marry and then this would be ours, to see us through. Even my mother wasn't very sure of how people might react, how our brother might feel since he divided it equally. But my father, he went against everything he knew, to do something he felt was right. It was the same when my sister was raped and everyone except the women's group was telling him to give up, but he didn't. In that fight, my mother and I were a hundred percent with him. But still, he must have been worried about not being able to protect us if the other men decided to harm us. But most importantly he wanted justice and that was his love for us. I remember the way his default facial expression transformed permanently after my sister's rape. His eyes would sometimes be red and I knew it must be because he had been crying a lot. That love which my father had for us and which my sister and I share is what propelled me to work for other girls in our position.

That is how I worked in the mahila mandal for a long time, when I lived in Kullu and even after I came back to Lahaul. My days seemed so much more worthwhile when I could be part of the support system for women who had all these terrible things happen to them—*balatkaar, mar-peet, zabardasti biyah* . . . When we could challenge forced marriages; question the men's logic in village meetings, it was as though I was able to do something for my sister. It felt like through those cases I was fighting back against the injustice she experienced, and that we all faced throughout our lives in different ways.

PARVATI

I want to start with my first husband—he's a good place to start because he's no longer part of my life. I am from the Ghara community, even though my mother's side had someone marrying into the Thakur caste, who in turn have some link to the Khangsar Thakurs. I suppose if I hadn't faced any "special" treatment for belonging to an untouchable community, I could say I was mixed. I have papers for both, SC and ST and this man, my first husband, he is from a higher caste. But he thought I was beautiful so he carried me off a field near Tholong. I had to marry him—this was how our Lahaul had become—with most cases of *kuji biyah* being forced. And then we were also inter-caste. But what he did not know was that I had a medical condition and I was *baanj* (sterile). So I hid it from him. Why tell him the truth about my body when he forced me—that was what I decided. I have never menstruated, so I never really became a woman in that way. I had learnt how to hide it, it was necessary to survive and not be ridiculed by everyone, so even though I went to meet the doctors regularly for this problem, it was still something that had to be kept a secret. My mother always worried that marrying my sisters would be hard if people found out about my condition.

My ex-husband spotted me at the August fair in Keylong when I was barely seventeen, just having cleared my tenth class exams. He was drinking with his friends and when I walked by, he tried talking to me. I avoided his questions about my village and our family's whereabouts and excused myself saying my mother was waiting. He came up to me at the fair the next day again and asked if I liked him. I said I was not interested. He asked if I would say yes to him if he sent me a *ngya* and I said no. This made him very upset. He thought I was too proud.

But the reason I had said no was because I didn't want to get married at all. My parents had very little land, and very few animals. We were not from a landed caste. My mother could hardly find enough wool to weave shawls through the winter months. In the summer, my mother would work on the highway to earn daily wages and my father would find small jobs in Manali. So, from a very early age I took care of my siblings, even worked on the highway once I was a teenager. I used to think that maybe someday I could get a government job, as a cleaner in the district office or some other post at the hospital. I had completed high school, so I wanted to do something with my life and support my family.

After his proposition at the fair, I received a *ngya* which I returned through a friend. My friend was scared for me because I had rejected him. She asked how I would escape the inevitable and I said I had to at least try. My life changed drastically after I rejected his *ngya*. I was constantly looking over my shoulder. It was a common thing in our Lahaul at that time, much much more than now. If you said no to a man, you had to be careful. Walking back after sundown from the fields that I labored on for daily wages, was now a completely different experience than before. In the past, those few minutes used to be mine, for me to think about whatever I wanted, to dream, to look at the sky, the mountains, hear the sounds of the river. But now all of this changed. And as I had feared, one such evening I was abducted.

A group of men had parked a jeep on the highway, but they had the lights off, so I didn't know that anyone was climbing up the mountain as I was coming down. They waited on the side, and as soon as I arrived, he picked me up and put me on his shoulder. I attempted to stop him, flailing my arms and legs. I tried biting his shoulder as he carried me but to no avail. When we reached his house, he molested me, over my *cholu*. I hit him quite hard and when he tried again, I got so fearful that I fainted! He got scared, he told me later. He ran away without doing anything further, left me locked in the room and went downstairs to hang out with his friends so nobody could blame him if something went wrong. The next morning, I woke up next to him. I wanted to kick him hard, but I said nothing instead. My parents were so poor, I knew they wouldn't even have the money to come looking for me in a jeep. We were not a (Dalit) caste family, but we were not thakurs or baniyas either. I had to adjust to this reality, and I told him that someone from his family should contact mine, and offer to bring them to his village. At least he had to give me that much. He agreed and sent his younger brother with a message. My parents came and I cried my heart out. But I knew it was over and that I would be married to this man. My mother said at least they were a better caste, had much land and sold hundreds of sacks of potatoes to the traders from Punjab.

After that, any time he touched me I would think of the sacks full of potatoes and the traders from Punjab who bought them. And before I knew it, my husband would be done!

This was how my first marriage came to be. And this was why I chose not to tell him that I could never be pregnant. He lived many years not knowing if it was his problem or mine that caused us to remain childless. I pretended to have my monthly period regularly for the five years I was married to him. He worried constantly about being infertile, sometimes even took it out on me. But I never told him about myself; it was my secret and I was not going to give him the chance to demean me even more. But eventually he did find out. Someone from my maternal village confirmed his suspicion and he asked me directly. I admitted it. There was no way I could lie and get away with it any longer. If he went to Keylong hospital and asked for my records the nurses would share them with him and he would know.

He was livid and threatened to divorce me. I was just fine with that possibility, so I told him to do so. Not only would I not have to work on his agricultural fields, I would also not have to look after him and all his family! That was my first thought and I made it clear that I wasn't going to be heartbroken if he left me. But I also felt certain that he would not make a big public scene of it, because he kept saying that I was not a real woman, that I was a half-woman and he was ashamed he had spent so many years being married to me. He hurt me with his words. He said it all made sense to him now as to why I did not have a soft and feminine appearance. He suddenly made it sound like he had never considered me pretty, which I knew wasn't true. He made it sound like I had not helped him through life at all, like I had no value, now that he had this information.

It made me feel sad. Reminded me of how when I was a teenager I spent years waiting for my period. My mother was certain I would start my period like the other girls. She would assure me saying many girls start late every time a friend or cousin started theirs. But then at some point her hope changed into despair, I didn't even realize when this shift happened. I was fine, I felt pretty like the other girls, so what if I didn't have my period; so what that I had big shoulders and arms and hands. Any case Lahauli women, including the Thakur women, all have rough skin on their hands and feet. It's because of the hard labor we have to do. This is just the reality of the mountain life. And my never-quite-a-woman life wasn't too different from everyone else's, except for the missing period. In fact, I was the only girl who wasn't crying in pain every month! My mother began taking me to doctors from my seventeenth birthday onwards. First it was the Men-Tsee-Khang *chomo* (nun) doctor. Then it was the amchi in another valley, where our family would not be as easily identified. So we took long bus rides to Ladakh and met the best amchis, but nobody could cure me of my problem. I look back at that time in my life and can never understand why everybody around me thought I was ill. It was the opposite, I was among the few girls who never got sick from the monthly blues and periods. I could work on the agricultural fields like everyone else, in fact I never had to take a break!

Gradually my mother began to suggest that I lie about my condition. That I not only never mention my condition but that I actively participate in conversations about periods, cramps, mood swings and such. It was such a heavy burden—what can I say. I was always scared that someone or the other would find out. But my friends were kind; even if some of them had figured it out they never said anything. Sometimes others in school or mean cousins would say things like "Oh, she's a man. Maybe this one will be the best *Ghara* warrior of Lahaul—look at her hands and her feet." My mother's family had some Thakur lineage, but really we were just Ghara. My mother always praised my fair skin, and told me to care for my long beautiful hair so I could look better than most of the girls and I did.

That first year with my first husband was the hardest year of my life. But after that it was generally ok. I didn't care much for the sex with him though. He was not too active in bed. He would start and finish in a second! It was not good like how it is with my current husband. I will tell you about this one some other time. Nobody would imagine it, but this old guy is really good at his business in bed. After that first year, my life with my first husband wasn't the worst. I didn't like doing so much work, pretending to be getting a period when I didn't, the constant cooking and cleaning for his entire extended family—but much of that is what all Lahauli women have to go through. And the divorce brought relief because he did not love or honor me.

Yet it is not as though after the divorce life was easy for me. My secret was out. People used to talk behind my back. Sometimes to my face they would call me *baanj* (sterile) and that I had manipulated my husband into staying with me. Everyone it would seem, had forgotten that I had been abducted;

that I did not have much choice but to marry him. They also forgot that I toiled on his land for years and got no piece of it, yet he got everything from me—agricultural worker, housekeeper, lover, wife: the only thing I couldn't give him was a child. And I would even have understood and encouraged him to have a child with another woman if he hadn't forced me to marry him, if he had been good to me. But he wasn't. He hit me in anger and frustration—maybe once a year or so—but it was humiliating, no matter how few times it happened. He would get angry and say things about my parents being poor and how I would have been working on the highway if he hadn't "saved" me. Therefore, partially because of my anger towards him, and partially out of my fear of the aftermath, I never did disclose my secret to him.

And after he found out I did not want to face the humiliation and his wrath thus I agreed to the divorce without any protest. He left me with nothing, not even what my parents gave me at the wedding and which, by Lahauli custom belongs to me. He said it belonged to his new wife who was the same caste as him and I didn't protest. What was the use? I was relieved to be rid of him. After the divorce, even though my parents had passed away, I lived in my maternal home with my uncles and brothers. My mother sat with all the brothers in my father's family. They were in a joint marriage, so the entire family still lived on the same land and worked on it together. I stayed there. That is, until my second husband proposed. He was very direct; said he knew about my condition but didn't care because he had grown children from his first wife who had recently passed away. He is much older than me, but I was drawn to him. He promised that I wouldn't have to work in the fields or care for the animals all winter long, and that he would bring me to Keylong where I could stay with him in his quarter. He was smitten by my beauty, and would quote lines from popular love songs.

I knew people spoke disparagingly of him, and of us as a bad match—he isn't conventionally good looking. He is quite dark complexioned compared to me, and is also much older. Finally, there is the fact that my first husband was of higher caste than me while my second husband was in a similar, if not lower caste, because people on my mother's side like to bring up their Thakur lineage, even though it is a very distant one. My parents did not have an inter-caste marriage. They would never have allowed it in their time. Nowadays people just avoid it, it works like an unspoken understanding.

But really, we are both Lahaulis, both tribals. What difference does it make? When we step out of Lahaul, we are placed in one "box" as *paharis* and tribals because of our facial features. And even when inside our beautiful valley Lahaul, we are made of the same flesh and blood. The same heart, yes?

We are Buddhists. Then why should caste even enter the picture? But people are so small minded that they care about all this. So many people just made fun of us, wished us ill. These jealous unhappy people of my village said I was marrying him for his job and pension. I want to ask those people what the difference is between them and the people of the plains? Why do they complain about how the plains people treat us different, like we have no idea how to live? Why do they feel bad when some Lahauli marries a person from Kullu or Chandigarh and that person's family discriminates against us? Aren't they doing the same with my husband and me? Why would a tribal person pretend to be placed socially higher than the Dalit caste person? I don't understand this. On the one hand we want to be united as Lahaulis and not let the plains people and the government make us feel bad or take away our land, our customs and such. On the other, inside the boundaries of our beloved mountains we will discriminate against each other—exactly like the plains people do to us, we do to each other! That just does not add up—do the *hisaab* (math) yourself, I tell people.

And of course because of this attitude Lahaulis adopt on this side of the top, so many folks could not comprehend that love was possible between my husband and I, or that either of us even deserve it. He because he is Dalit and me, for being both, a Dalit, and also a "freak"—never a real woman. I wear a cholu and a scarf. But they can only see a freak. So no, our love and how we have built this love in bits and pieces, through pain and joy, has never been understood or even accepted by society, except for those who have eaten with us, entered our home and touched our untouchability. Because when you do love a person, you love who they are as much as how they are. I love his being—that includes everything that makes him. I love all the things he is—as caste-person, as older, as Lahauli and as a man. That he is the one who stormed into my heart and brought me the most peace I have ever known.

And honestly, here we don't have as many bad caste cases (atrocities) as in the plains. You know, people may exclude you silently, or just keep their distance and such, but they don't beat you up or kill you like they do in UP and MP for inter-caste marriage. But it is important to address mental torture and social shame, those are also atrocities. I mean for example, a group like the one in Delhi, *pyar ke commandos* (Love Commandos) isn't really needed for the physical protection and safety of inter-caste couples in Lahaul. But it would be great if we could have our own Lahauli version of commandos who would bring the issue up and tell people to just stop discrimination at all levels. I had an inter-caste marriage the first time, but I did not choose it. So if we had Love Commandos here they could work on this issue—to encourage inter-caste marriages with consent of all parties.

Many Lahauli Dalits have land, even if outside the main village, but who cares about that nowadays. My husband's family has land, outside the village, and they grow a lot of potatoes. And you know, this means a lot of money. Even if he did not have the government job as a watchman he would be fine with money, but yes, in that case I would have had to do a lot more hard agricultural labor. And then, there's also the fact that his having the government job helped his children with their schooling and other facilities in Keylong. It helped him with his first wife's medical treatment, given that the hospital is in Keylong. Poor woman suffered quite a lot in the end.

Most importantly though, this job allowed him to send his daughter to Kullu. This makes me very proud of him, and of her. She's very smart, closer to my age, and also very pretty. We get along very well. I talk to her about her mother, her future plans and such. And a little bit of distance from Lahaul has surely helped her. She is in Manali, where people don't already know her family and caste. So she can mingle in the crowds there without anyone talking about her father's new younger wife!

Sometimes I think of what it would be like if my mother had been around and she knew that I married this guy. Would she mind that he is so much older? I doubt she would care about his caste, though I know that she was quite glad my first husband was higher caste. I think her family would start praying to Ghepan immediately because there is some distant linkage on her side to the Khangsar Thakurs and you know how that goes. Even now people walk backwards, doing their nonstop "Jule-ji," not wanting to show their backs to the Khangsar Thakur family members. In this day and age if these people want to behave like this and live under the Thakurs, as though they are still the *sarkar*, then let them. What can one say—all they have to do is come out of the village, walk in to the district headquarters and know that the law prohibits all such things. But no, they want to call it "reverence." So let them.

One of the Khangsar younger sons married the daughter of a nono from Kashmir. And their daughter is now the rani of Ladakh. So of course with all the raja-rani related excitement within the extended family they act as though they are all actually connected to the queen of England.

At other times I think my mother would be happy if she saw my life. She knew what a burden it was for me, to carry my secret around even from my own husband that first time. If she saw me this free, it would be beyond what she or any of us had expected as possible for me. She would be quite delighted I think, if I told her this: Ama, every winter, without fail, this man brings me from the village to the district headquarters Keylong. I don't stay with the animals in the cold like the other women in our village. He and I cook together in the little government quarter, get water from the tube well nearby even in the winter, weave shawls, watch TV, and listen to the radio together. His daughter is my friend and she respects me. I did not take him away from anyone that loves him.

I spend days and nights with him in the quarter, listening to songs, to the news. We walk about the streets when the sun is up and spend our nights next to each other. We hope that future generations will not discriminate so much. We protest, talk, fight, even get a few tomatoes in the winter when the district officers give some to my husband—this is how we love. I couldn't ask for more. It's a small quarter but it's cozy and warm. And our window looks straight out at the Saptapadi. It is as though our room faces the seven steps that complete the wedding ceremony to celebrate us every day, despite all the adversity. I feel I must have done something right. Some day in some life I made Raja Ghepan happy. So he brought me my life-partner to end my hardships.

DOLMA

I was born right on that mountain which you can see in the back, behind Tholong, the village that comes before Khangsar . . . When we stood on our side of the village, we could see the snowcapped peaks on the mountains across the river. There was always some snow on the peaks, no matter what month, or how much sunshine there was. And in the winter of course, it was just snow, snow, and more snow everywhere.

From the time I was a little girl I wanted to study, but it didn't make sense to anyone in my family. In those days there weren't really any schools at the village and what would I do with that in any case, since it was understood that I would spend most of my life doing agricultural labor. I guess they were right. My father was from the Khangsar Thakur family but not a direct descendant. So we did not have as much land but still we were never without anything we needed. I always knew I wouldn't inherit any part of whatever land my family had, given our Lahaul's customs. Some families give their daughters a small piece of land, if they remain single in order to continue looking after the family property, which otherwise gets handed down from father to son. But I knew my brothers wouldn't even inherit much land, so sharing with me was not an idea anyone would entertain. Despite the fact that our family did not receive as much land as they deserved from being part of the Thakur family, across generations we have continued to believe and trust in the nonos of that line. My sons have raised some of their concerns about the unfairness of the land inheritance with me. And even though I agree that my family deserved a better, larger share, I told my sons to look ahead because they would not get any land from my side of the family in any case because I wouldn't inherit any. So I told them to make a life out of what they have, get employment with the government and find financial security through education. They will inherit some share of their father's land, though when my husband was alive he did not participate much in the family's decisions. If he had lived and we had stayed with his family, it could have been a different situation, but in his absence I did the best I could.

My husband was killed over a game of *chholo*. I found him, carefully placed in a sitting position under the tree a few kilometers away from here, on the other side of the highway. I was beside myself with grief. At first I didn't know what was going on that fateful evening. I thought my husband was just late because of his gambling and drinking habits. So I thought maybe he was still playing cards with his friends and that afternoon he was simply delayed coming home. Then closer to sundown I got a little worried and someone from our village said there had been a fight near Gemur village where my husband usually hung out and played. I panicked and put on my scarf, my shawl, washed my hands and ran towards Gemur to see what might be going on.

It was one of the Thakur brothers who helped me. He said I was his sister (cousin) and convinced me to not spend time and energy trying to find the killer/s. He said to not give up on the idea of a future for my children because of this tragedy and to look ahead. He explained to me that there would be no point, since the killer/s had to have been from among my husband's friends who were playing the game and drinking with him that day. To help me get by, he gave me this piece of land by the river and suggested I grow my own crops. This way I would not have to return to my husband's family and work on their farms to survive. I took the offer and have always been grateful to him and to the Thakurs for this. They visit me whenever they come in from the city and bring their families too. They treat me like one of their own.

I have cultivated on this little patch of land ever since my husband died. I had three children, and since that awful day when he left us, numerous times I just wanted to jump into the river with my three babies to end it all. But this little piece of land, and the possibility of a future for my children even though my husband had such an unfair and untimely death, helped me survive. And of course as you well know, I survived also because of all the *chhang* that runs through my veins.

When my husband was around life was very different. We had problems like other couples, and sometimes his behavior was not acceptable. For the most part I could never say anything harsh to him in those moments, even though at times I really wanted to. In any case as a woman, even though related to the princely family, I knew that I would have spent my life working on agricultural fields—large or small, what matter. And more than anything else, during our difficult days, I would remind myself that he was only one love in my life. I had so many other loves to cherish, to live, and to learn. Despite him playing chholo so regularly we were happy. I prayed to Ghepan for this to become possible some day, that my husband would leave his addiction to chholo behind, and that this cycle should end.

And then it all did indeed end—abruptly and violently—not quite how I had imagined it. Someone just killed him with a knife, over a game. That is all I heard about it. Even if I wanted to know more and longed for justice, I knew I did not have the resources for that. I was a widow with three very young children. Most men were like vultures, trying to sweet talk me into sitting with them after my husband died. I kept a very stern exterior and warded off the men who tried, even though I lived in fear of violence.

Many people suggested that I settle down with another man since I was young and pretty, and because the unwanted attention may not end soon. But I had decided to live as a *chomo* (nun). Having this small piece of land right by the river allowed me to do so, without having to sit with one of my husband's brothers. One of them tried convincing me that he would look after us if I stayed. But I knew I would have to take him as a husband to stay in the family. My life with my husband over the years and my grief over his death were both too much for me to bear. I did not think it would be possible to live with another man.

And now when I look around, this is what I see: part of my little mud hut is *pucca*. Slowly I have built a concrete section. I even have a little guest room upstairs with glass windows, from where you can see our mountains. If I can build a toilet separately then maybe I can even run it as a guesthouse someday. I have this little shop, selling basic groceries and chhang which I make at home. I built every bit with love, with my own hands. This hut, by the *Bhaga* (river) facing the mountain on one side and the highway on the other, it is the fruit of my love.

I even keep the communal Yak for our village, even though I live alone, because my location is so good. The tube well is so near, the bus stop is right here, as is the Men-Tsee-Khang. The big hotel is across the highway, so a lot of foreign tourists stop by. The chomo and her assistant at the Men-Tsee-Khang are always around and we're friends. Palmo is so nearby too—she is my dearest friend, we are sisters. So being in this little hut, on this small patch of land has been the best thing for me. I have never had to look for company or felt lonely. Even in the winter, it is the perfect place for me. Now my oldest son has helped me build a small room in Kullu, since he has a bank job in Dharamsala. I have severe pain in my joints—arthritis. It is very common in Lahaul, especially among women, because we spend so much time climbing up and down the mountains, and also work in the water. So it is a luxury to have a room in Kullu where I can stay warm in the winters. My daughter is married; she had a mangni biyah, even though she always wanted to go live in Shimla. And my youngest son, I just want him to finish high school without going astray. He's simple and people are putting ideas in his head—that he can marry some fancy tourist in Kullu and go to London or something. When he told me I just threw the glass I was holding in my hand in his direction. He dodged it of course! What fancy tourist is this fool dreaming of! And he doesn't even realize that his "friends" are just making fun of him, using him to do their bidding because he's simple. I already told him that he can manage my shop. That's it for him, unless he gets a job of course. It's a wonderful thing, this shop. I have such a small piece of land that often I work on my friends' farms, or in the communal land. Here we don't think about land like it's only mine or only yours. Though now things are different than when we were younger. Now it's all very modern. But still, the important thing is that after I work with my friends on the fields, we cook and celebrate together. Right here. How many times you ate here, can you recall?

The best thing that I worked on, from scratch, is this little shop. I built it myself. I met so many different people from different parts of the world, all sitting right here in Stod valley. How lucky am I! I met Americans even before you went to America! Ha!

My best days are right here, when I cook huge pots of *thukpa* and host the fanciest momo parties for the mahila mandal in my little home—I am famous for this! In the end, the rest of my life did not turn out so bad.

4 ❧ NARRATING LOVE

Kavita[1] and I are walking through the streets of Kullu[2] town, discussing her decision to move out of Lahaul[3] permanently. "I had to hide. I needed to start afresh, in a place where I would not be recognized through my status. My daughters are growing up now—it is necessary that they learn to think highly of themselves, as girls and as Dalits,[4] as girls who deserve love, from everyone. But for these formative years of their lives I just want to protect them. Say you're a 'Sharma' if they ask you—who will know in Kullu—Sharma[5] or Lohar, I told them. Who will find out here?"

Keerthi[6] an Adivasi-Dalit woman, tells the story of how she came to inherit an equal share of her family's land despite the customary law of Lahaul, which does not grant property rights to women. She says,

> What my father did when he left equal share of the land for us that was love. He knew that the land he had inherited from his ancestors was land, which was never considered the rightful property of Dalits. It was land that at one time belonged to the *Jajman* and was given to my ancestors on account of having pleased the *Jajman*. So really, if you think about it, my ancestors knew what it was like to be landless, and thus their love for this land came from their struggle within the unjust *Jajmani* system. This is why my father left my sister and me some land.

Love, in these quotes from interviews with Kavita and Keerthi, and throughout the women's narratives appears as a verb, a frame—a thread even—with which the women weave their stories. For both Kavita and Keerthi, love not only operates as self-worth and affirmation, but also as a condemnation of caste and caste-based discrimination. Kavita moves to the neighboring district of Kullu to avoid multiple discriminatory labels—a Dalit single mother of two with a history of caste-based rape who is estranged from her husband—which are inescapably and identifiably mapped onto her in Lahaul. Yet in talking to me about it, she resists these labels and rejects caste. Instead she discusses the everyday strategies through which she negotiates these labels. By choosing a location that provides her (caste) anonymity and by directing her daughters to use the privileged-caste last name "Sharma," she rejects the interpellative strength of the violence of caste enacted through such an identification. While she uses another name for her daughters to avoid being identified as Dalits from a need to protect them from the discrimination that she believes will follow such identification, she also adds that she wants them to love *their* selves, as Dalits. Once again, by *choosing* to love the self that has historically been the object of hatred, she connects love of the self to a love of the community. In telling the story of how she resists and rejects the name-based identifications of caste-society in this way, Kavita demonstrates how love is necessary, especially in the face of hatred. In this way, this narration of self-love is in fact a form of resistance. Therefore the mode of storytelling she adopts is in fact the labor of love—the process of recognizing the self as a lovable subject.

Similarly for Keerthi, the fact of inheriting ancestral land, as an Adivasi-Dalit, transforms the inheritance-related decision her father makes into an act of love. And this love is the mode through which she chooses to tell the story of her inheritance. By connecting the love that she believes her father acted upon, to the long history of landlessness, bonded labor on the Jajman's[7] land, and disenfranchisement of Dalit communities in caste-society, she articulates her inheritance as an act of resistance. By choosing to narrate such everyday enactments of caste-resistance through an articulation of love, both Kavita and Keerthi demonstrate the workings of love as a politic (Nash 2014).

Their call to love is a call to not only resist caste domination, but seek justice. Such an articulation of love, especially in the face of hatred and violence makes it a political project and transforms what might otherwise be understood as "ordinary love"—that between a parent and child—into "radical love," which rejects hegemonic constructions of self and community (Jordan 1978; Lorde 1979). Kavita, Keerthi, and others in storying their lives through a range of such re-articulations of love, demonstrate the overlaps and inseparability of "ordinary love" and "radical love" through a focus on seeking justice.

Such a linking of love and justice has a long history in the context of social movements the world over, including those against caste and racial injustice. Dr. B.R. Ambedkar in his 1932 letter to the general secretary of the Harijan Sevak Sangh, attempted to convince the *Sangh* to include members of the Dalit community in the organization which was created solely for the purposes of ending untouchability. His primary arguments centered around linking love and justice, "The touchables and the untouchables cannot be held together by law. . . . The only thing that can hold them together is love. Outside the family, justice alone in my opinion, can open the possibility of love . . ." (B.R. Ambedkar 1989 [1932], in *Gandhi and his Fast*, p. 371). Beyond his call to love as the only route to ending caste injustice, Ambedkar also extensively discussed love in the context of compassion and humanity, through Buddhist principles, in everyday life. In discussing love as central to justice and humanity, Ambedkar quotes Gautam Buddha's doctrine of Love, among others, while critiquing and distancing himself from, the call for love Gandhi sought between oppressed and privileged castes, as a form of liberal caste-Hindu benevolence to end caste-discrimination while still maintaining caste heirarchies (Ambedkar 1943; 1989). Within much of the scholarship on the link between love and justice transnationally, there is little discussion of Dr. Ambedkar's discussion of love as necessary in the struggle to end the injustice of caste. Like Ambedkar, Martin Luther King linked love, justice, and theology in several of his civil rights and anti-apartheid speeches (Davis 2016). Oscar Romero framed El Salvador's armed struggle through love (Thompson 2014); "Betita" Martínez in her work within the Chicana/o and Civil Rights movements in the 1960s and 1970s grounded the political potential for collective transformation in the lived everyday experiences of people—a "love-praxis" (Havlin 2015). There is a longstanding discussion of love transforming concepts of attachment, community, and intimacy among women and queer of color theorists in the United States, who in pushing against theories of abjection, have positioned the theory of intersectionality as crucial to imagining the collective potential of love (Muñoz 2009) in search of a utopic future. In more recent times the rhetoric of love has been central to social movements transnationally such as #Blacklivesmatter, which draw upon Black feminist and U.S. women of color legacies of approaching love as a politic, a belief, and a form of practicing solidarity. It is within this broader transnational epistemological refashioning of love in seeking justice collectively that I locate the seemingly quotidian acts that Lahauli women (such as Kavita and Keerthi) perform, where love is constituted through its collective dimensions (as Adivasi *and* Dalit *and* women). In using love as a tool of narration the women reflect upon how self-love via its (dis) identifications (Muñoz 2009) can transform not only the self but also communities.

Along with approaching self-love and love of individuals/family members as a response to histories of caste injustice, the women often also articulated non-oppositional notions of love throughout their stories. I present these articulations of love through three women's stories, followed by a discussion with the local deputy superintendent of police (DSP), who relies upon hegemonic ideas of love. I close the chapter with a discussion of what such a non-oppositional articulation of love offers.

I include the following women's stories below—Abeley Yangchen, Pema Choden, and Dechen Palmo. The women highlight different ways of *doing* love through the temporal performance of marriage, death, and community in their stories. In both, dismissing romantic/sexual notions of the normative love-plot (Dechen Palmo's critique of the "two-person couple") and defining love as a mode of understanding the self through the collective (through responsibility toward tribe; duty toward ancestors; and through love *as* tribe), they offer a different epistemological approach to love, along with rich details about the region and deep reflections about the relationship between tribe, caste, and state.

I

"Love is something to be done"
Ama, one of the key Thakur families is in her late-eighties at the time of this interview. I address her as Abeley, which translates to "grandmother."

ABELEY (A): Oye, Himika. What do you want me to tell you? I met my husband so long back that even *I* cannot remember what year it was. But yes, it was long before the war with the Chinese. He was a descendant of the Wazir's family and died soon after the war. By that time we had had my youngest child. And my oldest was a teenager.

    I had a *kuji biyah* with him; he took me from my village when I was twenty something. What more can I tell you, look at how young you are, and then you are not even married. Ooooh you, what can I tell you now about the men I loved. (*utha liya tha na ri, aur kya bolna tu badi chhoti hai jo ri, shaadi bhi nahin ki toe areeey ri, abhi kya bolna ri. Kitno ko pyar kiya ji, lekin kahani to ek hi bani*)

HB: Abeley, you know you're young at heart, and you know only too well that I am neither so young nor so innocent. So there were many love-stories? (I ask only half-jokingly)

A: (laughing and slowly standing up) Oye, I got no teeth—look! Now who's old! Yes, many love stories! Now let's walk and sit outside under that tree. Maybe there I can tease you better and tell you some juicy stories. Hah, I know all about you young girls and boys. Like my grandchildren, you too must be so free.

Abeley walks slowly with her cane, stepping out of her home, grinning widely as we walk to her favorite spot under the tree. Half-winking, she says "Ooooh look at you all grown up! So now you must be ready for a joint." (we both laugh.) "Oye, sit here, you. Right in front of me so I can see how much of my story you can digest! Oooooh sorry ji (and grinning even wider, emphasizing the ji, Abeley continues) I am so sorry *ji*, Dr. Himika I should call you, eh? Now you have become a doctor and a college teacher. And you are so 'old.' Where is your cassette player today?" Abeley Ama refers to my recording device as a "cassette player," which I then take out of my bag and place in front of her as we both sit. Finally, this interview is beginning, or so I think.

A: Oye. Areeey. Now there you go. We forgot the most important thing!
HB: What?
A: Oye, I forgot the *namkeen chai* (butter/salt tea) inside. I shall go inside and bring us some.

I convince Abeley Ama to let me go inside and bring it out on a tray—two cups of butter tea and a huge thermos full of more.

    Abeley, sipping on her tea, perched on a seat made of a stone and the roots of the tree we are sitting under, begins talking:

A: Oye, it's all in my skin. See how paper thin it is? See these folds? These wrinkles and folds aren't about ageing, they are about the secrets I have tucked into them over the years. (AA says while pulling on the wrinkly skin on her wrist) If you try hard enough, you could see my life through the folds on this skin.

HB: Abeley, if only I could see through your skin!

A: Oye, don't be a smartass! I will tell you, slowly. But first you tell me: what will you do if I say I don't feel like answering questions you ask me?

HB: I shall not ask anymore then.

A: Oye, don't be so sensitive (*nakhra*). Ok then, ask a question to start me off, or I have to ask the questions too! (laughing)

HB: How did you get married into the Thakur family?

A: Aah. Those days were something else *beta*, oye. My husband took me from the fields. He never sent a *ngya*, but I knew he had his eye on me because he told my friend's brother how pretty I was. I was older than him and very strong, with beautiful long hair. In our Lahaul it is important for us women to be strong, have strong arms and legs. Even though we don't till the soil (the men do that, with the Yaks), we need to be strong, to do all the agricultural labor. In my days, we were also growing *Kuth*—it was a much slower and tougher crop. People came from Chhangthang and Zangskar to trade with us. Our men went there too, Tibet, China, all over the mountains. Not like these days, quick (cash) crops only—potatoes and peas—bought by traders from Punjab. He knew I would work well on the fields. And he was from the waziri, so when my family heard he might be interested, they were quite happy. But they hoped he would try for a *mangni biyah*.

HB: And you? Were you interested in him? Or a *mangni biyah*?

A: Oye, what matter what I thought? I was the girl. I knew somebody was going to marry me and I would be working on that farm the rest of my life. My only probable thought was that he is from a big family, it will be ok. Maybe he will take me to Kullu and other places. But still, as a girl I was a bit scared. I thought he would do a *kuji biyah*, because otherwise people may think we are in joint. And in their family, people hid joint, even in those days, for fear of being judged by people from the plains. After all, they were the samant/rulers.

Any case after he took me, there was a big party. I was mostly indifferent. He was not unpleasant or rude to me. But slowly we got to know each other. These days they say love-marriage and all. But love is not something you just wake up with! It has to be done. (*pyar karna parta hai; bas ho nahin jata!*)

HB: How did you *do* love?

A: Again you are trying to get some juicy story from me, aren't you? (laughs)

Hmm . . . it is something you make. And something you have to learn to *do*. You know, it's how I won't give up my land because I love this land. I have learnt how to love it. I know all its stories, how its texture has changed, how planting cash crops for so many years is changing the soil because of the water that is being channeled to it. But it's needed they say, for a more modern world. I must not be modern at all oye!

But I did learn love to (do) love. And he, my dear dear husband, we created the ways to love our Lahaul more, our people, not just having these children, but raising them with our Lahaul in mind.

That first year after we got married, it was just he and I. We were doing alright. I worried a bit that he might find someone younger when he went back to his posting in the plains. But I wasn't too worried because what non-Lahauli girl will come and work on these fields and live in this climate.

HB: And after the first year, did someone else join you all?

A: Oye, you want the best part right away, don't you! (Cackles again, and continues without pausing). After the first year, my husband's younger brother visited us from Kullu where he was trying to start a family business. Some hotel-*shotel*, you know. In those days we didn't think so much would happen; that the family would have so many businesses and orchards and things in a couple of generations.

But yes, I thought we had a *kuji biyah*, so none of his brothers would try for me. This younger one was a major looker though, with a smile like Guru Dutt and Shammi Kapoor oye! So I didn't mind him trying . . . (Cackles again)

Then, after my husband left for his posting, his brother returned to support me. That is how things happened. I sat with him because it felt right, as part of our Lahauli system. But he assumed that we would be in a joint. I did not want to be in a joint though. Even though we kind of were, you know, he was helping me when my husband was away. I had only my oldest child at that time, so it was good to have someone around. My in-laws lived far—managing another part of their land. My husband said we shouldn't make it a public thing. He worked in the military, and people would never understand our Lahauli customs. You know, it is different for us within the tribe but most non-tribals from all over—Kullu-Manali, Mandi, Kangra—saw joint as a negative thing.

Still, we went on like this for years. I told the younger one he should find a wife, we couldn't go on this way, people would know and we would be seen as a joint and I needed to be careful for the family's sake. He loved me and said it didn't matter what anyone else thought because this was how our ancestors wanted us to be. He tried hard to convince me because many families were in joint marriages at that time. I explained how my husband, his older brother felt that as part of the samant family, we had a greater responsibility to the people and our *maan-samman* (dignity and respect) had to be intact. My husband felt strongly that some of our old customs were not going to bring us respect as Lahaulis and we should give them up. His brother of course didn't share this view.

And then, one day I got a telegram saying my husband was dead. I could not believe it. I thought it must be someone else who died in that air crash and they just didn't know yet, because they couldn't find him. He was so young and I really struggled to accept it. For many days and months I did not believe it because they never found him.

I was grateful though, that my brother-in-law was with me. He supported me, explained to me that my husband wasn't going to return. I was so distraught. How was I to raise three children by myself? What about my husband's dreams for our sons to be government officers? My husband's younger brother stood by me. The love we learnt together was really something, but I couldn't give him what he wanted despite everything.

HB: Because of your husband's wishes ... ?

A: Yes, but I could not accept the idea of giving up on the ideals of the samant family, which I was now a part of. I had to think beyond myself. Times were changing. Now, we were the face of the Lahaulis to the rest of the world, and we learnt to love differently. With his older brother it was love for the tribe, the children, our people. I had to do all of my loving at once.

II

"My son died for his love of our people, our tribe."

Pema Choden is in her mid-sixties at the time of this interview. She has worked in the DRDA (District Rural Development Agency) for much of her life and raised four children. Up until her retirement a few years back, she was very active in the local community as an organizer.

We have known each other since my very first trip to the valley, and during my trip in 2011, we ran into each other on the mall road in Keylong. When she heard I was conducting these life history interviews with women across age and caste groups, for a book about the valley, she grew very interested and expressed an interest in participating in the project. Her younger son was not happy with this decision, and I discuss this later in the epilogue. Her older son, Kranti, I found out had been killed in a motor accident the previous winter. In her own words, she will never recover from this tragedy and now just wanted to do things in her life that she had never before done, including this interview, so that someone would read her story even if she wasn't around anymore.

This story is one brief part of several interviews with her.

PC: My husband returned to live with me in this house after all these years. Now that he is old and retired, he wanted to come back home. I told him right away though that he may return to live here because he still is part of this family, but that I have no desire to live with him, after he abandoned me for so long. And so, he must stay in the annexe. He tried talking about our love and I said no, all the love we had done, to keep this family, to keep our land, to stay true to our ancestors, you set it aside as though it wasn't part of you. It has been too long

FIGURE 4.1. Gemur Monastery

now and I will only accept you as the father of my children. So yes, he lives here, but in a separate section.

HB: How did you both meet?

PC: When I was twenty years old he courted me, after he set his eyes on me at the Kardang Gompa during the lama festival. I thought he is good looking, so why not. And of course a lot of *chhang* (rice beer) was also involved in the behaviors that led to that decision! (laughs)

Mostly though I was indifferent to his romantic gestures. There was also a district officer who was trying to woo me—from Mandi. He was quite good looking, and presented the option of an escape—from a life of hardship in Lahaul. But I decided to go for my Lahauli. I liked him of course, but it wasn't like they show you in the films. It's like this: I knew I could only love a Lahauli, because we are tribals. I was clear I would marry only another Lahauli—not because there was something wrong with the others but that was just how we had to hold on to our dignity—through sharing love and life in a way that would uphold it—towards our ancestors and the land—not only towards one person (*apne logon se pyar kiya na ji, apne pushton se, is zameen se—kewal ek insaan se nahin*).

He had a government job in Keylong and I moved with him after my older son Kranti was born. My husband's brother was in Shansha and would visit often. We didn't discuss it because that just wasn't part of how it was done in those days. But we all knew that we were going to be in a joint. First I sat with my husband, then whenever he had to be gone to Spiti for long stretches, his brother would visit from Shansha, help me manage the kid, the farms, the animals. And it just fell into place. You know, we weren't so bothered by what the government officials would say, or what people from elsewhere would say about us, especially the non-tribals.

Nowadays people have to consider these factors too. There are hardly any joint marriages, and in the few that there are, people have to be so careful and secretive. If the officers find out they will laugh, if the friends in Kullu get to know they will be shocked, so on and so forth. And these days they watch all these films and think love is meant for two people only! For example, consider my children. My son Vikam has married Kranti's widow now, but when Kranti was around, he did not do joint. Vikram at that time wanted to marry someone else. He said this is my sister-in-law. I cannot be with her. It was only after Kranti suddenly left us that Vikram proposed to his sister-in-law and she consented. She works in the police and was so devastated when Kranti passed away. Vikram's love has brought her back to life in a new way, and their son, little Kranti keeps us all sane. Now she is pregnant again—I am not sure if you noticed when you went to the police station that day.

HB: I did. She and I chatted for a few minutes but we talked about other things since it was at the police station.

PC: Ha ha, yes. That is not the best place to discuss joint! But in any case, that is my point. Kranti, his wife Reena and Vikram were not in a joint. They could not think like that, even though this is what our ancestors handed down to us—this was the way, the love, which would save this land, these mountains and our tribe from breaking apart. But nowadays nobody pays much heed to such things. They all want these relationships which involve two persons as a couple (*abhi toe ji sab ko* two-person couple *hi chahiye*) and mostly because that's what people from the plains call love. It is nonsensical if you ask me.

HB: Could you tell me how it was in your time, for you?

PC: I was in my early thirties when I qualified for a job at the district office in Keylong because I had completed my higher secondary education. I got a permanent job with the government. My husband got a posting in Spiti. Then, next thing I know, he has found somebody there and is living with her. I said to him, fine then. I will declare your brother as father of all my children. This got him all scared and he didn't father more children in Spiti. That woman was also so naive. Why did she marry someone who would leave her when she was old? What a rotten situation it must be for her. I told my husband not to leave her because I am fine here. At least until Kranti's death I was.

I retired a few years back, and let me tell you something: I have faced many terrible things in my life, but the two worst things I have lived through are my son's death, and my daughter's abduction. You know all about the latter, you were here then. But at least Raja Ghepan has given her a healthy life and she is here, in front of my eyes, has two beautiful children. But Vijay, my son—when he died, I thought my world would end. He was so young.

These mountains are everything to us because they give us life. But they can also be cruel and take life too. On that cold, snow-filled winter afternoon, when a constable from the police station walked over and knocked on our door I thought it must be about the weather getting worse and Kranti getting stuck in a landslide or a storm. But when he began saying the words, that my Kranti's jeep had just gone off the bridge and fallen into the gorge on his way back I thought my world had ended. I have no idea how long I was unconscious. When I regained consciousness, everyone here at home was crying. The air in my house was so heavy I thought I couldn't breathe. My Kranti, who had gone to ferry a patient because the government never sends a helicopter on time for such things, was dead. And I had to come to terms with it.

There he is now, our little Kranti (she gestures toward the very young boy playing in the hallway), who brought hope and sunshine back into this house.

HB: He looks just like Kranti too!

PC: (now laughing) He does, yes! Maybe by the time he grows up the government will care more for Scheduled Tribals like us. Maybe they will learn to respect us and our needs.

HB: Do you mean the chopper needs for winter, or in general?

PC: It's everything. See, we are told that we are lucky because government's tribal development financial allotments are so large for scheduled areas. But do the math. Schedule tribal regions are mostly in very remote places. No hospitals, no regular amenities and such. On top of that, in the upper Himalayan tribes like us, the population is not so dense, so of course the allotment seems bigger when you only look at how much money government allots and how many people there are. But it is not enough to only consider that. How about infrastructure? How about the fact that construction and building infrastructure is extremely costly in these parts? How about distribution—among ST and SC? And what about manpower? An entire district, including Spiti, and we get only one surgeon. What are we supposed to do? So many people die every winter because we are unable to transport them—even internally—within the valley. My son died doing the job of our government. Can they bring him back? Instead, they will laugh at me or pity me, if I even say this to them.

Kranti died for his love of our people, our tribe. It is rare in his generation. I encouraged him to go. I said Kranti yes, you have a jeep and this person needs to be taken to Kullu hospital, so you should drive him to this side of the top. And some good people offered to walk from the other side of the top, to carry the patient over, where they had another vehicle waiting. They did it and took him to a hospital in Kullu. He got treatment and survived, but had some permanent damage—his mobility is highly restricted now.

HB: How long had he been ill, this patient, before he could be transported out of the valley?

PC: He had a heart attack, beta, the previous night and the two junior doctors at the hospital here said he had to be treated at a proper hospital. The CMO

(Chief Medical Officer), Tshering was not there. He is a big "hi-fi" man, a senior doctor, but not as reliable. And the DC was away from Lahaul for yet another training—you know how the senior government officials always leave Lahaul during winter. They always find trainings to be at, in Pune or somewhere far and warm so they don't have to face the winter here. That is Ghepan's test for any plains person who works here—can they stay a whole winter or not? Can they cross the top on foot in the winter or not?

HB: So whom can people contact when the DC, SP (Superintendent of Police), surgeon and such people are away? What happened after that?

PC: The Sub-Divisional Magistrate (SDM) was requested to place a call to Shimla, early in the morning asking for chopper service. But they said it was not possible because they were not prepared. Can you believe the gall? They were not prepared—what does that even mean? It was not as though the winds over the Rohtang were too strong and they couldn't fly. No, they have all the technology in this day and age to figure out how to come here even despite the winds. They are prepared to go to Siachen if they have to, I am sure, in order to keep the border secure from the Chinese. They are scared of the Chinese so they are prepared. It is a matter of will. And for us tribals, the government lacks will, because they don't respect us. That's it.

I know our mountains bring a lot of hardship and this impacts even the governance of our region. I know because I love these mountains more than my own life, and yet, I have been struggling to live with them my whole life. The mountains are in my blood, and still I am often frustrated by the power and size of these mountains—even as I revere them. Our very survival, this breath, is contingent on their presence. These mountains and these rivers—this place is part of me, just as it has been part of my ancestors. You have to first respect this place, its mountains, its rivers, and its people. Only then can you hope to govern the region in a fair and good manner. Look at what our *samant* did. The British finally took the *waziri* away for a reason, right?

How much worse can it get when a government forgets its duty to its people in such a fundamental way: when they leave our weakest to die, winter after winter, not changing the situation?

HB: Has there been any discussion about this through the Panchayats? And how frequent are the flights when they run? How is the list of passengers determined? Could you talk a little bit about this process?

PC: Hmmm about Panchayats intervening, I believe there have been some letters written. There was also a protest outside the DC office some time back. After

Kranti's death, some locals from Keylong wrote a petition and requested the DC to urge the higher ups in Shimla. But not much has changed. I am not even sure it is the DC office's fault. I know the current SDM is a very eager officer who tries to get these things organized and appears to help people. The problem for us is that the district officers all change very quickly, because most of the officers are non-tribals and upper castes from the plains or from other parts of Himachal. They cannot stand being here. Not all of them are bad, or look down upon us but it is just too difficult a posting for most of them. They have to live far from families, in this climate, so high up in the mountains, so dry and snowing all the time and to top it all they don't speak the language—it is not easy for the officers also. I mean it would help them if they learnt to respect us (laughs). But I also appreciate their trouble—they did not join the army, they joined the state government through civil services exams. And after that to get this hard posting, it must be a lot. They are not trained to mingle with the locals. During my DRDA years I have known many government people who have been posted in Lahaul. I felt sad for most of them. But at least they get a lot of support from Shimla. The problem for us lies there, with the state government in Shimla—you want to take care of your own, but you don't consider us equally worthy and do not want to work any harder for us. So we stay in this place with such little help during the winter months, meanwhile the rest of the country is marching ahead, no matter the season!

And when the chopper schedule is declared, the seats on the chopper are all taken almost immediately. If you have some family connection then it's the best. But if you are from a Lohar family and you have no connection with any government people, what will you do? They will never put you ahead on the list for the chopper. Though these days the ST population is more careful in how it treats the Dalit caste STs. Still, when the chopper brings some fresh vegetables in the winter, the officers get those tomatoes, and a few other people they know well. The current army CO[8] is much nicer to the locals in these matters—they just leave bags at the local shops, and then it's free for all, first come first served. So the kids all make a run for the tomatoes!

III

"Love is love . . . how can it be divided/it can only be shared."

Palmo is an Adivasi-Dalit woman who is in her late fifties. She and I are to eat breakfast together in her home. This is the venue she has requested for a formal interview to tell me the story of her life in "joint." The following excerpt is from a much longer conversation that occurred in mid-June 2011.

"We will find the old pictures for you to see—of us three—and then place them next to the new ones." We search everywhere. Inside the wooden box where she stores her letters, old canvas bags where she hides her jewellery, under the carpet in the bedroom, for nearly an hour, but the pictures are nowhere to be found. "We must find those old pictures. Seeing the two pictures together will really *show* that our marriage is love; you can see us when we were younger and now as we are older, but still living with love" she says as she continues looking for the old photographs. I assure her that we will find it another day, that I shall be back to see it.

FIGURE 4.2. Village Jispa, Stod Valley

PD: I have been very lucky in my life, to have found true love—not with just one man, but with two of them. I had a *mangni-byah* (engagement followed by wedding) with the older brother. And then a few years later, I sat with[9] Rigzin. In our Lahaul these days, many women have bad luck—the second one usually goes away and finds another bride eventually, for himself, breaking up the family. But I was lucky—both truly loved me and did not break our family. We have loved each other, and upheld our ancestors' toil, not divided the land and shared a lifetime of love.

Though now it's changing here too—so many families don't want joint, they sell the land, the ancestors' land without permission, to build guest-houses for tourists. Our sons too, but we shall not live to see the land destroyed. We are under "tribal" category[10] but still, the officers, the police, the communities of the plains all think differently and judge us. So we hide joint. Often they laugh at us—people from the plains—they think women of Lahaul have no honor because we sit with more than one man. But they don't really think about it.

HB: They don't think about what ... ?

PD: That, what does love have to do with it—loss of honor, loss of land? They only worry about losing love, somehow lessening the love. Even our new generation of Lahaulis no longer want joint.

HB: What do you say when people ask whether your love is reduced, gets divided?

PD: Yes, this is one regular question—can you love enough if you love more than one person? What about the children? Doesn't the love get divided and reduced. Blah, blah, blah. And I say well, how can love be divided? Or reduced?

Love is love. We are connected in love to one another and to our ancestors through this love and through our land. If we don't have this love, this land, we have nothing. So it can never be divided or reduced. It is either there or not. And it is true, or not. The main question is if the love exists[11] or not. It can be shared, but how can it be divided? How can it be less (honor) to love and do right by your ancestors?

Let me give you an example:

You know, we went on a group holiday to the plains—from our valley—twenty people. Both my men came with me, and we were clicking pictures, in Bodh Gaya—like they say *"miya-biwi"* ("husband-wife") only I had two miyas [laughs]. It was so much fun, because all these plains people were staring at us—wearing our *cholus*, posing like a couple—three of us.

I was so happy during that trip—we were all together like that on a trip after so long, eating, drinking, sleeping in the same room—and I know what you're going to ask me now, *achi,* you have that look in your eyes. But I won't tell you everything yet.

HB: (At this point I teasingly ask) And so did you? Did you love them both then, in Bodh Gaya?

PD: Sure I did, we were in the right place for *moksha*! (grinning, her eyes twinkling.)

All three women talked about love in the context of marriage, particularly what is locally known as "joint," and referred to as polyandry in the official and anthropological literature about the region. And it is this practice of "joint" either rejected by part of the ruling caste and class (as in Abeley's case), or partially embraced (as in Pema Choden's case), or in an active celebration (as in Palmo's case). It is through their discussion of love that the women offer different vocabularies, while they also navigate hegemonic scripts of violence and love determined by caste society. It is important to note here, that in their articulation of love, the women are not "redefining" or "resisting" contemporary hegemonic scripts of love in the context of the state. Rather, they offer a radically different epistemology. This non-oppositional discourse of love signals an epistemological shift, one that understands self and community relationally. It does not rely on understandings of self and embodiment through self-contained dualistic notions of personhood entrenched in Western epistemologies (Seawright 2014). Yet, such a positioning of self within community produces a discourse of love as communal, as a social relation, rather than as a resource as it often appears in the state's function of love. These love-stories then, do interrupt, resist, and indeed expand current understandings of tribe as community.

To provide an everyday example of the discourse of love as it operates within a Brahmanical framework, I present another interview excerpt here, with a representative of the state—the Deputy Superintendent of Police (DSP), District Lahaul-Spiti. [This interview was recorded on June 30, 2011 in DSP Gurdev Singh's office, Keylong, and the notes contextualizing the scene are part of my fieldnotes.]

HB: (note to self) I continue waiting for the DSP's permission to gain access to a few case files that I have finally managed to locate in the storage room of the police station. I'm waiting; it feels like, for the hundredth time. Each file I find, they make me do this. The DSP is sitting right in front of me, checking cricket scores online, I am certain. As I drink the tea served to me, I finally decide to break the awkward silence in the room.

HB: (speaking to the DSP) Sir, so how do you like being posted in Lahaul? Or should I not ask?

DSP GS: What choice do we have—we just have to go wherever the government sends us. We are just here to serve the locals, make them happy, serve our time and return someday.

As if on cue, he begins enlisting the problems the administration faces, and suddenly begins discussing joint/polyandry.

DSP GS: And then, just see this whole polyandry business . . . they are still going on with it.

HB: But how do you know that people are still practicing polyandry?

DSP GS: Oh well, that . . . you know (*yahan ke mahilaon ke chaal chalan mein apna bhi toe interest haina ji*) the local women's modesty is a subject we have a lot of interest in. (And then added, laughingly.) Even the administration has local friends (*sarkar ke bhi yahan dost hain ji*).

HB: But why is there a problem then with polyandry, if people are not complaining? It is a Scheduled Area, and customary law applies here, right?

DSP GS: Look, Himika*ji*—I'm older than you, and let me explain something. It is also the administration's job to do the right thing. We are in a cultured society. In a family unit, if there is more than one father, there is confusion. How will the kids get any love? But then they have these tribal customs and laws that they want to hold on to. Women want to drink. They want more than one man. Do you think this is right? That one woman should have more than one man? Then they say we respect our women, we value our women, and this is only so that land is not divided, listening to ancestors and all this. I ask, how do you know whose child it is? And when we try, they don't listen. We have workshops. But they don't listen. They deny it, like they deny the alcohol.

And again, I ask, how will you decide whose child it is?

At this point seeing how agitated he was with this question of undetermined paternity I provide some information about the customary law of Lahaul.

HB: As you surely know sir, per the customary law of Lahaul, and as often clarified by community members themselves in meetings—the woman's statement decides the paternity of the child, and in the case of a dispute, irrespective of claims about the biological father, the child refers to the oldest brother (in the joint/polyandrous marriage) as "father" and all the other brothers as "uncle."

DSP GS: Well, so now that it's free for all, we have to listen to the women, and believe everything they say. Their culture is very tight you know, they don't include the administration. Except for wedding invitations where too, the women drink booze—*chhi chhi*—in our Mandi[12] women don't even go near the booze section, forget drinking it themselves. Only promiscuous women do that. But here it is the rule to be promiscuous (*yahanh to niyam hi ulta hai na ji—chaal chalan theek na ho to behtar hai*). And then they come and complain about force and *kuji biyah* to us—what is the administration supposed to do? This is your custom so you decide on your own then.

Embedded within deeply casteist and paternalistic discourses, DSP Gurdev Singh's words succinctly connect marriage to the state's function of love, which Palmo and others in joint interrupt. The DSP presents a view only too common among government officials in the region supported by the state as it protects certain kinds of sexual citizens and deems irrelevant, unmanageable, and unruly those that do not fit its mandate. This then produces the women of Lahaul as sexually deviant, promiscuous polyandrous tribal women, who are violence-deserving and whom the state can neither control nor wishes to protect, despite/in spite of its "honest agenda" of delivering a "cultured society"—the civilizing mandate of caste-society. By thus placing the Lahauli community within the purview of Other subjects it cannot manage nationally—such as Dalits, a range of indigenous sexual subjects, and queer-identifying communities—the failure to protect becomes the failure of the other.

Herein lies the paradox that Khajana Ram highlights—the very source of the higher moral responsibility is also the source of dismissal. In the same breath that he claims the state's authority, Khajana Ram also negates it by blaming tribal "culture," and the women's promiscuity for the state's failure to *civilize* or render *cultured*. Thus, the DSP introduces us to a discourse of promiscuity entrenched in colonial and Brahmanical logics of race and caste, whereby the state's failure to protect (Adivasi and Dalit) women is due to the unruliness of *their* communities. In other words, disciplining love via monogamy in marriage is another way of enacting caste dominance. The social legibility of tribal identity, when based on this violent discourse of caste purity, also requires the erasure of indigenous ways of being.

Such an erasure of Adivasi identity in this instance hinges on sustained monogamy (in the interest of both, romantic and parental love), and the promotion of linear developmental narratives of familial and national relations, into which the unruly sexual and caste subject must be made to fit. Locking "tribal sexualities" within this deviant form then not only adds insult to injury after violence, but is in effect the underlying structure which legitimates gender and caste violence.

The Hindu Marriage Act of 1955[13] does not apply to areas designated as Scheduled Tribal. Thus it is not considered "illegal" to be in a joint marriage, and yet its social implications in Lahaul via (Brahmanical) patriarchal codes of honor and shame have across the valley normalized monogamy and exclusivity as the only acceptable social norm when it comes to marriage. In following colonial ideologies about native sexuality, where tribes were the "most primitive" of all natives, contemporary discourses of state and media continue to ground their "civilizing" mission on colonial registers of ("tribal") sexuality as especially deviant.

On the other hand, for a number of Lahauli women who have been active in "joint," like Palmo, love is something that can be shared, but not divided. And marriage thus becomes one kind of relational practice that casts romantic love as community via its connectedness to ancestors and land. Thus the undivided land, while also significant for survival, is more importantly tied to its communal use, rather than ownership and use-value, within a capitalist Western approach to land. The love of land is yet another form of communal love. It is further linked to intimate family histories and kinship structures which include ancestors. In different ways the three women in this chapter offer an articulation of love and familial structure that doesn't adhere to the recognizable heterosexual social norms which uphold upper caste hegemony. Thus, the women's ruminations about their lives through ideas of love conceived in such varying ways raise important questions for how we could understand love as a politic. Their stories demonstrate how caste marginality and violence can also indeed shape meanings of love, and illustrate the processes by which we enact a political concept of love (Berlant 2011; Jordan 1978; Sandoval 2000). And when juxtaposed with DSP Khajana Ram's interviews, the women's stories illustrate the illegibilities that emerge when state discourses of love (and marriage) are juxtaposed with the women's experiences of the same. Further, their articulation of love and the increasing resistance to such ways of loving, which are also expressed by the DSP, offers us a way to think about the delicate links between tribe as community and caste as a system of domination within a wider, publicly emergent consciousness about gender and violence in India.

Their stories therefore are not a simple redefinition of love. To cast it in such a way would be to fall into the trap of normalizing Brahmanical epistemologies. Their stories offer an understanding of love that is communal, enacted through social relations that emerge from kinship alliances of land and access to land. Yet, through different rhetorical tactics, each of them forcefully compels an interrogation of Brahmanical patriarchy, and its role in defining love. It is important then to consider that the love they discuss itself operates on different terms. In this sense, "joint" provides a way of thinking about love, which interrupts the normalization of Brahmanism as the default epistemology. This requires that the project of anti-caste feminism should not be a project to include forms of difference into existing structures and epistemologies, where one is always only speaking back to Brahmanism, but that it be internal to the deconstruction and decolonization of knowledge to actually position itself in relation to indigenous knowledges and Dalit epistemologies.

5 ❧ MAGIC TRICKS

This chapter elaborates upon the relationship between tribe and state—by demonstrating how violence (against "tribal" women) becomes the register on which the otherwise oppositional patriarchies of state and tribe collude and produce the "tribal" woman as both, an unreliable subject and a target of violence. I trace how the violent death of one woman—Bina, in Lahaul, Himachal Pradesh India—is remembered across official and community discourses. To this end, I reflect upon the self-definition and self-positioning of the Lahaula tribe through an analysis of different sets of memories surrounding her death within the tribe. By focusing on how the memory of this case also evolves in the official and legal realm, this chapter sheds light on some key issues within the complex web of tribe and state politics in India.

In the winter of 2005, Bina Devi's husband set her on fire during an argument at their home in Keylong. She eventually succumbed to her injuries less than a month later at a hospital in Shimla. The official and surviving narratives surrounding her death shifted from murder to suicide until the case was finally legally resolved as an accident (CD No. 47).[1] During my fieldwork in Lahaul in 2011, I collected relevant ethnographic material[2] to trace the shifting contours of the memory of her death, and my analysis illustrates the collusions that exist between two competing patriarchies—those of state and tribe. Both discourses, while framing gendered violence in different directions, also co-constitute each other and "magically" transform the case from one of violence, to one eventually dismissed as accident.

Thus my broader goal here is to demonstrate how violence (against tribal women) becomes the register on which the otherwise oppositional patriarchies of state and tribe collude and produce the tribal woman as both, an unreliable subject and a target of violence. In concluding the chapter, I discuss feminist counter-memory as a means to re-articulate and re-frame the memory of Bina's death where her subject position is that of a believable agent, one that is not (pre)determined (as unreliable) by state and tribal patriarchies.

Within the overarching framework of decolonial, transnational and Dalit feminisms which are at the heart of this book, I discuss the memories of Bina's death as necessarily located in socio-historical specificities of the Lahaula community rather than within a broad generalizable categorization of Adivasi/tribal[3] as "minority" in India. Violence (against Adivasi/tribal women) is the register on which these otherwise oppositional patriarchies of state and tribe appear in sync with one another.[4] Ironically (tribal) women's bodies serve not only as the site for contestation of ideologies between these dual patriarchies, but also as the site for collusions. This attention to both, collusions and contestations between specific aspects of state and tribe in co-constructing the memories of the case—officially, and socially—continue to produce (tribal) women as targets[5] of patriarchal violence. Finally, I turn to feminist counter-memory as a means to re-articulate the memory of Bina's death where her subject position is that of a believable agent.

In understanding gendered violence as always produced within and sustaining intersecting structures of domination, such as race, caste, class, sexuality, and disability, several feminist scholars have called for a move beyond single axis approaches to studying and addressing such violence *within* marginalized communities (Crenshaw 1991; Fregoso 2003; Hill 2011). To this end, my discussion of this case has two specific goals. First, I hope to draw attention to the often-contested fact of violence against women *within* the Lahauli community. Second, I do so to illustrate the intersections of state and tribe in the circulation of memories of violence as I explicate the relationship between these dual patriarchies, which collude to silence, deny and conduct (gendered) violence. The case I examine here illustrates the dual processes by which violence against women *within* tribe is mandatorily silenced on the one hand, and yet how the memory of violence continues to live (albeit, in denial) through the circulation of what Michael Taussig

(1999) has called the "public secret"—that which is never really a secret, yet "cannot be spoken," thus always remaining un-knowable.

For this chapter, I have chosen to focus on this case among several others that I have researched because it exemplifies how normative codes of gender, sexuality, and tribe determine both, official and community memories of Bina's death and continue to produce tribal women as targets of violence. Thus this case is not only about the death of a (tribal) woman. Rather it is illustrative of the social forces that shaped an entire life finally brought to the event of a violent death (Loomba 1993). By tracing the shape of one woman's unspectacular death as it appears in official and community memories, this case also presents particularly vexing questions about agency in the recall of everyday forms of violence. For example, what does the memory of violence look like when there is no survivor and who gets to determine that? What is the relationship of the individual subject to the collective subjectivity of the tribe? How does violence get re-articulated as accident and how is its subsequent dismissal put to *use* by multiple patriarchies through official and community memories?

FIELDNOTES

I begin with a journal entry below, written sometime in the summer of 2011, to situate the official memory physically in the police station where I accessed the materials (thus forming the basis for one kind of feminist counter-memory). Here I present this journal entry as a deeply ironic fieldwork moment—one which I later illustrate as co-constituting the memory of several members of the community (mostly active men of the local tribal manch/chapter). This incident occurred when I had returned to the Keylong Police Station after days of waiting for official approval from the police department to gain access to their case files for the official records of violence against women in the district. I had already carried a list of the cases that I wanted to trace based on previously conducted research[6] in the area. My plan was to start following up on cases one by one, and see which ones I could get complete access to, finally making copies of the relevant and permissible files. The first case I was looking for was that of Bina's murder by her husband. The following incident occurred at the Police Station, Keylong, district Lahaul-Spiti sometime after I did gain access to the files.

JUNE 22. 2011, MAGIC TRICKS:

Constable Anil Kumar, my sole sympathizer at the Keylong Police Station offered to help me go through the numerous files stacked on top of each other in the storage section right next to the munshi's office. Tied with tough red threads, layers of dust collected over months, possibly years, lay hundreds of thick files with old tattered sheets of paper in them—right from petty theft to murder—precariously piled on top of one another, with barely enough room for Anil Kumar and me to stand together. Bina's file was hidden somewhere here, so we began bringing the files out to the "common area" of the police station and placed them on the floor. After doing this for three odd days, and after numerous old files had been sifted through, today I found the dusty old file I was looking for, the complete file apparently, but each sheet of paper in tatters. I parked myself on the floor and began reading.

The file read exactly as I knew it would, up until the point at which suddenly the case changed, from suicide to accident. Somewhere at this point, all the prosecution's witnesses turned hostile, the court decided to dismiss the case and all possibility of further appeal was dismissed. This, despite two family members who testified repeatedly to Bina's last attempts at disclosing the violence of what happened with her. As I reached the section of the file where the case suddenly lost steam as murder or domestic violence,[7] I kept reading the changed witness statements over and over, thinking to myself that this was odd—almost like a magic trick.

As this thought about how all the evidence had magically transformed was going through my mind, I noticed that the constables had all walked out of the room to the adjoining area. I called out to see what had happened and one of them casually responded, "*madamji jadugar aya hai. aap bhi dekhiye*" ("madam, the magician is here ... you should watch this too").

A little thrown off by this information, I walked outside to see this magician who had indeed come to the police grounds to perform magic tricks for the constables. That he appeared at the very moment when I was thinking about how magically all the witnesses had turned hostile was unnerving to say the least, and chillingly added another layer of irony to the case. For the acquittal of the accused, a state-tribe sponsored magic trick was indeed necessary. And here was a real magician, as though to mark this moment in my memory.

In discussing this "magic trick," I explore three different types of memory, in connection with Bina's death. The first type of memory I explore is that of the state/judicial structure which legally establishes her death as an accident with certainty, leading to the acquittal of her husband and an official resolution of the case. The most notable aspect of this kind of remembering is the end result, also considered the "truth" by the courts.

The second type of memory I explore is that of the local community in Lahaul. I discuss how her death is remembered through the circulation of a particular phrase that I found repeated in multiple re-tellings of her death: "it is what it is" (*hai to hai na ji*). A phrase that produces a definitive and complicit (with the state and its patriarchal machinery) discourse about violence as rooted in not what might have happened with her, but to how the case is resolved officially, and more importantly how the denial of violence is as crucial for the tribal patriarchy as for the state.

Finally, the third type of memory I discuss is the ethnographic feminist counter-memory which constitutes a feminist reading of the case. Here, attention is paid to aspects of the narrative which the state doesn't consider "evidence" or truth, thus creating the space for a counter-narrative. While this feminist recall too relies on the details documented by the state (my analysis is also based on the court's case file), it focuses on aspects of the records which have been dismissed and don't fit the neat memory path chosen by the state, and rendered as karmic intervention within the community.

My interest in thinking through these memories and the way in which the case is remembered is not to enter an impossible debate around the veracity of each narrative involved. Rather, I'm interested in the discursive practices that become visible in the curatorship of the memory of gendered violence (in this instance, Bina's death).

BINA'S NARRATIVE[8]

Bina was in a violent marriage with her husband, a Himachal Pradesh homeguard (member of the Indian paramilitary force which functions as an auxiliary to the Indian Police). He suspected her of having an affair with the neighbor and regularly abused her on this pretext. One night when particularly enraged, he set her on fire. It was the first week of January, and there was a lot of snow outside. She ran out of the house and began rolling on the snow, to stop the fire from killing her. Their neighbor saw this and ran up to help. By then Bina's husband himself had begun to help her and sustained injuries himself. However, she was badly burnt, and when taken to the district hospital, the only doctor on duty recorded an initial statement where Bina said that the fire occurred as a result of an accident. She received basic care at the Keylong hospital and the doctor asked for her to be sent to a hospital with better facilities. Being winter, all access to the valley was shut off and they had to wait before the scheduled government helicopter arrived and transported Bina to better care first in Kullu, and eventually in the state capital, Shimla. Within some time after being moved to the hospital in Shimla, Bina passed away. Her parents were there with her, and in the week preceding her death, she made a dying declaration to them stating that her husband was the one responsible for her death. After Bina's death and during the legal proceedings, the court decided to count as a "dying declaration," her initial statement, recorded in the presence of the doctor at the Keylong Hospital the night the incident occurred and where she had stated that the fire occurred due to an accident. Thus her final declaration made to her parents was finally legally dismissed.

THE STATE'S MEMORY

In conversations with the then Superintendent of Police in Lahaul (referred to as SP from here on), and later when reading the case file, I found out that the police had first registered a case of attempt to murder under the Domestic Violence Act of India, Section 498A (PWDVA). In a meeting with the SP that same year when I asked if Bina's husband was therefore in custody, he was evasive (eventually I found out that he had applied for a bond bail, and been granted one by the sessions court). Within a few minutes the judge of the sessions court of Lahaul walked into the SP's office. This was my first meeting with the judge, and he joined our conversation. I brought up the case we had just discussed, and here is what followed.

The judge at first couldn't recall which case I was talking about. Then, he remembered and started out to "correct" me, "This was not an attempt to murder case, Madam, it was registered as a suicide . . . The woman, Bina had committed suicide . . . Such things don't happen here. There is no violence against women here." Quite taken aback at this new piece of information, I turned to the SP and asked him to correct the judge, as he knew best, and he had just given me different details. However, at this point the SP quickly changed the subject and asked for my leave (meaning that I should leave his office) as the judge had come to meet him to discuss some extremely urgent matter. I thanked him, got permission to go through the police records once again and left.

At another point, I checked the hand written records at the police station. Bina's case was indeed registered at first as an attempt to murder. However, sometime later, it was changed to suicide. While these changes involved legal proceedings, the speed with which some of these changes in the file occurred was surprising to me. It didn't take much to understand the significance of the fact that her husband was a homeguard, affiliated with the police.

This case demonstrates how the state (mis)remembers violence via the process of silencing and denial. Her husband set Bina on fire. She made an effort in her dying moment, to speak, which became a kind of silence, because it could not be heard as "legal" speech and evidence by the state. Separately, when Bina was taken to the hospital in Lahaul the night she was set on fire, a police report was filed based on what the doctor at the hospital stated. In her initial statement to the police and the hospital, Bina did not state that the fire was a result of her husband's violence. In a subsequent statement she made to her parents, when she briefly regained consciousness at the Shimla hospital, she admitted that on that first night she had been scared of what might happen if she did speak the truth, and that she gathered the courage to tell her story only when she knew she was safe. Further, she also stated that she had stored large amounts of liquor illegally in her house and didn't want the police to find it, which they would, had they searched the house looking for evidence of violence. The irony of Bina's attempts to be "safe" from her husband, and police intervention in the hours right after she was set on fire, appears tragically naive at first glance, but was also the product of the social and structural conditions in which she was living up until then. Had she known she wouldn't make it alive out of that entire incident, would she have stated what happened that night differently than she did?

Repeatedly in conversations with me, members of the police department, the judiciary, and administrative staff at the district offices of Keylong, alluded to the possibility of violence, but undermined it by talking of how it could as much have been suicide as murder. In yet another conversation in the summer of 2011, the then Sub-Divisional Magistrate (SDM) of Keylong sums up perfectly the circular logic of the state, focused, at all costs on disavowing violence, "But you have already made up your mind in advance . . . For you, it's not about the evidence. How do you know she or her father weren't lying just to get her husband into trouble? And if she wasn't, she was initially trying to protect him, obviously. Then how do you know this is what she would have wanted?"

In the moment the SDM said the above, we were both aware that eventually the case was dismissed as an accident, primarily based on the fact that all witnesses (who had taken an oath in the initial phase of the trial that Bina's death indeed appeared to be due to violence) had suddenly all turned hostile. For the SDM Bina's narrative/dying declaration can and must only serve the interest of her husband. This imperative is entrenched in an understanding of conjugality as both, "women's refuge" (Basu 2012) and duty. If she claimed violence, she wanted to punish him unreasonably; if she claimed accident, she did the right thing, and when there is no way to know what happened beyond the evidence available to the state, we must assume that her husband's welfare is indeed what she would have wanted. Thus, Bina in both, her death and her life, is positioned simultaneously within this construction of marriage as (heterosexual) privilege and "women's refuge," where they are entrapped "within cycles of violence and impoverishment" (Basu 2012).

Further, the SDM's comment also marks the state as objective, while my position as a feminist/researcher as already biased. In following Foucault (1977), Srimati Basu (2012) discusses the "judges of normality" as referring to not only "the actual judges but to the omnipresent policing and judging from other agents of the state" (p. 470). Similarly, in these multiple verdicts pronounced by these "judges of normality," the seeming "neutrality of the state" is invoked to render Bina's dying declaration as unreliable as in it she accuses her husband (and breaks the codes of conjugality).

In no version of the official memory is there space for relying entirely on the woman's story as she narrated it on her deathbed, and the reason provided repeatedly is that she gave two contradictory statements. Yet, when all of the prosecution's witnesses who had formerly testified in court claiming violence suddenly turned hostile and retracted their statements the courts did not dismiss their shift in status as unreliable. Instead the court ruled the case to be an accident based on these new statements. Thus the production of one kind of reliable subject for the court necessitates dismissing Bina (and her family) as the unreliable subject(s). The collusion of representatives of different arms of the state—the police and the juridical structure—in remembering her death only through a denial of violence is clearly illustrated in this one example.

Further, what I read in the case file at the police station in the summer of 2011 (the section on witnesses turning hostile) after the case had been judicially dismissed, cements this denial of violence completely. What purpose is served by the official memory, which is grounded in the denial of violence? What structures are kept from crumbling? Wouldn't an acknowledgment of the prevalence of violence against (tribal) women bring to crisis interlocking/multiple structures of tribe, family, and state?

THE PUBLIC SECRET

This leads me to the public memory of this case and the interplay of denial and concealment within the tribe. In the summer of 2011, two full years after the case had been legally dismissed, I spoke to several people locally about how they remembered Bina's death. This included interviews with local men, members of the district administration and local women, including some members of the *mahila mandals* (women's groups). Here I discuss how one particular public memory of the case is constructed through the repeated use of a phrase—"*hai to hai na ji*/it is what it is"— something Lahaulis use for a range of events, from inclement weather and devastating snowfall to the temperature of tea. Thus it stood out as particularly meaningful when I heard this phrase being invoked repeatedly when I asked people about Bina's case. I present three quotes[9] in which this particular phrase is used to recall Bina's death publicly.

SHAMSHER, EMPLOYEE AT THE DC OFFICE:[10]

It is what it is *ji*. Now what's the use. Earlier they did indeed say that, you know that it's a murder. But then who really knows what went on, who can tell for sure. And then, he's a homeguard, so one has to be careful about what one says—especially in my office. The person who I share my office with is from the man's (accused) village . . . And you already know, that we Lahaulis are different from the plains people . . . And what can anyone find out now, you know. He's alive, she's dead. Their story is over. *It is what it is.*

MEME, SHOP OWNER, KEYLONG:
No, no—this man was framed for sure. In the beginning they did say it was a murder and all—quite shocking for our Lahaul you know, these things don't happen here, we Lahaulis are not violent by nature. And eventually they proved it—that it was an accident.

At this point I asked, ". . . but you do know that all the witnesses turned hostile, right—what do you make of that?" His response,

In these matters it's always hard to tell but then, *it is what it is.*

WATCHMAN, GOVERNMENT GUEST HOUSE, KEYLONG:
I heard something like that, you know (that she was killed). Then, I don't know what happened except they proved it was an accident. You know there is such little violence among us Lahaulis . . . so what her family was saying about murder was a big surprise. But then you see him now, happy, well-settled . . . *it is what it is.*

These quotes are representative of the general response I received as I spoke to a number of people in Lahaul about this case. Through a series of rhetorical tactics, which are at once ambivalent and yet certain about what happened with Bina, each person eventually denies the violence. Yet, it is important to note that the eventual denial and concealment of violence is repeatedly derived from the premise that perhaps (or indeed) her death was a violent one. Yet, the circulation of this discourse, which at once marks the possibility of violence and denies it, works like Taussig's (1999) "public secret." For him, the public secret "is that which is generally known, but *cannot be spoken*" (p. 50). Following Taussig (1999), Nayanika Mookherjee (2006) has argued that the public secrecy of the 1971 rapes of the Bangladesh war reasserts normative codes of power and dominance through an interplay of revelation and concealment in the circulation of rumor and judgment in public memory. Secrecy surrounding the (already publicly declared) rapes while impossible to achieve, provides the grounds for the "public secret" to be "actively not-known" (Mookherjee 2006). Similarly, in this instance, the public secret (that Bina's death was indeed a violent one), is made possible through this discourse of "it is what it is," which is at once confusing and clear, constantly moving between revelation and concealment, and always determined through an attention to what *surrounds* her death. Further, here too, it is normative codes of gender, (heterosexual) family, tribe, and state that determine the denial of this public secret.

Let me begin with the first quote from an interview with Shamsher, an employee of the DC office, an active member of the Tribal Association of Lahaul, a person who has been actively supportive of women in his own family in the face of violence and the accompanying social and legal aftermath. For him, the case is murky not because of what might have happened to Bina (whether her death was a violent one or not) but because her husband (the accused) is a well-connected man affiliated with the Indian army, generating some anxiety among several local people of the consequences of discussing the death as violent, and finally because she is indeed *not living.* The emphasis is on what surrounds her death, in terms of the *use* of discussing her death, which in parallel constructs her husband's new life, now marked by conjugal bliss, thus returning the (tribal) familial unit to natural (heterosexual) order. In her death and through his new life, Shamsher says, "*their* story is over." Further, he invokes the difference between Lahaulis and people of the plains. When I probed him further on this, Shamsher responded by falling upon essentialist logics of the (Buddhist) "tribe as peaceful" and a masculinist impulse to stick by a fellow Lahauli man in trouble. The former is articulated through his insistence on the very little likelihood of violence among Lahaulis on account of being a "peaceful tribe" [*shant hain ji, humare log*], and the latter is expressed through his comment that there is no way to really know [*pucca to pata nahin hai na ji, aur phir ab khush bhi hain*], then why bother with revelation, especially when he (Bina's husband) is now happily ensconced in his new conjugal life.

For Meme (quote 2), the case initially has no room for doubt. For him the man was indeed framed. Meme speaks only of what he considers the "hard facts"—that Bina's husband was framed, and that then he was proved innocent—the court's decision *must* be right, especially when coupled with the fact that Lahaulis "by nature" are non-violent. Falling back on the same essentialist logic espoused by Shamsher above—of Lahaulis who are by association with Budhhism *naturally* peaceful—his statements produce the tribe as always peaceful, not violent, setting it apart from the rest of the country, but also reinforce a complete faith in the juridical structure, in denying the possibility of violence against (Lahauli) women. Eventually, when asked to consider the context of the witnesses turning hostile, Meme falls back on the same fatalistic discourse of *it is what it is*. Once again, the conversation ends with alluding to the possibility of violence, re-centering the initial denial of violence, through this seemingly ambivalent statement.

In the watchman's (quote 3) statement too, the same pattern is repeated. He admits to first having heard about the case as violence/murder, but immediately follows it up with the court's decision on the matter, and finally relies on the same logic of a non-violent Lahauli temperament to reinforce what on the face of it is an ambiguous statement—*"it is what it is"* but which once again effectively denies the possibility of violence.

Almost every individual I spoke to was invested in the present—emphasizing the relevance of focusing on the one that is alive (Bina's husband), over the dead and gone (Bina). Further, the picture of the living is rendered complete with him having re-married, once again a family man, happy and settled. And finally, the state proving his innocence aligns perfectly with the broader imperative of tribal pride for Lahaulis—expressed in these quotes through a repeated reminder that Lahaulis are *not* violent. Further, within this (hetero) patriarchal rhetoric of *usefulness* invoked by Anil, the performance of being a "family man" overshadows all else. She pays with her life for his new life, which we (must) accept, since *it is what it is*.

The *value* of the life lost and the life lived determines how the community remembers the death of Bina, always in the context of the life her husband continues to live. In this pitting of the dead against the living, his life triumphs as *more* grievable and wronged than hers. While her death appears easily forgotten it is the public secret that gains its own life and constructs these new old narratives of tribe, family, and state.

The public secret moves between restoring structures of kinship (through a unified emphasis on heterosexual family and tribal masculinity) and tribal pride (through the repeated assertion of the tribe as "peaceful" no matter its essentialist, colonialist underpinnings). It constructs an all too familiar progress narrative—one which looks to the future with the state and does not destabilize normative and interlocking systems of domination (tribe, sexuality, and gender). In constructing these narratives, the public secret lives on in the memory of the community through this interplay of revelation and concealment.

NECESSARY FICTIONS: STATE AND TRIBE IN LAHAUL

In these and other interviews with Lahaulis, especially men actively involved in the tribal manch, one recurrent theme has been that of self-distinction of the hill tribe from the caste communities of the plains. By insisting on the absence of discrimination[11] and violence (caste, class, gender) within the tribe which follows its "own customs" distinct from non-tribal parts of the country, Lahaulis draw upon notions of difference reinforced by the postcolonial Indian state via the Fifth Schedule of the Indian Constitution (Kurup 2008) to counter decades of racialized representation of tribes in India as "barbaric." Within the complex politics of tribal autonomy and state-defined parameters of *backwardness* (a term used by the state to mark tribal communities across the country as against the *progress* of non-tribal *savarna* caste communities in Peninsular India), the Lahauli community falls within the purview of the Fifth Schedule of the Indian Constitution. Like many tribes in peninsular India, tribal self-definition here too is balanced precariously on this play of tradition and modernity.

While it is crucial to hold on to notions of authenticity via a claim to the requisite markers of tradition that qualify tribal subjects as worthy of being recognized as a Scheduled Tribe (Agarwal 2004), it is equally important to participate in modernity, defined through the state's forward-moving progress agenda. This self-definition of the tribe as embodying the best of both, tradition and modernity, is solidified through a positioning of the Lahaula tribe as internally pure and clean from the violence found *elsewhere*, thus maintaining tribal superiority over the (non-tribal) state. In this careful balancing act, (tribal) women's bodies become the site where tribal patriarchy claims its place (via denial of violence and the claim of superiority vis-à-vis the non-tribal) in the progress narrative set forth by the state in its claims of development of *backward* tribes while maintaining border security.

This self-distinction of the hill tribe from the plains is necessary as it serves the tribe in two key ways. First, the reconstruction of the tribal self as "different" from the non-tribal Other (never violent towards women) provides a counter to decades of material and cultural dispossession[12] of tribal communities/men in India (Bhabha 1994), as engaged in barbaric practices of violence, in need of "reformation" and "rescue" by the (non-tribal) state. This discourse of the tribal self as traditional and yet non-violent rejects popular conceptions of tribe as Other and allows for its participation in modernity. Second, it becomes the basis on which the tribe claims non-violence, sets itself apart from the rest of the nation, and yet maintains its positioning as invested in India's safety. Further, as previously mentioned, due to both, their historical role in British India's army and their contributions to postcolonial India's wars against China and Pakistan, the Lahaulis pride themselves in playing a key role in India's border security (especially as a geo-politically significant region located on the Indo-Tibet *and* Indo-Pak borders) thus positioning themselves carefully as *integral* to India.[13]

It is useful here to consider other similar yet different ways in which such self-representation of hill tribes as distinct has appeared in other tribal contexts in India. In her research with Nepali women in the tea plantations of Darjeeling, Debarati Sen (2012) demonstrates how *Pahadiness* (loosely translated as identity of the hills/hill) is constructed through similar essentialist cultural tropes of tribe (as evidenced in Lahaul) and ethnic pride to produce a gendered (ethnic) identity which women workers of the plantations experience as both, empowering and disempowering. For Sen (2012), this construction of a gendered ethnic identity through participation and inclusion in the sub-nationalist movement for Nepali autonomy makes it possible for the women to negotiate and enter a terrain of respectability previously denied to them while simultaneously being used to serve a masculinist political agenda within the ethnic movement for Nepali autonomy. Thus what appears is the inseparability of gendered ethnic identity from the (tribal) struggle for autonomy, especially in the self-representation of the community within the nation-state. While the impetus for both contexts (in Lahaul and Darjeeling) is similarly marked through a politics of respectability in relation to tribal status in the broader context of the nation-state, what sets the Lahaula tribe apart is that this move towards respectability relies on the construction of a *superior* tribal identity in relation to non-tribal caste communities of the plains.

The history of dispossession and disenfranchisement of hill tribes in India is central to the Lahauli attempt at re-positioning their tribe as committed to non-violent, gender-just ideals, above and beyond the caste communities of the plains which are seen as notorious in terms of the ubiquity of violence against (*their*) women. Furthermore, this denial and concealment of gendered violence as part of a rejection of their status as a racial Other is aimed towards a stronger integration with the state which includes a desire for an affective shift in the racial imaginary of the nation-state, rather than a demand for autonomy or even a call for respectful inclusion.

Violence in particular, is one register where such a repudiation of Brahmanical (casteist, sexist) and racial ideologies whilst simultaneously embracing the state's pronouncement of the accused's innocence, becomes a necessary fiction for the tribe as well. Such a denial (of violence) can be understood as fitting with the tribe's broader goal of staying true to its imaginary of *never* violent, especially when positioned against what is seen as rampant (domestic violence) in the plains.

To return to the case at hand, yet another important layer in this continuum of state and tribal patriarchy is the social location of the accused as a Himachal Pradesh homeguard and its role in the production of this memory. In this instance the perpetrator is a member of both state and tribe, and both have an investment in his "innocence." Thus it might appear that the state and tribal patriarchy come together on proving innocence only when the perpetrator is situated at the intersection of both, tribe and state. However, in my research I found that not a single case of domestic violence led to a conviction between the years 2005 and 2011. The few that were even registered as domestic violence (under "cruelty to woman" in the official records), fell into three categories: pending further investigation; dismissed due to an absence of evidence; and changed to either suicide or accident. Multiple interviews with state officials and local community members (mostly men active in the tribal manch/chapter) over the years have repeatedly illustrated the insistence of both, members of the state and tribe, on the absence of violence against women in the region. This emphatic agreement between members of both state and tribal patriarchy occurs irrespective of the status of the perpetrator (whether as member of both, state and tribe, like in this instance, or whether as member of tribe alone). This takes me to my initial argument, that violence (against women) becomes the site on which this consolidation between these dual patriarchies becomes possible.

In other words, something is served for both, state and tribe through a denial of violence, and while the end goal for both might be different, violence opens up grounds where these discourses collude.

The state operates within a broader set of end goals, relating to administration and governance in yet another border tribe. For the state, on the one hand the Lahaulis present themselves as yet another "unruly" tribe, with their own "tight customs," with "rampant promiscuity" and "uncivilized marriage practices (such as polyandry)" often cited by district officials as reasons for the state's denial expressed through a "helplessness" in effectively controlling sexual offences/harassment/assault locally (Bhattacharya 2008). Yet in the instance of domestic violence, the denial of violence again becomes necessary. My contention is that on both counts it is imperative that the state machinery not intervene in violence within the community, and in fact either dismiss (as with sexual violence), or disavow it (as with domestic violence). This, despite its otherwise protectionist and reformist logic toward tribes allows the state to achieve several of its administrative goals, including two directly relevant ones. First, it continues its strategy of not ruffling feathers within the tribe, since as mentioned earlier, Lahaul occupies a liminal yet significant place in India's border security. The climatic conditions being harsh and severe[14] for much of the year, the state machinery *needs* Lahauli co-operation to survive in this border area. Further, this denial and dismissal of violence continues the construction of domestic violence (highly prevalent across other parts of India as well) as part of "women's problems," without needing to acknowledge its own complicity and active participation in violence against tribal communities all over India. This allows a broad, nebulous category of "domestic violence" to continue to exist within the realm of the "private"—a de-politicized position on (domestic) violence that the State machinery remains deeply invested in, nationally (Baxi 2012). Thus, not addressing similar forms of violence across the (Lahauli) tribe allows the state to continue to at once discriminate via and protect the hierarchical structures of tribe, caste, and gender nationally.

Here we find that both state and tribe seek a narrative that aligns with a set of broader goals committed to such a re-positioning of tribe. This obligation of the state and tribe for an unequivocal, consistent, and causal narrative constructs the denial and creates what could be termed necessary fictions. This then leads me to ask, what of the memory, which both state and tribe obfuscate, even deliberately write over? How and why might it be relevant for a feminist project to write the alternate versions of the narrative that appear through this web of state, tribe, gender politics, and that both official and community discourses obscure?

DEAD WOMEN TELL NO TALES

In her 1993 chapter titled "Dead Women Tell No Tales," Ania Loomba cautions us against reading feminist analyses of individual cases of violence (whether *Sati* or dowry murder or any other form) as only about representing an individual. Rather, she demonstrates how the representation of one instance of violence can also represent the politics of gender and community identities, for a repositioning of the individual subject within a set of collective subjects which, in this case includes the postcolonial feminist intellectual (Spivak 1988) as well as the varying positions taken by local women active in the women's organizations in Lahaul. It is in this spirit that I discuss feminist counter-memory and my own location here.

> JUNE 23, 2011, OLD CIRCUIT HOUSE, KEYLONG:
> Earlier today, when I returned to the police station, Anil informed me gently that some people at the station had been asking about me—about why I was there, that people are worried because they think I'm going to file a public appeal or make a big media fuss about it. Why do I want to know what happened, he asked? She's dead. And he's acquitted, has had a fresh start in life, didn't even need bail the second time around, yes? Why rake up the past? What has happened has happened, isn't it? What is the use? (*kya fayda?*)

The question that Constable Anil Kumar raises—*kya fayda?*/what's the use? is one that several others from the Lahauli community (some of whom I have quoted earlier) too brought up in interviews. For example, as mentioned in the previous section, all three men raised the seeming pointlessness of talking about this issue now that she is dead—why rake up the past? Repeatedly during my fieldwork I came upon this question—what is the use of remembering the narrative as Bina *possibly* told it to her family, in the last days of her life? What then, is the point of a feminist counter-memory? And *this* particular feminist memory? Even as we are aware that a quick reversal of the magic trick is not possible with such a counter-memory, it does raise several significant issues as to why it matters to remember *intentionally* (Alexander 2005).

The first issue I would like to reflect upon relates to the possibilities that are opened up by feminist counter-memory. Following Judith Fetterley (1978), Hirsch and Smith (2002) in their discussion of feminist counter-memory call for "'resisting readers' who interrogate the ideological assumptions that structure and legitimate coherent linear narratives … have learned to question claims to narrative reliability, seeking instead to understand alternative ways in which truthfulness may be assessed and used … learned how to analyze and document the practices of private everyday experience, recognizing that they are as politically revealing in their own way as any event played out in the public arena" (p. 12). As my discussion of the official memories of Bina's case illustrates, the focus of official archives remains the narrative of the powerful (within both contexts—of tribal patriarchy and state), "those who control hegemonic discursive spaces."

What such a counter-memory opens up is not just the possibility of an alternative memory of what happened with Bina, but a space to discuss memory contextually, across different discourses, fleshing out an alternative method of remembering, of offering another choice, beyond the mis-rememberings and misrecognitions (Bourdieu 2004) that the official and the public memory of the case present. For me then, the point is to re-consider the terms of the curatorship of memory, to re-center the *use* (*fayda*) of recalling Bina's death, in order to open up the grounds for more dialogue.

However, before I explore the potential possibilities that a feminist counter-memory presents, I would like to discuss how such a recall too, is not pure. Such a feminist counter-memory too is fraught with dangers and difficulties, which include the politics of location, questions of agency, and the politics of representing violence. Ethnographic feminist counter-memory is also marked by the risks of writing the body (Minh-ha 1989). First, there is the literal problem of writing the body consumed by violence, i.e. the difficulty of writing (about) violence when (Bina) the woman in question is not around to tell the tale. Second, there is the difficulty of writing violence back into marginalized and historically disenfranchised (tribal) communities. This then raises the question of *who* (re)presents the feminist counter-memory? Spivak, in her famous 1988

chapter, "Can the Subaltern Speak?" urges the postcolonial feminist intellectual to own this task (of representing the subaltern) with flourish. Yet,
this process is, and has always been marked by the shifting and multiple
subjectivities of those engaging in this representation. For instance, here, in
the absence of the agent herself, the counter-memory can only be presented
by those willing to believe or (re)tell the narrative in a way that remains true
to Bina's statement in the hours preceding her death. Her absence runs as
the central thread in how her life/death is remembered. And, as Loomba
(1993) has cautioned us, it is not only the tale of the dead that bears being
told, and being heard. While Bina's absence allows for the responsibility (of
her death) to shift[15] for both, the state and the tribe, research on domestic
violence in India has long demonstrated that denial of violence, even when
the agent in question is living, is only too common (Basu 2006, 2012; Baxi
2010; Bhattacharya 2008, 2013).

Thus, the question is not whether we discuss questions of agency and
injustice with this instance in mind because Bina is dead, rather, the question is *how* do we address it, and to what end. Further, if a recovery of her
narrative is a possibility, it leads me back to my initial set of questions: Why
is such a recovery important? Thinking about Bina's agency, subjectivity and
the question of injustice matters because there's a broader context—it is not
just for the individual in question; rather it reflects the contextual issues
that determine how we remember or don't remember the violence Adivasi
women face, whether enacted by the state, by members of the non-tribal and
savarna caste communities, or by other members of the tribe in question. At
the same time, working with the (im)possibility of discussing agency in the
event of death presents a particularly potent challenge for feminist ethnographies of violence. Obviously, in this case, there is no recovery of the event
made possible by talking with/interviewing the woman[16] in question—that
possibility has been foreclosed by her death. But the possibility of a resis-
tant reading, a recovery of her story is indeed possible. The feminist exploration of her case is made possible through an attention to elements in the
case file which are ignored or set aside as irrelevant material by official and
community records; an attention to the fragments of Bina's own narrative
offers such a counter-memory.

Even though the official and community memories need to present the
narrative as a whole, the boundaries of that false wholeness are stretched
when we pay attention to the fragments of the story, which are being written

over by these records. So arguably, even when I'm relying on the very same records, how I'm listening and who I'm listening to changes how I look at or understand what happened that day when Bina was burnt, eventually leading up to her death.

What possibilities open up with a counter-memory that centers the violence leading to Bina's death? What are the processes by which the memory of her death gets reshaped and reconstructed by both state and tribal patriarchy? The struggle over remembering at all—how to remember, why to remember—transforms the memory of violence. The memory changes from a single-dimensional account of what happened on the day she was set on fire into a history of what follows in the form of her narrative in her remaining days leading up to her death, something that accounts for her social location as a tribal woman, within the larger context of tribe, gender, and sexuality in India.

Further, loss and injustice are not *only* produced by the state. In this instance, the collusion of the tribe with the state is crucial in producing a particular memory—that of Bina's death as an accident. Yet, given the complex and long history of disenfranchisement and struggle for rights of tribal communities in India, another question that needs attention pertains to the risks of writing violence back into marginalized communities. While a detailed examination of these dangers and risks is beyond the scope of this chapter, I would like to reflect briefly on the politics of location in my broader discussion as I reflect on the dynamics of ethnographic accounting of violence *within* the Lahauli tribe.

On the one hand, this counter-memory presents the possibility of a story being remembered and re-articulated, rather than dismissed as an untruth; and on the other, it carries the risk of being misused by re-inscribing men of the tribe as violent, a stereotype of the *uncivilized* tribe which the Lahaulis are countering by claiming non-violence and non-discrimination as discussed earlier. In the epilogue of her book, *In the Shadows of the State*, Alpa Shah (2010) follows Talal Asad (1973) in reminding us that "writing ethnography is a political act." She draws upon the potential of ethnographic analyses to demonstrate both, the failings and successes of indigenous movements in moving toward radical political goals. My project too is carefully balanced between these two places—struggle and injustice—and works in solidarity with *both*, the tribal women's call to end violence that they are targets of *within* tribe; and with the broader goal of the Lahaula community in resisting the racialized construction of tribal as Other in India. The key question for me has been instead about how to discuss violence in this context *despite* the limitations and risks it poses. For me this also involves continually evolving in terms of my research practices to work in (situated) solidarity (Nagar and Geiger 2007) with the women's groups in Lahaul who actively work against the violence within their communities despite the backlash that it presents for them.

In conclusion, I would like to return to the issue of what and who then constitutes this feminist counter-memory? By no means is this memory only the purview of the feminist postcolonial intellectual, or of the family of the woman in question. Despite the local women's collective's active presence in the community as fighting gender injustice in Lahaul, a large number of women members of the Keylong Mahila Mandal (women's group) and the Tribal Manch did not believe Bina. They decided to support her husband and the local male leaders in the positioning of this case as an accident. However, there were two members in the Keylong Mahila Mandal who actively disbelieved the state and tribal patriarchy's narratives. I shall end this chapter with another rendition of feminist counter-memory as it appeared in conversation with one of the two women—Parvati.

In conversation with Parvati (a very active member of the local women's group), I asked her what she thought about the case, how it had proceeded and the reaction of many people within the community. She responded, "These people (the man in question and his family) must have bribed everyone in the picture, *ji*. All these people—the witnesses—who've turned hostile, are all lying now. Who cares now, you know, they're thinking she's gone so what matter! Let me tell you, that's how it is. All these people being true Lahaulis thinking 'who knows' but they don't care. For them everything is 'it is what it is.' For everything our people say it, you know that . . . But God is the true witness, no matter what the courts say . . . All these people will also serve their time."

Whether or not we agree with the call for divine intervention and vengeance that Parvati issues here, it bears significance that of several members of the Lahauli community that I spoke to (with the exception of Bina's extended family), Parvati was the only person who actively called out the state and the accused's family directly—for lying and bribing—two commonly used strategies in proving innocence within the juridical structure. She chose to remember the narrative, which the state and many in the tribe chose to forget. Of several members of the community who had heard details of the case as it was playing out in court, she stood out as the only one who believed Bina.

6 ⇀ REMEMBERING FOR LOVE

This chapter weaves memory, ethnography, and solidarity in the context of caste and gender violence in Lahaul. It takes into account different aspects of ethnographic memory by focusing on the notes, journal entries, and different relationships of remembering that were formed during what I call fieldwork/lifework. I understand ethnographic dialogue (Madison 2008) and the recall of violence as embedded in different notions of love, resistance, and solidarity. I approach memory as at once dispersed and layered. This dispersal and layering is illustrated through an analysis of my own memories of fieldwork and the memory of caste violence shared by one of my interlocutors, Kavita. I then close the chapter with a discussion of the politics of location as salient to the construction of a feminist counter-memory, in dialogue with my interlocutors. Such a method accounts for the process of remembering violence through an attention to everyday aspects of Lahauli women's lives over and above the official and state memories of singular events of violence.

As mentioned in the prologue and the first chapter, it was my early work as an organizer that led me to many conversations with local women who wanted to organize around questions of violence (against women) in the valley. Eventually I stayed on in the valley after a group trip with local women to different organizations in North India, to continue working as a community organizer with the local women's groups, collectively called mahila mandals, working on anti-violence campaigns led by the women. My role consisted of supporting the group with filing cases of violence that arose on a day-to-day level, strategizing for future conversations, planning anti-violence campaigns, and valley-level meetings with everyone in the community to address issues of marriage practice, honor, and violence.[1] It was during this time that Kavita and I grew to know each other better, as she quickly became one of the key local organizers for the initial activism of the women's groups in the region.[2]

Thus, while this book is based on oral history based ethnographic interviews, field notes, and journal entries from 2010 to 2011, my relationship with Kavita is much longer. For me, remembering my fieldwork is inextricably intertwined with memories of Lahaul and all of those years of my life in general. By this I mean that my memories of fieldwork, as my life's work, go beyond the formal fieldwork periods I spent in Lahaul for both, my doctoral work and subsequently for this book. Additionally, the memories of the period that constitutes the official fieldwork too are not only interview-focused. Rather, my field memories, like for many researchers before me are deeply entwined with my daily experiences and political–emotional connections with those who had an impact on my life during that time. By political–emotional connections, I mean the relationships I had with different people in and around Lahaul—people who deeply influenced my work and politics. Kavita, who began with me as a co-worker in the collective, wanted to eventually be an official interlocutor in my research, a collaborator and participant in conventional terms; but she was not only that either. She was, and remains, a comrade, supporter, feminist community, and research collaborator for me in Lahaul. Remembering my fieldwork, then, is not only about analyzing interviews, events, and archival documents, but also involves love and political commitment to and with those who repeatedly welcomed me into their circle. To quote Jacqui Alexander (2005, 275), "Love inspires remembering." So here I am, finally, remembering for love.[3]

KAVITA

At the time when I was working in the valley, Kavita was living with her husband in Manali, often coming up to Lahaul to meet her family and work in their agricultural fields during harvest season. She became one of the key local activists for them. She was committed to strengthening links between the larger Dalit and Adivasi movement in the state and the activities of the local group. Kavita is from the only Dalit family in her village, and her life experiences include various forms of (caste) violence. Further, as elaborated in the previous chapters, the Lahauli community positions itself as simultaneously historically disposessed via the Brahmanical structures of caste hierarchies, while maintaining a strict caste order internally. In various formulations of caste structures in India, both Dalits and Adivasis fall under the purview of historically disenfranchised groups. However, in Lahaul, the tribe itself is further stratified along caste lines, constructed loosely around the regulations of caste purity usually found in non-Adivasi and mainland communities of the hills and plains in India. Thus, while Kavita is a Dalit woman herself, her location as also an Adivasi further complicates the dynamics of how caste violence plays out socially, legally, and politically in her life.

Over the years that I have known her, Kavita has had to move in and out of the valley several times. She left the home that she had shared with her husband primarily because of domestic violence–related circumstances, and then by the time we were talking in 2011, she had moved back into the Kullu valley. Upon her return to her parents' home, having left her husband, she began looking for work to support herself and her children. She worked a few odd jobs at the local school in the village. This was the period during which our relationship strengthened—both through our shared history of having worked in the women's collective earlier, and our shared goal of addressing multiple layers of violence in Lahaul. During this period, she clearly expressed her desire to talk about her experiences of violence in a formal interview. I documented her life history for this book, as part of this particular history of Lahaul, and our camaraderie strengthened over this period. Our time together also included long, detailed discussions about our lives, current affairs, poetry, other people's lives, the local administration, the army, and numerous other topics of conversation often shared between confidantes and friends.

A theme that repeatedly emerged in conversations and interviews with Kavita was her sense of loss, especially the loss of bodily integrity within and beyond the context of her experience of sexual violence. In an interview I briefly discuss later in this chapter, she used the metaphor of being "trampled" in describing her experience of rape at the age of sixteen by the village priest. In the same conversation, she talked about breaking social codes and talking about her rape publicly. Her reason for wanting to do this emerged from a desire to enable other women in the same position to speak out against violence. She repeatedly spoke of her love for her daughters, her love for her community as a Dalit woman, and her wish to speak openly against these injustices. Through such a resignification of her victim status, Kavita's memories offer a range of resistive possibilities. In narrating her story, Kavita goes far beyond any singular event of violence in her life, thus locating her experiences within larger social processes already in motion—processes that she repeatedly negotiates and wrestles her way through—such as when she herself turns her victim status on its head through both her daily life and her desire to speak openly about her rape. By thus choosing to speak out, Kavita destabilizes what Sharon Marcus (1992, 389) has discussed as the rape "script." However, this move does not necessarily achieve the physical prevention of rape on her body as Marcus has called for, but constitutes a political refusal to accept the discursive power of rape. In the end, however, she decided not to tell her story openly,[4] in light of the backlash and shame it could bring on her daughters. Kavita decided instead to wait for divine intervention in the form of karmic justice, according to which the universe operates on cause and effect of actions/deeds, hence no deed goes unpunished or unrewarded.[5]

She asked to be interviewed, and wanted to be a central "character" (her word) in this book about Lahaul. She named herself "Kavita" for the reader of this text, literally meaning "poetry," "Don't you think it's an apt name for me in your book? I'm dreamy, and quite like a poem . . ."

In interviews, Kavita talked extensively about her relationship with her ex-husband. Although she loved him deeply, she eventually ran away from him to save both herself and her daughters from his violent and destructive moods. Repeatedly she struggled with the idea of having loved him, and that she still thought of it as love. She struggled with her own entrenchments in what she considered a shameful love, routinely pushing against the (heterosexual) love plot which often sanctions violence as the fallout of too much love, reasoned as jealousy. For example, we were meeting after over a year in 2011. She ensured we ate at the new places I mustn't miss, and that I become acquainted with the new neighborhood she lived in. It took me more than a year to find her again—I traveled to Kullu and Lahaul over two breaks from school (summer and winter of 2010), looking for her as carefully as I could. I called all the old numbers, old e-mail addresses, looked through new government records—knowing her parents wouldn't know where she was. Until suddenly in January 2011, just as I was leaving the States I received an e-mail from her. Here is another piece[6] of that first conversation in 2011.

K: I had to hide. I needed to start afresh. I didn't want my ex Sunil to know where I was. Especially that I was so close by, with our daughters . . . love like that is hard, you know. He treated me so badly, beat me so much that I had to leave, run away, but I have never stopped caring for him . . . he was there when nobody else was. So this time I had to hide—not let anyone find out. And then my brother said he saw you in the village, in the winter that too—I couldn't believe it—I have missed you! (She smiled.)

H: I was so relieved, really, to know that you're ok. I missed you too. Is he still around in Kullu then—Sunil? (I'm looking worried, frowning.)

K: Nah, thank GOD he left—now I cannot be tempted to return to him—and I can move around freely. What about you? Do you stay in touch with your ex?

H: I don't think I could, even if I tried—it would be too difficult.

K: Oh but that's the thing with love, it makes you do the hardest things . . . I'm not being a fool here, I know Sunil was violent, and I love(d) him despite that . . . it was not easy—to love him—it took a lot of work to not be filled with shame for loving him.

Love, in its popular romantic conception, is part of a heterosexual dream plot reserved for the individual (Berlant 2012). Yet it can mean different things to people depending on their location. To love literally can mean to labor/work, and it can also be used to explain intimate partner violence. Loss of such love however, can sometimes be freeing. Throughout her narrative, Kavita emphasized the themes of loss, love, and resistance that for her existed simultaneously in the face of violence. She moved from discussing one kind of loss associated with (caste) violence to another. And each little story within her overall story was woven around her feelings of love—love for her daughters, her ex, her family, her co-workers, and for her community. She would begin sharing one part of a violent moment in her life and move onto something else, like her daughters, reiterating why she needed her daughters to love themselves, as Dalit and Adivasi girls.

Remembering and forgetting in the context of violence are both durational, but non-sequential; that is, they both operate outside what Lawrence Langer (1996, 55) has called a "stream of time." However, how time factors, either linearly or nonlinearly, into acts of remembrance and forget-ting is also determined by who does the memory work, what it pertains to, and the processes that are at play in the overall scheme of understanding the memory of violence.

DISPERSED MEMORY

This leads me to a key aspect of how I began to understand the narrative as a cohesive whole: namely, that memories of violence—those remembered by myself and my interlocutors—may be durational, sometimes even sequen-tial, and yet, are dispersed. The memories that the women shared with me are dispersed and remembered in pieces that are not necessarily linear. Add-ing yet another layer of memory, the narratives that the memories offer are also remembered by the women themselves, the state and police officials, and by me, each time a little, and at times a great deal, differently. Further, there are different entry points into the conversation for each person that interrupt the direction and sense of chronological continuity. For example, this is the case in terms of my recall: some pieces of each narrative are remembered from journal entries, interviews with my collaborators, con-versations with colleagues, and so on.

In relation to Kavita's recall, the amount of disclosure in each instance of remembering also varied for her, depending on whether she remembered to the police, to the courts, to her family, or to me. All these memories, how-ever, appear at once, often as overlapping life histories narrated at different times in one document. The memories, in other words, are dispersed.

While the official memory of a violent event may tell one story, the woman who experienced the violence may remember the story differently. Because I remember both sets of memories, I invoke this idea of layering. Furthermore, a memory of violence that has literally been written over by the state, police records, or community memory can still shine through in the process of feminist ethnographic recovery, thus challenging the offi-cial memory of the "same" story. This is particularly significant because all of these memories—the stories I heard and the stories I tell—are either directly about or somehow connected to memories of violence. These are mostly about memories of material and discursive violence, rendered inseparable because of the underlying scheme of caste, and thus in their narrations too, they appeared as such—whether in how the women shared them or in how the police records and officials chose to forget them. Therefore, these memories are neither linear nor chronological.

Both linearity and chronology impose an artificial cohesive wholeness upon that which is durationally non-sequential and, in fact, often dispersed. Langer (1996) has discussed the difference between chronological and durational witnessing, where the former is sequential and the latter continuous. So while testimony may sound chronological, for the witness, the memory remains non-temporal, "out of time," caught between an historical narrative that imposes chronology and a witness memory "baffled by a lack of language" (p. 55). It is important to note that none of these narratives or their memories are seamlessly tied together, precisely because they are memories of violence.

This understanding of individual narratives of violence as existing outside the "stream of time" (p. 55) is useful, as it reinforces the need to pay attention to individual narratives as equally significant to collective histories and memories of violence. This kind of violence hardly finds space in official history beyond police records, if even that. Furthermore, it is discarded within a large floating space of what is often considered routine—the rape of a Dalit Adivasi woman, a form of gendered violence necessary to uphold caste domination (Irudayam et al. 2011). This kind of violence in caste-society is all too often read as part of a general malaise, as something that is not socially memorable, and if it is so then the reason is that of "violence against a woman." It is, thus, not memorialized, not part of a collective history, and remains undocumented beyond a chronological recall of police and court records. To remember that it is in fact (caste) violence would be tantamount to acknowledging the violence of caste enacted through state and community, which would dismantle the very backbone of a social order being upheld through the existence of caste hierarchy.

Because violence disrupts the everyday linearity of events, I argue that memories of (caste) violence that center feminist praxis must not follow—and must, in fact, reject—the artificial, seamless, chronological psychological patterns of order imposed on women by official records and literature.[7] This imposition comes from the foreclosure of the possibility of a certain type of faithfulness to one's own experience of violence. State and biomedical recordings of violence can partake in a certain type of forgetting of the subjective experience of violence; they can deny the social and political structures embedded in the visceral, embodied experiences of violence articulated in the caste and gender hierarchies remembered by the subject. Thus it is often the case that experiences of (caste) violence are altogether not recorded, and when they are recorded, the reductive chronological and psychologizing schemes imposed on the events of violence have no fidelity to the lived experiences of the subjects who were violated.

Additionally, my ethnographic recall is also dispersed as I travel through field memories—memories that are always intertwined with my own life. What might I mean by this dispersed nature of ethnographic recollection? While ethnographic fieldwork is chronological insofar as it fits into a programmatic version of linearity, the doing of fieldwork, as it connects to my lifework is often dispersed and discontinuous. For example, most conversations I had with collaborators, even those conversations that were official interviews, did not follow a chronological structure. In other words, conversations and life stories were narrated and shared with me over a period of months, shared while we went about conducting the rest of our lives and businesses as usual. I say this to emphasize that intimate conversations about life, caste domination, violence, and our histories are obviously never planned into any exact linear order of fieldwork; instead, they appeared in unexpected and dispersed ways.

My own memories of fieldwork were recorded in my journal at different points in time: some were written late at night after a full day of work; others were written while traveling from one location to another or recalled for my interlocutors, friends, and colleagues over the telephone or in person. Eventually, several memories were recounted at community meetings in Lahaul, at conferences, in hotel rooms, and during various travels thousands of miles away from the valley. All of this further complicates the texture of ethnographic memory. This fragmented process of remembering my fieldwork, then, is what I refer to as the dispersed nature of ethnographic recall. But why is it important to pay attention to this fragmented process?

Because memory is often seen as an individual process separate from history, understanding the fragmentation in the process of speaking memory allows us to unsettle any idea of authentic history, any idea of authentic memories of violence. In her discussion of privacy and invisibility in gay and lesbian cultures, Ann Cvetkovich (2003) discusses why and how "in the absence of institutionalized documentation or in opposition to official histories, memory becomes a valuable historical resource." For her, unconventional modes of remembering "stand alongside the documents of the dominant culture in order to offer alternative modes of knowledge" (p. 8). In this vein, I seek to draw attention to the dispersed nature of recall and the fragmented structure of memory. I do this not to construct a "true" memory, but to illustrate how notions of authentic and linear recall, which insist on a cohesive structure and occupy the space of official knowledge, do a disservice to Dalit and Adivasi women's memories of violence.

By privileging a memory that is officially sought, the processual account of violence is lost, continuing to center events of violence. Unless there is an attention to the processes as remembered by the women who experience violence, it becomes difficult to understand what the particular events of violence might mean, especially when we consider the enactment of sexual assault as a means of upholding a caste society, thus severely limiting the possibilities of justice. Consider the official memory of Kavita's rape as an example of this disservice.

Kavita's father filed a police report stating that the local village priest raped her. The official record of her case included names of the victim and the accused, the date and time of the event, and some descriptions of the events leading up to the police intervention. Eventually, the official record stated that the case was resolved out of court. However, among several other things, this official record failed to mention the caste and gender nexus in which her rape was embedded; it also did not highlight that her father accepted compromise money, despite the fact that this was common knowledge both in her village and at the police station. Presumably, this was because, as Pratiksha Baxi (2010) has illustrated, compromise is not permitted in India for crimes like rape and murder; moreover, her father, and not Kavita herself, conducted most of the conversations with the police.

Thus, the official memory fails Kavita at multiple levels. First, it documents the events in an orderly fashion, but obfuscates the complex politics of caste, tribe, gender, and sexuality in India, something that Kavita herself highlights in her moments of recall in both her journal and in conversations with me. Furthermore, it produces the false narrative of an objective state apparatus that intervened according to the law—an apparatus willing to, and successful in, supporting the victim. This is a classic example of Pierre Bourdieu's (2004) misrecognition in which the violence contained in the legal and social practice of compromise is transformed into a seemingly "positive" event for the victim in question. The discursive violence of the compromise then gets turned on its head, becoming a moment of resolution that ostensibly "helps" the victim.[8] The records illustrate the state as finally "giving in" to her family's wishes to withdraw the case, but a closer look at this moment illustrates the politics of caste, tribe, and gender surrounding the compromise.[9] While it is clear that Kavita's rape was indeed an act of caste violence, but for it to fall under the legal purview of the (Prevention of) Atrocities Act of India, the violence would have had to be committed by a caste Hindu who was also not Adivasi.[10] Because the priest also hails from a disenfranchised community (as an Adivasi, and a member of a Scheduled Tribe), the police claimed that it was not and could not be a caste atrocity. Hence, the two options offered to Kavita's family were that of either legal redress via the registration of the assault as rape alone or an out-of-court compromise. This decision to eventually compromise, while made by Kavita's own family ostensibly for "her own good," is embedded in the same logic of caste violence that routinely subjects Dalit families to the discursive violence of caste both within the legal framework of "crime" via the misuse of legislations like the Atrocities Act and within the minutiae of everyday social life (Rao 2009). In this instance also, we see how the act is not applied and the rapist continues to serve as the village priest.

What emerges here is the particularly marginalized location of Dalit women, within Adivasi communities, an intersectional marginality which I have discussed in the introduction to this book at some length. The legal possibilities are further complicated because of caste–tribe politics, as the impunity granted in this case is to an Adivasi, and not to the usual caste Hindu member of society. Thus, via this trick of settling matters "internally" within what it names the SC and ST communities of Lahaul, the state continues its complicity and active participation in perpetuating violence against Dalit women by offering compromise in rape cases as a solution—both in this specific instance and in India in general (Kannabiran 2011).

A processual recall would have produced a different narrative, one that remained attentive and faithful to Kavita's experiences and her narrative of the rape and what happened after it, including the social implications of the compromise in further dishonoring a (Dalit) woman. For example, in a conversation with me, Kavita recalled that her caste status was invoked by the man who raped her, in the moments preceding and during her rape. Further, she recalled her grief and simultaneous anger at how the police approached the issue, and the injustice of the continuing presence of her rapist in the village, which finally resulted in her having to move away. All of this is entirely missed in the official record, which remained focused solely on the actual event of rape. Additionally, the fact that her father agreed to compromise—hence exposing her to greater social indignity—needed to be underplayed in the official record. Nayanika Mookherjee (2006, 440) has discussed how women with few economic resources often "might only have their moral selves and honor as symbolic capital." This is further lost when material resources are accepted by victims or their families as compensation for their loss of honor through sexual violence, which doubles the public shame of rape, especially for women of marginalized communities. In this instance, Kavita's father's decision to accept the compromise added insult to injury.[11] What is further lost in the linear narrative are Kavita's own thoughts about her father's decision to accept the money for her benefit. Here, we see that the memory of violence that constitutes much more than the event itself is never really captured in the official narrative, which fails to record the multiple temporalities of recall that violence sets off. Additionally, in Kavita's case, the official linear recording eventually allowed a forgetting, one that created a space where her rape could later be disavowed through a series of misrecognitions.

Arguably, one could say that the procedure of the law produces linearity; that is, the state's mandate is such that it can only produce a perspective that is rendered through chronology. Because such a mandate foregrounds the limit of these procedures, the bodily, sensory, and political complexities are always already lost. Furthermore, even a more sympathetic record—given that most police and juridical records are not always sympathetic to women, especially those who experience (caste) violence—when linear, will still be marked by omissions. Finally, an individual's memory can also follow a linear storytelling path. My point however, is that linear recall, which focuses on the event of violence alone, is insufficient because it is a singular approach that does not account for multiple aspects of her recall, including the ways in which bodily memory is metaphorically experienced in the moment of recall. Therefore, effectively, an official record misses the relevance of the victim's subjectivity, which, as Veena Das (2000) has argued, over time produces self-creations by the person who experienced the violence, while remembering through the everyday.

To understand the dense realm of meaning formation in relation to violence requires delving into questions of subjectivity as constituted by caste and tribe, and paying attention to how violence and memory co-constitute each other, without focusing on a search for facts as truth—what Michael Taussig[12] (1991, xiii–xiv) has called the "social being of truth." Instead, an attention to the processual, embodied, and fragmented process of remembering, which takes into account Kavita's subjectivity at the nexus of caste, gender, and sexuality in India, opens up the possibility of a political interpretation, one that is a departure from the official memory of the state. Following third world and women of color feminist critiques of second-wave feminists, Shailaja Paik (2009, 45) has rightly urged that there is a "need to understand the diversity of experiences of Dalit castes, the specific Dalit histories, culture and religion, class, personal lives and self-hood in their own contexts."

Thus, focusing on Dalit and Adivasi women's subjectivity needs to be connected to how it is and can be politicized. Several women I interviewed in Lahaul, including Kavita, wanted to discuss their experiences and include the violence in their own lives in what was to be my dissertation and eventual book, discussions excluded in prior historicizations. Still, I was and remain worried about the consequences this might have. Yasmin Saikia (2004, 279) addresses this fraught possibility of research "instigating more violence against" already marginalized women. While aware of the potential consequences of such documentation, the women seek to share their histories—sharing with the expectation that a representation of their experiences would eventually help them "overcome the silence that had been imposed upon them" (p. 279). The point I am making here is that the trajectory of how the women came to remember violence in and for this project is not merely incidental, but is the central motivation behind my research. Furthermore, in this case, the narratives of violence emerged as the women narrated several aspects of their lives and histories in interconnected ways. Thus, my emphasis on the processual aspects of memories of violence that account for women's narratives beyond the event of violence is integral to this context, and it constitutes what Kimberly Theidon (2007, 474) has called the "broader truths that women narrate." These truths must not be "reduced to the sexual harm they have experienced." My chapter is grounded in what Ravina Aggarwal (2000, 537) calls the "micropolitics of social struggles in everyday contexts," as I focus on women's lived experiences rooted in daily life, emphasizing the need to understand the memory of violence as always processual. My emphasis on process has at its roots an understanding of individual experiences of violence, and thus also its related suffering, as always already social. In discussing the significance of the experiential domain of suffering, Arthur Kleinman and colleagues (1996) emphasize the need to examine violence and suffering as "beyond a single theme or uniform experience." For them, "suffering is profoundly social in the sense that it helps constitute the social world" (p. xix). In particular, it is these very "routine processes of ordinary oppression" that I find particularly useful because I emphasize the importance of process in understanding forms of suffering as both collective and individual. Kavita's individual experience of violence and suffering is also social if we pay attention to the ways in which her rape is normalized and routinized by the state, thus obscuring "the greatly consequential workings of 'power' in social life" (p. xiv), which, in this instance, are the workings of caste and gender.

Moreover, since memory is also marked by loss, an attention to the fragmented processes involved in the loss allows us to think of these otherwise seemingly individual memories as remembering differently, creating a feminist counter-memory. This is what a critical feminist ethnography of violence seeks to build. In other words, memories are often fluid and dispersed; they become part of one's subjectivity through this dynamic process of remembrance and not-forgetting. Only a processually attentive remembering that engages with the memories and silences of those who lie outside the "parameters of the dominant" (Mohanty 2003, 83) can account for a full political project. To further illustrate some of these processual aspects of remembering and forgetting, I now turn to a journal entry from my fieldwork year.

REMEMBERING INTENTIONALLY

Over the course of my fieldwork, my journal became my sounding board for everything. In it, I processed my own feelings about what happened daily, in addition to describing details of the events and conversations that constituted my routine. Additionally, the journal kept the memories alive for me when I was writing. Returning to the United States after living a year in Lahaul and trying to get back into transcribing, translating, teaching, and other academic pursuits had me feeling lost and uncertain about what I was writing. The journal grounded me; it kept my memories fresh, even as they evolved with each round of retelling and re-remembering. I have provided below here a section of my journal entry from the first time Kavita shared the details of the sexual assault she experienced when she was sixteen . . .

Today Kavita and I talked for over three hours. I recorded the interview. We started at the Gompa (monastery) by the school and ended at the steps of the temple by where she had been raped by the priest years ago. When describing the details of her rape and the torturous walk back home, she used the words that I can best translate to "trampling" the grass as she dragged her feet. As she began speaking about it, she was crying, and I was too. For her then, and for us now. The Kavita of today who wants to reach out and save herself from more than ten years back, and who now hopes to stop it from happening to others. She used the metaphor of the trampled grass and her trampled body as she described how part of herself was crushed that day. I thought of how I could never articulate that moment in words—the sight of the new fresh green grass that she had once trampled—the clarity and confusion of that moment muddled in my own tears during her retelling. We sat inside for a long time after, crying and shivering.

She wants to talk about it to the world. She feels it could be her response to how the police forgot her case. She wants her story to stop others from experiencing her own ongoing suffering every time she remembers or is reminded of the rape. . . . I asked her if she could think about remembering publicly some more. It's a lot, telling and retelling this history . . . and the backlash that it might bring with it.[13]

We spent all day together. I returned home late and here I am now, with my words again, speaking my memories and hers; sitting in front of the Saptapadi.[14] The constant cheesy music from the dhaba floating in; the low murmur of voices streaming in from the main road; the clanging of the hammer against the stones; the sun against my neck and back; the sudden laughter from the neighbor's house—all reassuring me of their existence. Somehow each mundane detail reminding me, as she did, that all the violence contained in that one story cannot be, must not be, forgotten.

Remembering like this can be so painful. Yet, worthwhile because we remembered, those years of forgetting.

Kavita's remembering is one that actively seeks and engages a will to not-
forget. In Alexander's (2005, 277) words, Kavita "intentionally" remembers
as she chooses to not-forget, and fights back the deliberate forgetfulness of
the state in the initial police response to her rape. Remembering an experience of caste violence in this manner is different from looking back at violence; remembering the experience involves a recall of the perception of the
violence and what surrounds it—again. In this way, remembering is embodied. The violence that Kavita has suffered bodily is recalled through multiple senses in one act of remembering, and grounds the materiality of sexual
assault within the structural violence of caste domination in India. There is
the violence, which is experienced and stored as a violent memory. When
Kavita recalls this bodily violence, when she talks, for example, of "trampling the grass," she experiences this violence as it is remembered—not as
a looking back—but she remembers the suffering as what it means today
when she remembers. The memory of the violence as an act of "trampling"
literally and metaphorically[15] maps onto the enactment of caste domination
through rape against a Dalit woman, by a priest, a privileged-caste member.

Yet another way in which remembering violence is embodied appears in
the journal entry included above: the music from the dhaba, the sun against
my neck and back, the clanging of the hammer. All of these descriptions
lie entangled with the remarkable and mundane moments of remembering.
This is yet another layer of memory: I remember Kavita remembering her
experience of violence. There is something in that moment about the nature
of violence and its telling that jars the usual frames of cognition because
those two coexist in that one moment—the extraordinary site of remembering violence and the mundane things that surround the violence and
its recall.

On the one hand, the magnitude of the violence at first glance appears
so far removed from the everyday, so far removed from us sitting together;
and on the other, we remember it in layers, she to me, and I in my journal, alongside this other jarring sensory recall—as a palpable, real, present,
everyday experience of caste for a Dalit and/or Adivasi woman. There is
often a methodological attempt to separate the two because they are jarring, but one must remember that both are juxtaposed and entangled; they

are separate because they appear as different kinds: one everyday, and one not. Yet, it is important not to separate the moments of violence as isolated moments that either victimize or perpetrate such violence, because then we lose sight of the circular structure that enabled each particular violent enactment—in sustaining caste. Thus a binaristic, event-centered model of understanding violence, which relies upon a linear logic, is precisely what gets punctured when we pay attention to the process of recall.

In writing about histories of violence, it is methodologically important to note that when one remembers the violent narrative, one also remembers other things. Ethnographic recall thus entails dialogic performance—receiving the telling of an extraordinary violence in the context of all the extraneous sensory details—ensuring that we do not, cannot forget the violent nexus of systems of domination and subordination. As we keep journals, record on tapes, or make notes, these sensory details become part of that memory, as we perform these memories for different audiences, as we narrate and re-narrate, we co-perform these memories.

Remembering violence does not always have to be an act of resistance, and even when it is, there does not have to be one spectacular and celebratory moment of resistance. In her discussion of resistance, agency, and sociality, Chandra Talpade Mohanty (2003) says that "resistance accompanies all forms of domination . . . inheres in the very gaps, fissures, and silences of hegemonic narratives." For her, "agency is figured in the small, day-to-day practices and struggles of third world women" (p. 38). This is precisely how an emphasis on process, on the everyday details of women's lives, contributes toward an understanding of agency and resistance that "examines power" (p. 83). Rather than "locate resistors" (Abu-Lughod 1990, 41) and look for moments that clearly stand out as celebratory moments of resistance, Mohanty (2003), Mohanty, Ann Russo, and Lourdes Torres (1991), and Abu-Lughod emphasize the need to locate and examine women's everyday experiences within larger structures of power. They do this because domination and resistance occur at once. Kavita's recognition of the injustice of her violation and her struggle with how to speak about her rape in a way that would carry her story forward are indeed illustrative of resistance as a "diagnostic of power" (Abu-Lughod 1990, 41). It is dispersed and expressed through processes of remembering and writing her own memory, now entangled with mine.

Further, such a reading of Kavita's experience allows us to think of resisting today, the structure that enabled the violence, i.e. caste, with the memory of the specific act of violence, i.e. rape, that was yesterday—thus making the past and present inseparable, disrupting once again any linear order of time. This is only possible when we register the act of violence as part of the sociality of caste. In this example of Kavita's remembering, there is no room for forgetting. Why is this type of remembering necessary when there may often be a psychic need to forget? Part of her remembering is a will against forgetting; she holds on to her memory precisely because it is a political act and for her, even an act of love, of resistance. Thus, it becomes important to recognize multiple and competing memories as we think of resistance as always already present. What Kavita remembers may have been remembered differently or rendered entirely absent from official recall, hence reemphasizing the political potential of her memory.

In the journal entry above, I briefly mention Kavita first wanting to tell her story openly, followed by her final decision to not do so publicly. In the moment that Kavita and I were having that conversation, she repeatedly expressed the desire to break her silence and tell her story socially in an aggressive manner, where her voice and story could reach other women of her community. For her, remembering was a way of resisting the disciplining of Dalit Adivasi women through violence. In this very deliberate, self-conscious move of remembering for the purpose of resistance, Kavita turns a moment of vulnerability—and imposed victimized identity—into one of resistance. She felt the need to be actively engaged in a process of fighting the kind of powerlessness faced by her and other women in her situation. What eventually stopped her from going public, however, is the very real possibility of violent backlash. In those days, we talked a lot about what it meant for her to do this—that is, to tell her story publicly in a local/national newspaper. We considered the backlash within her community: her own family's position on this, the kinds of dangers to which it would expose her and her family and, in particular, her daughters. Further, we also talked about what her goals were and whether a newspaper chapter or television coverage could eventually achieve the same end.

Finally, she decided against it, primarily out of concern for her daughters and what it would mean for their future. However, she did decide to remember and talk about it to me.[16] While her case did not stand a chance in a court of law and was withdrawn by her father for reasons that still remain inexplicable to Kavita, she decided that retelling what happened to her during, before, and after her rape was necessary, especially since I was working on a book that documented Lahauli women's lives. Over the years and in different ways, Kavita has asked me to "tell for sure" ("batana zaroor") her story. She has always articulated her need to tell her story as necessary, such that it allows people who read it to not only know what happened with her, but also to register that caste violence does occur in Lahaul. This, then, is her way of ensuring a counter-history, especially in response to the state's deliberate invisibilizing of not only Adivasi women's experiences of violence, but of completely obliterating Dalit Adivasi women's narratives (by denying their very existence), in the region. Although this intentional act of remembrance may be negotiated, it nonetheless contains the possibility of feminist activism, feminist critique of caste and tribe, and actual practical changes with regard to sexual violence against Dalit and/or Adivasi women.

Kavita's will against non-remembrance is in opposition to a will to forget, which takes the form of a disavowal. This is the forgetfulness that the state and Brahmanical patriarchal modes of power will. For the state, the (caste) violence that happens cannot be happening; the state and the patriarchy must produce lies—lies that are too often produced through violence, lies that, in fact, beget more violence.

In Kavita's own case, caste and gender politics intersect in the most classic way to once again benefit the caste and gender–privileged male priest, who is "upper" caste, but Adivasi—a seeming contradiction in terms of his caste identity—yet caste-privileged within this context. This is yet another example of systems that will people to remember in ways that effectively emerge as lies. These individual lies eventually become the public memory through politicians, state officials, police records, families that have constructed narratives for future generations, and so on. If I return to my own field memories, the forgetting engaged by the state and its individual representatives about the rapes, murders, and everyday violation of Dalit and/ or Adivasi women's bodies locally in Lahaul is a clear example of the above. For example, in Kavita's case, it is in a sense because of the state's disavowal that Kavita must not-forget. Again, this is another way in which Kavita's remembering is a remembering of resistance.

Disavowal at once affirms something and denies it. The denial of what is initially affirmed is instrumental in allowing things to function according to the status quo. Forgetting always serves some purpose, it keeps the structure from disintegrating. So the question then becomes: What purpose is served by the disavowal, by this forgetting? What structures are kept in place? Would not a remembering bring to crisis interlocking/multiple structures of caste, religion, modernity, and state?

As discussed above, caste violence often produces forgetfulness. To quote Alexander (2005, 278), "a memory of violence and violation begets a will to forget." This will to forget works differently than the will to disavowal. First, there is the need to forget the very materiality of the violence in order to survive the embodied violence on the sex and spirit, and to forget the visceral nature of that violation on the body. This need to forget is seen in the narratives of violence enacted on the bodies of women/people on the margins everywhere. In other words, the duration of the remembrance of violence is often exactly that, a duration; it must have a terminal limit, and that limit is the point of forgetting. Here, once again, we see the mundane: the memories of violence must be forgotten so that there can be an everyday apart from the violence. The need to forget is so strong that we sometimes forget that we have forgotten.

A site of traumatized memory can also be a site of forgetting. Over the course of my fieldwork, and then during the transcribing, translating, and writing of my dissertation, I too often had to forget. There were journal entries that I forgot about and when writing this chapter, I literally excavated. Those are the entries that I had to reach back into each time I attempted to write and rewrite. This is not a looking back from the outside, but a reaching back into, into the visceral—into the bodily (Alexander 2005, 276). For me, then, there is no writing, no representing, without re-remembering; each memory of the re-remembering of the women's stories entangled with mine; each attempt at embracing the messiness of forgetting and remembering what travels through my body, my mind, my spirit as I attempt to retell these histories continually reworking my methodology. This is further complicated by the fact that with each different entry I bring into the conversation, my own subject position shifts.

LOCATION AND VULNERABILITY

These processes of remembering and not-forgetting violence often render both the ethnographer and the co-interlocutors sharing their histories vulnerable, even as they allow us to resist, retell, and remember. In one telephone conversation with me, Kavita referred to a poem we both love,[17] stating that the reason for it is ". . . because both of us are very vulnerable and sincere at once to our memories and to each other." As she stated so definitively, we render each other vulnerable through our relationships of faithfulness. This is deeply significant in understanding and further complicating issues of self, subjectivity, and location in critical feminist ethnographic practice. However, our vulnerabilities are also located differentially. The uneven terrain that marks my relationship with Kavita as a co-interlocutor, also marks this notion of vulnerability.

If one approaches memories of violence with a care toward the person sharing the memory, and an understanding of individual acts of violence as part of a process, one could argue that not-forgetting violence is yet another point where intervention is necessary. Often, as we engage in the feminist recovery of violent memories, what may get lost is that this process, while it contains the possibility of resistance and hope, also carries the risk of failure. Kavita's call brought home my own anguish about avoiding an engagement with my own epistemological crisis. My story, my life, my fieldwork all remain entangled, inseparable from the experiences of the women I am in dialog with. This deeply personal experience (Madison 2005) is one that I cannot and do not resist.

Yet, no matter what I choose to do methodologically, one sentiment constantly underlies much of this ethnographic process: the failure of fieldwork and representation, even as I understand my fieldwork as my lifework. If my epistemic journey is also my journey through life, then accepting the failures which are inherent in my solidarity practices, also requires that I work through those failures to find new paths or expand old ones. When I revisit my journal from the initial days of my fieldwork, one sentiment that repeatedly appears is my desire to return to Lahaul as if I had never left. My anxiety is one that is intertwined with my location and my fears of returning without being able to walk back as though I had never left, and it always contains the possibility of romanticizing and diminishing my life's work, and the mutual trust between me and my interlocutors. Despite the camaraderie and the clear articulation of trust, purpose, and solidarity between us, as I attempt to represent Kavita's life, I worry often about the complexity of my relationship with her. My concerns are articulated as this desire to have never left, and it is caught in my personal relationship with her and my knowledge that even when I did this fieldwork, I was returning "home," and when I left, I was always leaving my own "trail of longings, desires and unfulfilled expectations" (Behar 1996, 25). My choice in staying on in the United States after the project took shape organically in my own doctoral thesis changes how I position myself today. These field memories lie on this unsettling border of speaking memories for love and solidarity and the possible risks of representing the intimate workings of caste violence for academic consumption. Eventually, beyond the times we met in Lahaul and Kullu and talked on the telephone, the only place that Kavita and I appear together are in these pages. I write this chapter aware that it also helps my career in fulfilling tenure-related expectations at a U.S. university. I am left wanting more from myself and from what I finally do represent. Here, I write through and with the hope that my own retelling and remembering of my field memories will open up more possibilities for conversations about "that vulnerability we are still barely able to speak" (p. 25). Even as I recognize the colonial history of fieldwork as method, I, like Aggarwal (2000, 537) in my own "feminist commitment to situated and accountable writing," look for a way to stay hopeful through the messiness of ethnographic co-performance (Madison 2005). The "field" is also the "home" I return to, and the fieldwork is also lifework. As a woman of color feminist located in the States, for whom the word home still conjures up a memory on another continent, the relationship between field, home, and work always remains tightly knit, closely woven, happily entangled.

Several feminist scholars have emphasized the need to re-historicize third world women's experiences, and in doing so, have highlighted the importance of location in representation. For me, the process of remembering (caste and gender) violence differently is also an intervention. This form of feminist intervention keeps coming up short; it leads me to ask where this re-representation leaves Kavita and I as we continue to appear together in these pages, in my memories, and in my representation of her memories. On the one hand, our memories contain the possibility of a story being remembered when we appear together; on the other, we live materially and discursively worlds apart, separated by multiple borders. To clarify further, this dilemma is not one that should be read as a personal desire for "borderlessness,"[18] in fact, the challenge lies in walking across and among these borders, living across them in ways that allow for a feminist remembering/counter-memory. This difficulty of walking across and among borders also underscores the very process of writing this chapter. For example, the modes in which I choose to write this chapter need to speak to multiple challenges of crossing these multiple borders with what Richa Nagar and Susan Geiger (2007, 3) have called "situated solidarities"—with the memories that different people shared with me in Lahaul; with my own memories of fieldwork; and, finally, with the task of contributing to an archive of feminist counter-memory transnationally.

That Kavita was and remains vulnerable in this relationship—partly because of my ethnographer privilege, partly because of the very subject at hand, and partly because of our camaraderie—has not altered her conviction in having her story documented by me, nor has it changed my certainty to place her at the center of my project. The question for me has never been whether this story should be told, but rather: How do I remember and retell this story that has emerged from both, the commitment to documenting (caste) violence that is my feminist praxis, and the love that is my inspiration, what Gloria Anzaldúa (1999) has called "soul" and what Chela Sandoval[19] (2000, 135) described as a "hermeneutic of love." For me, this hermeneutic involves engaging with and continually evolving in terms of my research practices to work in solidarity with Kavita and other Lahauli (Dalit and/or Adivasi) women. My attempt here is not to list my privileges and identity-markers as though there is a distant landscape of structural inequalities that my research/writing can claim from the outside; rather, my attempt is to illustrate how and why Kavita and I co-inhabit this messy space of our varying structural realities, and what this means politically. To think about crossing these multiple borders politically, as several feminist ethnographers working through issues concerning self and subjectivity have argued, is not to enlist identities as discrete; rather, it is to acknowledge, recognize, understand, and work with the ways in which these stories are mediated through our own bodies, despite and in-between the structural, institutional, and sociopolitical disjunctures inherent in the practice of fieldwork (Nagar and Geiger 2007). Kavita's own memories—her memories as an oppressed caste subject having experienced violence—render her vulnerable—and yet she seizes herself as an agent of her own retelling from that structure. For her this is a clearly articulated act of solidarity toward other Dalit and/or Adivasi women in Lahaul. Through the choices she makes in her everyday life, we see an example of how her own remembering exists in opposition to public and institutional forgetting and disavowal—a disavowal that, in some sense, threatens to foreclose the possibility of a type of fidelity that a subject can wish to have toward her own remembering.

What possibilities open up with this kind of remembering that simultaneously render Kavita vulnerable, yet allow her to resist? The struggle over remembering at all—how to remember, what to remember—transforms the memory of violence. The memory changes from a one-dimensional account of what happened on the day she was raped into a history of caste violence. This processual narrative of what follows such violence in the form of her life, also allows the necessary inclusion of her own resistance against the event as part of a process, situated within the larger context of caste, gender, and sexuality in India. Her remembering intentionally, is a definitive political act, demanding attention, daring to love and hope for a radical transformative praxis, one that would prevent such violence against others. A critical feminist counter-memory seeks this transformation; it attempts to facilitate the processes of remembering for justice, for hope, and for that negotiated, uneven space, no matter how complicated, to build solidarities across difference. Carefully perched somewhere between hope and loss, both of which mark all of these memories, each interlocutor here (yours and mine), embodies such transformative possibilities. I too have intentionally remembered narratives of (caste) violence and my interlocutors' narrations of radical love, weaving through the many fragmented moments, of solidarity and failure, in this intimate "field" of memory/life/work (Visweswaran 1994).

EPILOGUE

In closing this book, I want to return to the beginning to tell a story that taught me early on in my work in Lahaul to grapple with failure as part of my feminist praxis. I learnt to face the instability of relationships and friendships formed across hierarchical social locations, and the unevenness of solidarity work across such power differentials. This experience taught me about the complexities and the difficulties of holding myself accountable to both, my friendships and my political commitments to the communities I worked with. The relationships that I highlight here were vital in teaching me the power of storytelling without romanticizing the struggles inherent in this process. Thus, I approach failure not as an end in itself. I understand failure as a means of grappling with the ethics of feminist research. As Aimee Carrillo Rowe (2008) has eloquently stated, ". . . reading failures becomes a methodology for locating the various fault lines and limit points that frame our feminist projects—the crises productive of our feminist futures" (p. 18).

This is the story of my friendship with a Lahauli activist and organizer, Lata, whom I met when I first went to Lahaul. The first part of this story takes place in the year 2000, after which I move to a moment in 2011 when I meet Lata's mother and her brother. The events narrated here led me to realizing the negotiatedness of my own feminist praxis as an anti-caste and anti-violence organizer working with a women's collective in Lahaul. It forced me to consider the significance of friendship in collaborative work where separating feminist solidarity work from the emotions, affections, and insecurities that constitute the rest of our lives, becomes impossible.

LATA

We met during my first trip to Lahaul, for a CAPART-funded handicrafts fair in Keylong. I had traveled to Lahaul to write a "monitoring and evaluation" report about the fair. Lata was the first person I spoke to about how the handicrafts fair was working for the women artisans. Right at the outset, she exposed the role of the middlemen in the fair. According to official documents, the fair aimed to exclusively support local women's handicrafts and entrepreneurship efforts. Eventually, Lata supported me in locating the women whose names were on the files, but who were not the ones running the stalls nor benefitting from the fair which had been hijacked by middlemen from nearby towns and districts. Over the course of the next few months, I moved to Lahaul on a fellowship and eventually began working with a local mahila mandal. Lata and I began spending time together. She helped me find a room, got me acquainted with my new surroundings, and we would often hang out in the evenings talking about all kinds of things—her growing up in Lahaul, me growing up in Jamshedpur; the state of the world we lived in, the possibilities that the worlds we imagined could bring; love and romance; the trials and tribulations of negotiating with family as we took decisions about our lives as adults; the list is endless.

Repeatedly Lata spoke of her dream of eventually moving to Shimla with a government job. She spoke about living close enough to Lahaul but away from the agricultural labor and life on Lahauli terms that she feared she was destined to live. We talked often about escaping our respective "homes" to realize our dreams; about getting away to find our own paths, to do things we believed we could, but just hadn't yet. I had left the home and town I was raised in several years before I met Lata. In our conversations, she would often ask me what it felt like—the taste of "getting away" and if I was lonely without the daily presence of the very familial relationships that I/she were trying to re-negotiate through acts/dreams of leaving. I hoped to make a "bigger" escape, to leave the hardships of my class background behind while being aware that my non-tribal and caste-privileged status made such a thing much more possible. Lata often talked about her escape-dreams but these were not only dreams; they were plans, which were central to her life until that moment when they (the same plans) couldn't be part of her landscape anymore.

We also grew closer because during this period she became more and more active in the *mahila mandal* that I was actively working with. Older and younger women who were from the region trusted her. She had completed a college degree, could read and write English (considered a major asset in many parts of rural India); was fluent in Hindi, and was often seen as more worldly than a lot of other local women. She began working on cases of violence—and with her passionate labor, the collective's impact on these issues only grew stronger.

An issue she (and the collective) was working on, was the locally specific form of violence prevalent in Lahaul—marriage by abduction. She had begun working on a few cases—supporting women who needed support after these forced marriages. The collective began a campaign called "*kiski izzat gayi*" (whose honor is lost), and Lata was among those spearheading it. This was followed by a valley-level meeting on questions of violence and in particular, marriage by abduction. The women's collective stayed active in organizing and seeing these events through to completion despite a lot of resistance and even direct confrontation with younger men from the community. The group began discussing the possibility of consequences (mainly in the form of backlash), especially for women active in the collective.

JOURNAL ENTRY

I took the bus to Manali early Wednesday morning. After I got in, I called Lata's home, to check in with her about next week's plans for the *mandal*. Her mother picked up the phone, crying. At first I couldn't understand what she was saying, between the bad connection and her crying. Then I figured out that Lata hadn't come home all night. Her mother suspected she had been abducted, exactly the night I left to come down to Manali. She was abducted along with a group of her other women friends by a man who had been pursuing her (and whose advances she had been rejecting) for over a year now. They abducted her and the other girls as the women were walking on the road right behind Lata's house, at around 7 P.M.

Her mother was beside herself with worry. I decided to travel back the same night. It took me seven hours to drive back, realizing that another night would be over before we could reach her, *if* we did so at all. We all drove to the house of the man who was suspected to have abducted her—as he had been pursuing her for a while. She had refused his advances and didn't want to marry him, and therefore he decided to abduct her with the help of some friends.

At his house, his family worked hard to convince Lata's mother to agree to the wedding rituals.

Her mother insisted that Lata come back home and that she should neither decide to stay with this man, nor feel compelled to marry him.

At some point during all of this, Lata agreed to go home and take a few days to decide.

Over the next few days at her mother's house, Lata finally decided to go back and to marry and live with him. She felt that facing the community and villagers as a dishonored woman was something she couldn't bear. Despite her mother's promises of support, one of her brothers agreed that staying back would be a big mistake. He asserted that Lata would regret her decision to not marry in the future given that shame and dishonor would always follow her.

In subsequent conversations, Lata shared details of what had happened the night she was abducted. She also spoke of his remorse. He had apologized the same night and begged her to marry him, blaming the abduction and her violation on love. He knew he had robbed her of her dreams and plans, and repeatedly asked for her forgiveness and promised to make it up to her.

Over the next few days, she decided that it was her karma that her life had taken such a turn. She accepted his love, and decided to forgive and marry him rather than face the shame she feared would come her way once the incident became known publicly. She decided to step away from the work of the collective, and moved to a different location to live with him. Over time they moved to Keylong from his village, and he has been a "decent husband" (in her words), over the last several years.

Within those messy and traumatic circumstances, this was the decision Lata took and I stood by her. Among the *mandal* members there were a lot of conflicting ideas about what Lata should have done, ranging from how dangerous her decision to stay with her abductor might be, and what was the point of all the activism prior to this if she was unable to take a stand, to what choice did she really have and she did what she had to do, and such. My own position regarding this issue was something that came up for some of the *mandal* members as "soft." In a meeting, the members asserted that I didn't push her hard enough to make the right choice of not going back to him, and that I even attended the wedding (none of the other women from the *mandal* did) despite the position of several others in the group.

This raised a lot of difficult questions—for me as a feminist activist, for those *mandal* members who were dismissing her decision as a big mistake, and for those of us who were close to her and knew her anguish but were not at liberty to discuss it publicly. Several other women who were not active in the mandal also supported her decision. I admitted that even if a fear of consequences had prompted her decision to marry this man, Lata was my friend and I wanted to support her, no matter how messy that decision. The group was split unevenly on Lata's decision. Some (including me) felt that unless we could really provide an alternative and take responsibility beyond the workings of monthly activities of the *mandal* that were no longer part of her daily life the second she moved away from Lahaul. Staying on in the valley after an abduction without a husband was not an option for most women—did we really have the right to judge her decision? In fact, now that she had decided to be with him, didn't we also need to share the responsibility of what happened to her, why she was specifically targeted at a particular time in the community, and most importantly, if she was walking into possibly dangerous terrain, shouldn't we stand by her, no matter?

There were several members of the *mandal* who did raise these questions, but were worried about voicing all of their concerns too openly. Further, the group included both Dalit and caste-privileged women. In this conflictual moment too, members of the collective across caste groupings were split. Indeed, I was deeply aware that it was easier for me to articulate these concerns, which some of the younger women may have shared with me in private, because my location as someone from the plains and caste-privileged always placed me as an in-betweener (Diversi and Moreira 2008).

The conversations within the *mandal* led to negotiations of various kinds. I was writing a report with/for the group and now we were split in terms of whether or not to include Lata's story as part of our "evidence of VAW (Violence Against Women) in Lahaul" section. This led to more discussions on what it would mean to frame these (real) abductions followed by marriage (which were in violation of the customary practice of "marriage by abduction" in the valley) as "violence." Questions about what constituted violence, and what kinds of names and categories the group needed to continue with their work in the valley now became an even bigger part of our discussions following Lata's abduction and wedding, and laid the foundation for a number of my subsequent work-related decisions.

During the course of those months, and subsequently too, I found myself asking a range of questions to which I had no straightforward answers and nor did the others in the *mandal*. These questions did however open up possibilities for negotiations and solidarities to be strengthened. Why did Lata do what she did? The choices we made, she and the others from the *mandal* and me—what did any of this mean for the future of women's organizing in the valley? What types of alliances did we each open or shut ourselves to/from and how did these varying ways of engaging with the same event create a complex space for solidarity, then, and what might that mean now as I reflect upon it here?

Further, as a caste-privileged activist in the context of India where tribes have been historically disenfranchised, marginalized, and dehumanized, the decisions I made always carried the aftertaste of a violent caste-society. Lata belongs to a caste- and class-privileged family, and my choice to support her after she made the decision to get married despite the fact that Dalit (oppressed caste) members of the women's collective were against it (there were also other Dalit members who supported her) posed a very difficult challenge to my feminist, anti-caste, and anti-violence politics. I was aware that Lata would not inherit any ancestral property, even though her family occupied a class status that many others who worked in/with the collective, myself included, did not. As she didn't work on the land, she wouldn't have access to it either, unless she decided to take on agricultural labor. Living outside Lahaul, alone, without a job yet was also a daunting possibility. It was a complicated and painful decision—to marry her abductor—even for her. As someone who believed that the onus of marking, thinking, researching, writing, and working against the violence of caste from a framework where the salience of caste is not just acknowledged but also challenged and disrupted in order to bring an end to caste society, *what did it mean for me to align myself with Lata's decision despite my own concerns on the matter?* I desperately wanted to find a way that allowed me to stay accountable to my friend, to the women of the collective who I was committed to, and to my own politics.

I made the decision to support her and continue the work with the *mandal* even more zealously, and some of the other *mandal* members also decided the same. It was clear to everyone that this was not really a choice Lata wanted to make. Yet, I also understood the *mandal*'s position on the matter as valid. Their critique of this decision arose from the implications for what the *mandal* members had built so carefully in order to fight marriage by abduction, to support women who were abducted, and to facilitate different decisions than the ones women often felt they *had* to make. And here was one of their own; someone who put so much labor into this movement; doing just the opposite of what the group had been fighting for and facilitating in the valley. Thus, it also made sense to me that several members of the collective felt they could not support Lata. Any way I looked at it, this crisis of solidarity was not one that had any clear answers and resolutions.

Over the next year or so while I continued working in the valley, my relationship with Lata changed drastically. She (understandably) distanced herself from the collective, and the friendships that she had formed there—something I could not blame her for, but that also worried me. It would not be true if I said I understood completely and didn't feel any pain that she withdrew from our friendship, but I revisit it here today to reflect upon what that meant. For me, the process by which the group (and I) negotiated our friendships, our feminisms, and our work with/in the *mandal* in order to remain accountable to one another despite differences is the most significant part of this process of embracing the situatedness of solidarities in transnational feminist praxis.

Lata's story stands in for the negotiations that occurred then and continued to circulate through various other friendships I formed in the valley, even as we may not have agreed on the specifics of her decisions. We did not include her story in the eventual report (there was no way by which anonymity and confidentiality could be maintained), and so we grappled again, with a different set of questions—this time about who represents whom and why? What did it mean to the *mandal* to eventually not include her story? I supported this decision made by the *mandal* members, even as it displaced Lata's labor prior to the violence she experienced.

I stood in the messy space of friendship then—in solidarity with Lata, and with the other members of the group while still going against the wishes of several members of the collective, knowing that I could not choose otherwise. I say I could not because Lata had been violated, and her decision was risky either way. She was in pain, in grief, in fear, and most importantly I (and others in the *mandal*) knew that while she was afraid to go down a path that would pose everyday barriers of herculean proportions to her emotional and spiritual survival in the valley, the path she had chosen would also be extremely hard and required all the strength she could garner. For some of us, the decision she made was and remains as legitimate a step as what the *mandal* had hoped for/wanted, wherein she would have fought back with the group's support.

In 2011 while in Lahaul again during the research for this book, I ran into Lata's mother Ane, at the mall road in Keylong. Upon hearing about this project, Ane expressed active interest in telling her story and wanted it to be included here. I reciprocated her enthusiasm and went to her house where her son expressed his reservations about this project, and I quote him here, "Why are you writing a book now? I don't understand why . . . You know what people say about us in the plains. So whether you write about our gompas and thangkas, or whether you write about how our women are suffering, how will it look on us?"

Over ten years later, with Lata's brother's questions, I found myself in a place similar to the day I decided to stand by Lata's decision to get married despite the collective's reservations. I understood her brother's reservations not only as arising from the events that led to Lata's life decisions, and my own social location, but also from the checkered history of activism and research across difference, in different parts of India, including Lahaul.

His concern about what a representation of caste and gender violence within the tribe from the women's perspective can mean to the world on the other side of the top is indeed an important one. On the one hand, this book presents *only one* story of Lahaul through the daily performance of theory by Adivasi-Dalit and Adivasi non-Dalit women of the region and on the other, it carries the risk of being misused by reinscribing men of the region as violent, a stereotype of the *uncivilized* tribe that Lahaulis routinely face, and which they often counter via claims of non-violence and nondiscrimination (as discussed earlier in chapter five). In quoting Talal Asad in her book, *In the Shadows of the State*, Alpa Shah reminds us that "writing ethnography is a political act" (Asad 1973; Shah 2010). She draws upon the possibilities embedded in ethnographic storytelling to demonstrate both the failings and successes of indigenous movements in moving toward radical political goals. In the same spirit, this book too is carefully perched in that space between justice and hope—and works in solidarity with the women's call to end caste and gender violence that they are targets of *within* the tribe; the tribal-Dalit movement to gain recognition and end caste domination within and beyond tribe; and with the broader goal of both Dalit and caste-privileged Lahaulis in resisting the racialized construction of tribal as Other in India.

It is not a revelation that power differentials between researchers and the communities that their work may be situated in are at the very least complicated and messy. Several feminist organizers and researchers who work across social, cultural, and political divides have written about it. Still, I tell this story here because this re-telling is also part of that unresolvable and messy feminist lifework/fieldwork, it also presents the limits of that leap of faith—through narration the story transgresses its own limits (Certeau 1986).

Choosing to remember these stories for a wider audience has often required self-contradictory methods (such as writing in English, a language most of the women here do not speak), but has also allowed me to create a space I now understand as lying between the legible and the illegible—Achi Yangmo's "phu-phu-phu[1]"—a hybrid representational space that grapples with ethics and demonstrates its accountability. Working with and through failures while still negotiating the story is then an inherent part of this methodology. In negotiating failure, I take my cue from Richa Nagar (2016, 78), who in response to a question about failure as part of the research journey said the following:

> I realize that your question about "efforts that failed" has actually proved to be quite generative. It has triggered a series of reflections that I hope have helped me to convey the point that if we learn to value mistakes—as moments that can teach us critical lessons about our assumptions, contextualities, methodologies, and epistemes—then it is impossible to declare anything in these collective journeys as failure. It is often the unforeseen risks and mistakes that push us to more clearly define our intellectual, political and creative commitments while teaching us to grapple with their inseparability from forever evolving practices.

The women who chose to tell their stories here chose an act of transgression; they show us the strength of storytelling. Somewhere between Yangmo's directive that I not make my ethical dilemmas about this project bigger than the women's stories, and Lata's brother challenging my decision to write these stories, lies the journey of this book. Through its uneven journey, the stories of the women in the book indeed cut across the story that *is* this book.

These stories offer ways of thinking about caste and gender violence; they disrupt and complicate the relationship between caste, tribe, and state, and insist that we acknowledge, recognize, and politicize their intersections; they offer us ways of approaching love, and most importantly they demonstrate that the women of Lahaul generate knowledge and in so doing, offer transformative possibilities beyond love and violence.

ACKNOWLEDGMENTS

This book weaves memories, tales, and lives shared by and with women from Lahaul. Kavita, Lata, Parvati, Keerthi, Dolma, Bina, Yangmo, Dechen, Abeley Angmo, your joys, sorrows, and love are the colors of this weave. Gratitude isn't best expressed through words; yet, words are all I have here. I hope this book, with all its hopes, desires, and failings can be my words of gratitude to you.

Over the years the stories in this book have traveled from Lahaul to different parts of the world, literally as well as culturally, linguistically, and politically. In Lahaul, after the women whose stories make this book, I would like to express my gratitude to several others who have guided me, worked with me, shared with me their immense knowledge of the region, and also lovingly communicated their honest critiques: Lal Chand Dhissa, Chhering Dorje, Tashi Yangzom, Ajay Lahauli, Achi Yangzin, Shakuntala Devi, Shamsher Singh, Sonam, and Sukhdayal ji. My first encounter with the region and community of Lahaul occurred when I worked with CAPART, India and I would never have embarked on that first journey if it weren't for Ashok Thakur. That support, from him and subsequently Sarojini Thakur, continued in Lahaul, Rangri, and Delhi. I have also received a huge amount of kindness and support from several people, families, and businesses in Lahaul, many of whom I cannot list here. These include Bir Singh, Ravi Thakur, the staff at the Hotel Jispa, the photocopier shops in Keylong, Tashi and the staff at Tashi Delek Hotel, those at the Old Circuit House, and many more. There are several institutions, official units, and their respective staff members that I owe a debt to: the Shimla archives, the district library in Keylong, the DC office in Keylong and its numerous commissioners and deputies over the years, and the police station in Keylong, Udaipur, and Kullu. I was immensely fortunate to have met and known Nalini and Shashi in Manali. Dharamchandji of Sunshine guest house in Manali offered me discounted rooms on numerous occasions when I was trying to go in and out of the Lahaul valley. In Delhi, during my fieldwork years for this, and earlier projects in the region, I always found a home with Teresa Khanna and Abhiroop Mukhopadhyay.

My feminist family, friends, and interlocutors scattered in different parts of the world, from Lahaul to Syracuse, have been my homeplace, no matter where I have been located physically, psychically, and intellectually. Pushpa Devi, Aisha Durham, Natalie Havlin, Celiany Rivera-Velazquez, Samidha Satapathy, Srirupa Prasad, Amit Prasad, and Linda Carty—you have stood by me, pushed me to stay honest, and seen the horizon when I could not. Much beyond this book, I am grateful because you bear witness to my story. I am grateful to the friends and intellectual interlocutors I found through my days in Delhi, Bombay, Urbana-Champaign, and Stony Brook who have all been part of the journey of this book: Deepti Misri, Vandana Chaudhry, Nisha Bora, Sreela Sarkar, Dhrubodhi Mukherjee, Desiree Yomtoob, Claudio Moreira, Devika Bordia, Sanjiv Dangi, and Diana Sands.

I will always remain indebted to my mentors in Illinois: Paula Treichler, Norman Denzin, Kent Ono, Ivy Glennon, and John Nerone.

At Syracuse, I was granted a semester for fieldwork that laid the foundation for this book. But more importantly, it is for these colleagues and friends I found here, that I am grateful: Paula Johnson, Chandra Talpade Mohanty, Romita Ray, Jackie Cuevas, Pedro DiPietro, Sue Wadley, Brian Weider, Dalia Rodriguez, and Isabella-Mia Rodriguez.

Among the several colleagues, friends and feminist family who have journeyed with me, Azza Basarudin welcomed me into her home as I was writing. Amit Sood generously assigned me a bed and a desk every time I needed to be in New York. Karl Laraque ensured the glossary was complete, despite a health crisis. And Alaí Reyes-Santos walked with me, as she led the book to its right home.

In Kimberly Guinta of Rutgers University Press, I found a feminist editor who walked the talk, and whose support and promptness were more than what any first-author could ask for. I am also grateful to others at the press who have seen this book through its different stages, and for the anonymous reviewers who provided invaluable feedback.

Finally, none of this would ever have been possible without the dedication and conviction of my parents, Alpana and Dilip Bhattacharya. For them, and for the rest of my family in India I am thankful every day.

APPENDIX I

Genealogy of Previous Work

This book has its roots in my early activist work in Lahaul which was followed by my earlier research to collaboratively document and facilitate anti-violence work with a local women's collective. The initial work of the collective was to generate awareness about, and prevent violence against women in the valley and the group's work began with the campaign around one specific form of violence[1] against women in the area: marriage by abduction or marriage by theft (Tobdan 1993). A longstanding[2] custom of this region, marriage by abduction in the valley often entailed seizing the desired woman from an agricultural field by the man who desired her, commonly helped by a group of his friends. She was then taken to a distant village, and locked inside a room with the man in question. By spending the night at the man's house she was considered dishonored, unless the man married her the next morning. Given little choice in the matter, she "accepted" the marriage proposal, and the ceremony was accordingly conducted. Customarily this practice was not necessarily violent, and operated within the romantic parameters of elopement.

Historically, marriage by abduction enabled the kinship structure of the tribe. First, it provided the groom an option to avoid bride price and sometimes the unaffordable wedding costs. Second, marriage by abduction was also a way for a couple to share an exclusive marriage, as the main form of marriage prevalent in the Lahula tribe was arranged and polyandrous. In fact this was the case till the Indian government officially banned polyandry through the Hindu Marriage Act of 1955. Despite the inapplicability of the Hindu Marriage Act in tribes following Customary Law, by the 1970s the Himalayan tribes had largely begun shifting toward the practice of monogamous marriages (Tobdan 1993). Third, marriage by abduction provided a social framework that enabled couples to depart from traditional expectations through mutual consent without threatening the tribe's familial structures. Since marriages decided through extended familial involvement entailed not only high wedding costs for the groom and his family, such marriages were often polyandrous. Thus, marriage by abduction provided an out to those who preferred to avoid these obligations. Consent was determined through the exchange of *ngya*, a token gift usually consisting of some grains of barley, or money (Tobdan 1993).

Until the mid-twentieth century, if a man wanted to marry a woman without paying the bride's family, he would first send her an offer with the ngya through a friend. If the offer was acceptable to the woman, she would keep the ngya, if not, it would be returned. If it was accepted, the man would then pick her up from a convenient and predetermined location, and they would elope. This marriage arrangement was more or less institutionalized: not only were consensual abductions and elopement carried out according to traditional customs, families and communities participated in the ritualized ceremonies after. For example, upon the woman's return to the village, she would stage a series of theatrical lamentations in public view, relating the story of her "abduction" and begging her family's forgiveness for depriving them of the economic gains expected by the bride's family. The circumstance of abduction accommodated differences in practice without dishonor. Hence, the practice came to be termed marriage by abduction, rather than marriage by elopement.

The practice of marriage by abduction is not unique to the Lahaul valley, or the other communities in the region, but it has also been documented in parts of China, Central Asia, and East Africa. Apart from its public acknowledgment within the community in Lahaul, marriage by abduction has no official status. It is either discussed in the customary laws of Lahaul as a kind of elopement, or, it gets categorized as rape and kidnapping, in government records. Marriage by abduction as it originated in Lahaul carried the romantic element of elopement between a man and a woman who wished to share an exclusive marriage in an otherwise polyandrous society. In Kyrgyzthan, Central Asia, as documented in Petr Lom's 2004 film, the current discourse around the practice of marriage by abduction is still one of romance and honor for the woman in gaining the status of wife and beloved. The element of force and coercion are rendered invisible in the moment that the woman gives her consent, and falls in love. The film attempts to narrate the stories of both men and women in tracking the practice, and offers a fresh look at how some men in Kyrgyzthan look upon it as tribal custom that is important to uphold, as a marker of their masculinity, and as a necessity. It also illustrates the tensions that exist in the women's narratives in the film, as being both a romantic episode leading to them falling in love with their abductors, and as being a violent, non-consensual act that has a definitive impact on their lives, even when it carries the social status of being married.

Lori Handrahan (2002), whose doctoral dissertation investigates the impact of gendered ethnicity in Kyrgyzthan, suggests that the region's long history of struggle with independence, identity issues, and the impact of diverse religious beliefs (primarily Islam and Buddhism) have led to an increase in marriage by abduction or kidnapping since the disintegration of the former Soviet Union. Handrahan (2004) in her article "Hunting for Women" discusses how gendered violence appears to be crucial in consolidating male ethnicity. She argues that the rise in abductions is a literal re-capturing of a post-Soviet tribal identity through a violent and traditional act.

McLaren's (2001) ethnographic work in Nanhui, China, talks about the historical institutionalization of the practice of "quingan" (seizing the bride) which continued in parts of China till the 1940s. She argues that the practice was not a "remnant" of the ancient past but that it fulfilled certain social functions in relation to the bride price system prevalent in those times. She illustrates that many men who were poor and not part of the elite marriage system (which was elaborate, expensive, and entailed a large bride price), were forced to abduct women to marry them or remain bachelors throughout their lives. One of the earliest writings on this practice in Central Asia is Green's (1938) book, which builds on colonial tropes of Cherkess men as violent, and their "culture" as "barbaric."

Whether in Green's colonialist writings about marriage by abduction, or in Handrahan's (2004; 2001) nuanced study of the relationship between the production of violent masculinity as an anti-colonial construct and marriage by abduction, there is a common thread that runs through all these texts. From Green's (1938) colonial research, to Mc Laren's (2001) rich description of the practice in twentieth-century China to Lom's (2004) attempt at documenting facts and tracking the practice as it occurs in Kyrgyzthan to Handrahan's (2004; 2002) nuanced argument linking male ethnic identity to the resurgence of abductions in Kyrgyzthan, all of this research approaches marriage by abduction as rape. In documenting their research all the scholars mention rape without elaborating on what it may mean or not for the women who are being abducted, and whose understandings may be rooted in frameworks that do not operate within Western categories of rape, sexual violence, and marriage. In contrast, the women in the *mahila mandals* in Lahaul do not discuss this practice as rape.

This is the most important distinction that emerged through the collaborative and participatory action research with the women's groups in Lahaul.

In Lahaul, over time this practice transformed into (non-consensual) abductions and was no longer a mutually agreeable way to evade joint marriages (polyandry) and the high cost of engagement-marriages. This transformation of a historically relevant practice into a violent form of marriage whereby prior consent of the woman (as mandated by the custom) was no longer necessary is precisely what led to the organizing work of the women's groups in Lahaul. By the time I was working in the region, the practice no longer entailed "abduction" in name only. In the cases we worked on, often even when a man did ask for a woman's consent, it was reduced to a token gesture, as force was routinely used in the event of a refusal from the woman. Gradually, even as polyandry came under heightened social scrutiny, and costs of marriages through bridal incomes were reduced, the abductions continued, eventually in these truly forced and violent ways. Also, as the research demonstrated, many women did not receive the initial marriage proposal from the man in question, including the *ngya* and instead were abducted from fields, highways, or elsewhere at the will of the man.

During the participatory research action project which had its first phase in 2000–2001, and then again in 2005–2006, when it took the shape of my doctoral work, I had come to understand that the women had a wide range of experiences of violence that they wanted to discuss when talking of and working against marriage by abduction. In listening, I became aware that distinctions among forms of violence often depended more on historical, cultural, or social context than on the precise nature of the account. Thus while (marriage by) abduction and rape shared limited, phallocentric legal definitions in India,[3] the women themselves placed their experiences of abduction and assault within the cultural discourses of rape surrounding them. Beyond caste, a woman's age may be a factor, or whether the act of abduction nonetheless preserved her honor (e.g. whether there was assault and/or if it was followed by marriage), whether it permitted legal redress, and whether there was a vocabulary available to articulate their experiences. The research was challenged by the assumptions that underlay the project.

The women raised a number of significant questions in this attempt to contextualize, understand better, and end the practice which in its contemporary avatar had taken a violent shape. What was the relationship between this very regional form of violence (marriage by abduction) and other forms of violence also prevalent in Lahaul, which are/were more widely observable across India? Situating any specific form of violence within a wider mosaic of violence illustrates the ways in which these different forms of violence articulate with each other, and the disjunctures between them. Looking at it as a mosaic, with different tiles, which refer to different acts of violence, loosens up the cultural assumptions that in fact conjure up a mosaic. The terms of the acts that fit into the mosaic can be changed, but by whom? How do we categorize specific acts as rape, or sexual violence or domestic violence and on whose terms? Are these separations among different forms of violence productive? And in that case, for who? Who decides how each form is defined and what the redressal mechanisms are? What are the structures and systems which are upheld through the circulation of certain meanings of violence, and which are the institutions that are threatened by any challenges posed to the structures that uphold the everyday injustice of caste and gender violence?

My initial work specifically focused on and documented this practice, and its presence in the contemporary context of Lahaul, as part of a larger participatory action research project with the collective goal of ending the practice of marriage by abduction. As discussed in the prologue, this was in fact the issue around which women decided to organize when visiting the Mahila Samakhya activists in the Garhwal Himalayas. Thus, after the successful campaigns on the issue in the early days by the mahila mandals, there was a substantial reduction in these violent abductions. Local village Panchayats and the men of the Tribal Samiti of Lahaul and the Stod Valley Kalyan Sabha, took this issue up actively after the initial campaigns. I documented the practice with the women's groups through extensive fieldwork. The interventions made by the mahila mandals with regard to real abductions were successful, especially since various community groups and individuals, including influential members of the once-ruling castes of Thakurs, took it upon themselves to address the issue. Additionally many of the younger women working in the collective themselves got married, or moved away, and gradually the activities of the groups on this issue reduced and eventually dissolved. However, the women's groups were still very active on other issues, including different forms of violence. By the time I returned to Lahaul in 2010, marriage by abduction was no longer a central focus for any village-level mahila mandal.

APPENDIX II

First Information Reports

CASE I: F.I.R

5/05 (23-1-05) Under 302 in F.I.R. but was deleted vide. CD No. 47 (this case diary is only available in the case file) noted in F.I.R . . . instead 306, 309 added. 306 IPC—Sunita—set on fire, died on 22/01/05 then why filed under Section 306?

> Complainant—Sohan Lal complainant s/o [son of] Basant Ram, Mohila, PO Pangah, Manali Police Station, Distt. Kullu 50 yrs.
> Accused—Suresh Lal (31 yrs@ time of reporting), s/o Prem Chand r/o [resident of] Jasrath (near Jalma). Deceased Sunita 27 yrs.
> ("*tel chhidak kar aag lagayi, jo bahar bhagi to girne se chot ayi aur mar gayi*"/"she caught on fire due to some cooking oil spilling on her, and when she ran outside to roll in the snow, she fell, got hurt and died")
> As a result, the accused was acquitted on 27.06.07 on fast track Kullu court.
> Even the witness that eventually turned hostile admitted that her husband called her "*kutia*" or "*kutla*" (meaning "bitch")
> F.I.R. received by fax from sub-inspector, Shimla Mr. Prem Lal

> *Sunita lower Keylong—Bodh caste; married in September 2003 to Suresh Lal, s/o Hira Lal of Jasrath, p.o. Jalma [this is the chowki where*

he is currently posted]. She lived with Suresh Lal in his quarter as he was/is home guard employee. On 3.1.05 a relative (maternal uncle's son), Prem Nath, called me at 12:30 P.M. and told me that she was burnt and injured and had been admitted in Keylong hospital. Upon hearing this, I contacted our relatives in Keylong and asked them to find out what happened. My relatives saw my daughter and son-in-law Suresh boarding the helicopter from Keylong for Bhuntar, Kullu. From Bhuntar I took both, Sunita and Suresh to the Kullu hospital. Due to severe burns Sunita was in a serious condition. The MO (medical officer) recommended that she be transported from Kullu on 05.01.05 to IGMC Shimla which is a bigger hospital. My wife Yekki Devi and Dinesh, who is Sunita's brother-in-law took her to IGMC Shimla on 6.01.05. Sunita was admitted to the hospital on 06.01.05 and she died today, on 22.01.05 at about 6:10 A.M.

On 20.01.05 around 5 P.M. two days prior to her death, Sunita provided my wife and me with a detailed account of what had happened. She declared that Suresh Kumar had poured kerosene oil over her body and then lit a matchstick with which he set her person on fire. Sunita stated that when she tried to escape, he held her down tight. However, after some struggle with great difficulty she managed to get out of his grip and ran out the door. We are aware that our son-in-law has been violent with our daughter Sunita in the past too. I have seen Sunita in a highly injured and burnt condition. I am convinced that my son-in-law Suresh doused my daughter Sunita in kerosene and set her on fire which ended her life. My statement has now been recorded by the police.

Signed Sohan Lal. 22.01.05
Prem Lal Chowki Incharge, Lakkad bazaar; Karyawahi Police Shimla.

22.01.05 On this date, Prem Lal and Om Prakash (constable # 1352) have attempted to get more details. Report # 5 Daily diary PP Lakkar Bazaar, at IGMC Shimla.

Mr. Sohan Lal (complainant) gave the above statement to my S.I. (sub-inspector) Prem Lal. And those words written were read out for the complainant, which he agreed to, and then signed on the statement. The statement is also signed by SI Prem Lal. As per the complainant's statement, the crime is being filed under Section 302 of the IPC.

The police station in the jurisdiction of Lahaul and Spiti is currently inaccessible due to heavy snowfall. All roads are currently closed. An application for a legal case is being sent via fax. The corpse of Sunita, the deceased is also being sent for a post-mortem. Original statement, fingerprints and post-mortem reports are being sent by post to Lahaul and Spiti. ICP Lakkar Bazaar@ 22.01.05

Prem Lal (S.I.) sent it. The proceedings have begun.

The fax was sent word by word, based on which F.I.R. carbon copies were also created.

Documents were prepared for further investigation for a complete surveillance. The issue is of special interest due to atrocity against tribal woman. A special report will be issued.

CASE II: F.I.R

20/05 (23.5.05) under 306; 498 A; 34 IPC—suicide of Bina Devi (age: 25/26 married in 1997/98)

Complainant—Hari Singh s/o Kishan Datt; r/o Shipting, PO Muling
Accused—Ashwini Kumar(27) r/o Wokta; s/o Jai Singh also accused (51); Shakuntala (w/o [wife of] Jai Singh, 52 yrs.)
Dead body untraceable. Initial proceedings under sec 174 CRPC were conducted thereafter case got registered. Untraced. Case dropped.
She jumped from the Ghushal bridge, Kothi Ghushal, Distt Lahaul and Spiti.

Married to Ashwini alias Sanjay 2000. For first seven years of their marriage the in-laws did not mistreat Bina. But subsequently they began harassing her. She often complained about this to her parents. We kept sending her back to her in-laws and this is how their son, Anmol, who was 3 years old, was born. After he was born, the harassment from Aswini, her husband, and Jai Singh and her sis-in-law (Kuntala Devi) increased quite drastically and they insisted that she work longer hours on the agricultural fields.

In Feb 2005 Bina Devi came to our place. She explained in tears that her parents-in-law were really harassing her. We just got her to calm down and unfortunately convinced her to return and make up with her in-laws.

She narrated these details to Tinzin Dolma, r/o of Tandi about this too. Bina Devi's husband is employed by the army, he was home on leave. Bina Devi on 20.05.05 went to visit her parents during the day and because of this her in-laws and her husband began yelling and cursing at her. On the same day Bina Devi's parents calmed her down and sent her back to the in-laws to pacify them. On 22.05.05 I left my place at about 11 A.M. and walked to Tandi bridge at about 11:30 A.M. when I saw a big group of people collected. Ranjeet Singh, r/o Kardang informed me that Bina Devi's scarf and glasses were found lying on the Ghushal bridge, and that she had taken her son along with her and jumped into the river Chandra from the bridge. At this point others around the bridge at that time embarked on a search for Bina Devi and Anmol, along the river. Her body couldn't be found. Today, on 23.05.05 one more search party consisting of police and local villagers attempted to locate the two bodies. Bina Devi decided to end her life along with that of her son's on account of the abuse she suffered at the hands of her husband.

I was going to report to the police station, but I ran into you at the Tandi bridge. Please record this as my official statement.

Signed: Hari Singh.
In the presence of Rajendra Kumar of the police force—ASI (Assistant Sub-Inspector)—Investigation Officer (Karavahi police) Keylong

Hari Singh told my SI and got the formal statement. Myself, the ASI Arakshi, constable #100 and #113 (Mohan Lal) went to Tandi bridge for the investigation of this incident, and ran into the complainant. We read out statement to the complainant and got their signature in English. As per the statement, the crime is being logged under Sections 498 A, 306, and 34 of the IPC.

This is the original copy, under the watch of constable #100 Surendra Kumar, who is carrying this to the PI in order to file an F.I.R.

My SI was also present at that time, Rajendra Kumar, dated 3.05.05
@4 P.M.

Also sent to the ASI from the police station.

Special reported case, so F.I.R should be considered special.

Registered cases under SC/ST (POA) Act 1989 from 1st April 1993 to
31st March 2009.

NOTES

PROLOGUE: FROM FIELDWORK TO LIFEWORK

1. The Council for Advancement of People's Action & Rural Technology (CAPART) describes itself as a "nodal agency for catalysing and coordinating the emerging partnership between voluntary organisations and the Government for sustainable development of rural areas."

2. The Lahaul valley is part of the northern most district of the state of Himachal Pradesh (H.P.) in India, situated along the Manali–Leh highway (which leads into Kashmir), bordering Tibet on one side and Ladakh on the other.

3. Dussehra is a ten-day long major festival celebrated in different parts of India, including the Kullu valley of Himachal Pradesh, neighboring Lahaul. It usually follows the week after the harvest season in the valley is over, and large groups of people from Lahaul travel to Kullu to participate in this festival.

4. Marriage by abduction evolved from being a historical practice of marriage by elopement, to marriage via violent abduction in Lahaul. I discuss this and provide a brief trajectory of my previous work elsewhere.

5. Literally translating to "engagement-wedding."

6. The term draws on Devika Chawla's eloquent discussion of fieldwork as "home/work," in *Home, Uprooted* (Chawla 2014).

7. A village near/in Lahaul, where I spent much of my time during my fieldwork.

8. Here I use Homi Bhabha's (1988) conceptualization of theory as the temporality of negotiation or translation, emerging from the process of articulating in-between contradictory positions.

9. "Dalit" refers to a politicized identity of members of the most oppressed castes in India, previously known as untouchables. Literally "Dalit" means "ground down" or "broken" in Marathi.

10. Adivasi literally means "original dwellers" and translates to tribe in English. While the usage of the term tribe when referring to Adivasi communities in most parts of India is a complicated and contested issue (Baviskar 2006), in this context, as in parts of my work, I have opted to use both tribe and Adivasi based on what my interlocutors opted for in interviews.

11. I deliberately use "non-Dalit" here, as a social location that refers to a genealogy of participation in a range of non-Dalit social configurations (caste-gender-sexuality-race-class) premised on an understanding of "Dalit" as referring to much more than caste-identity. My interest in not conflating markers of identity with social location is embedded in an Ambedkarite and Dalit feminist intersectional framework and is not meant to obscure my own caste-privileged status as per the ideology of Brahmanical patriarchy—that of being raised in a nuclear and heterosexual savarna family. I detail my own location as well as the contested terrain of nomenclature in different parts of this book.

12. In the tradition of Chandra Mohanty's articulation of what such a praxis could offer.

13. Jacqui Alexander (2005) discusses remembering intentionally as a political step, often enacted in resisting violence.

14. I had returned in 2010 for a shorter period.

1   CROSSING THE TOP

1. The first academic research I conducted in the region was a collaborative ethnography focused on marriage by abduction and was also my doctoral work.

2. For more on this see Vijay Prashad's 2000 book *Untouchable Freedom*.

3. It is important to note here that Rege (1998; 2006, 2013) and Dalit feminist activists and writers do not conflate the Indian feminist movement led by savarna caste activists and U.S. women of color and transnational feminisms.

4. In documenting the trajectory of feminist anti-violence, particularly anti-rape organizing for a future research project, I found unpublished exchanges among feminists of different constituencies in India questioning this, in various documents and conference proceedings and such between feminist activists discussing rape law reform in the 1970s and 1980s.

5. Such as the Prevention of Atrocities against SC and ST Act of India, 1989.

6. A detailed and rare discussion of the complex relationship between caste and tribe, colonial usage, and constitutional nomenclature vs politicized vocabularies regarding caste and tribe is found in Soma Chaudhuri's (2013) ethnography of migrant laborers in Jalpaiguri, West Bengal, India, and I build upon her work.

7. I am referring here to early sociological distinctions *and* constitutional/governmental language, following those of the colonial civilizing mission, where tribal communities were/are necessarily understood as anthropological categories, existing *outside* caste and caste communities of Hindu society, placing tribal communities squarely within the racialized savage paradigm.

8. I discuss these distinctions, intersections, and challenges posed by using such terms interchangeably, in greater depth later in chapter two, in the section titled "Politics of Caste and Tribe."

9. The hegemonic underpinnings of "tribe" in relation to Adivasi subjectivity has been discussed in depth by Rycroft and Dasgupta in their 2011 edited collection titled, "The politics of belonging in India: Becoming Adivasi."

10. For example, there is a burgeoning body of research that traces the origins of tribes in India to an ancient Hindu caste order by orientalists such as Koenraad Elst, whose scholarship upholds the notion of a Hindu Nation in India.

11. Virginius Xaxa has critiqued the tendency among sociologists of caste and tribe to read the Hinduization of tribes as a process of Sanskritization.

12. Debjani Ganguly in *Caste and Dalit Lifeworlds* (2008).

13. In 1846 after the first Anglo-Sikh war, Lahaul passed into the hands of the East India Company who placed the administration of the region in the hands of a Wazir. This is how the head of the Kolong family, Amar Chand, was appointed the Wazir of Lahaul, which ensured the participation of Lahauli men in World War I for the British. The fort of the Wazir was in Khangsar, thus often the male descendents of the family are referred to as Khangsar Thakurs. These descendents went on to serve in World War II, then in the Indo-China war, and current male descendants of the family not only hold huge landholdings in Lahaul and Kullu, they are often employed in the higher echelons of the government, such as the IAS, IPS, and some have also been elected into the state assembly. Thus, in several interviews, people continue to refer to the Khangsar Thakurs as the *samant*.

14. Refers to the Scheduled Castes and Scheduled Tribes Prevention of Atrocities Act of 1989 (also known as the PoA Act) which was a constitutional amendment that is meant to provide protection for Dalits against caste atrocity/violence. The PoA Act of 1989 and the Civil Rights Act of 1955 are not applicable in Lahaul.

15. Through the Panchayat Extension to scheduled areas Act, 1996, tribes in Himachal Pradesh fall under the Fifth Schedule of the Indian Constitution. The Panchayat Act was extended to these areas in 1996. While it was meant to grant autonomy to tribal areas, it had many shortcomings, including those posed by the question of caste striations within tribe.

16. For a detailed discussion of the interdependence between theories in the flesh and specialized knowledges, look at Soyini Madison's 1993 article in *TPQ* titled "'That was my Occupation': Oral Narrative, Performance and Black Feminist Thought."

17. Later in this chapter I discuss in some detail the use of both, the term violence and the notion of love in this book.

18. While in the prologue to the book I have attempted to provide a shortened narrative, which traces the trajectory of my work in Lahaul and discusses the tensions between fieldwork and lifework, some of these questions also appear in the last chapter. However, it is in the epilogue of the book that I discuss specific moments of failure and related details about my story and social location.

19. Several feminists of color including Angela Davis, Faye Harrison, and Chandra Talpade Mohanty (to name a few) have discussed the politics of knowledge production across disciplines in the U.S. academy, and I follow the path they have carved out here without entering those specific debates in the book.

20. For a more detailed discussion of the relationship between the scholar and caste in conventional disciplines, wherein scholar translates to "Brahmin" (ranked highest within an essentialized caste order), look at Guru and Sarukkai (2012), *The Cracked Mirror*.

21. See Map 1.1.

22. The Jajmani system is an exploitative institution entrenched in rigid caste hierarchies, which maintains an unequal system of labor, skill, and service flow (ostensibly labeled as "exchange of service based on hereditary trade") between different caste groups in India.

23. For further information about demographic details about the region, please refer to the District Census Handbook for Lahaul & Spiti, Himachal Pradesh, Census of India 2011.

24. Dr. B.R. Ambedkar converted to Buddhism in 1956 because he believed the principles (*Dhamma*) of Buddhism to be the best. He was disillusioned with the centrality of caste and gender inequality in the principles of Hinduism.

25. Raja Ghepan is considered to be the indigenous deity of the region worshipped equally by both, Hindus and Buddhists.

26. *Chhortens* are miniature stupas, also used in Tibetan Buddhist death rituals. These small stupa-like structures are found in villages and often they hold the remains of lamas and other important people.

27. Men-Tsee-Khang centers are Tibetan Buddhist medical centers, connected to the main institute first started by the fourteenth Dalai Lama as a nodal institute for Tibetan medicine in Dharamshala, India. In smaller locations such as village Jispa in Lahaul, they are often run by a lama, or a chomo and a trainee assistant.

28. Amchis are doctors and practitioners of classical Tibetan medicine.

29. Shishir Gupta discusses this at length in his book, *The Himalayan Face-Off* (2014).

30. Much of the conversations I had with people about the tunnel were speculative, as thus far the tunnel construction is far from complete.

31. This relationship between the dual patriarchies of state and tribe (including tribal Dalit) does not mean that hierarchies and systems of domination do not play out *within* tribe, nor should it be read as a position that *all* tribal and tribal-Dalit identifying members of the community opt for. I refer here to the interviews and conversations with a range of community members across caste, class, and gender hierarchies and leaders of both, the Tribal Manch and the Janajatiya Dalit Sangh.

32. For more on the general propensity among non-Dalit feminists to apply Ambedkar's theory on caste and gender as applicable only to Dalit women, see Sharmila Rege's (2013) discussion on reclaiming Ambedkar's feminist legacy in *The Madness of Manu*.

2   SHADES OF WILDNESS

I have borrowed the title of this chapter from Ajay Skaria's (1997) discussion of colonial discourses of savagery, which operated in "shades of wildness," whereby the entire population of India was considered "savage" but tribes were seen as more primitive than the caste-society Hindus.

1. Here I am borrowing from Spivak's (1988) essay, "Can the Subaltern Speak?" the discussion of "the white man saving the brown woman."

2. Chaudhuri (2013) discusses the representation of Adivasis in popular cultural texts in India that allow for a continual circulation of "wildness" along different points in the continuum of the savage paradigm.

3. Caste in India is upheld through rituals of caste-based purity and pollution, which include rules of touch, proximity, sharing food, utensils, and caste endogamy. It is

through these rules that untouchability was and continues to be practiced across both, varnas and jatis.

4. For more details read Tanika Sarkar's "Rebellion as Modern Self-fashioning" (2011).

5. Rupa Viswanathan (2012) clarifies some of these distinctions succinctly, especially those pertaining to the usage of "Dalit" and "SC" in her essay "The Textbook Case of Exclusion."

6. I am referring to the Poona Pact of 1932, when under the threat of Gandhi's demise due to another fast-unto-death, Ambedkar, on behalf of Dalits in India, signed a document that denied the political recognition of Dalits, supported Gandhi's plan of "inclusion" of oppressed castes, and deeply regretted this move that definitively set the tone for even more discriminatory caste politics for decades to come.

7. H.P. Govt's letter no. TD (F) 10–3/93 dtd. 23.02.2004, granting dual status to the Dalits of Scheduled Tribes.

8. http://kafila.org/2013/01/18/remembering-laxmi-orang-and-the-gender-question -in-assam-mayur-chetia-and-bonojit-hussain. Accessed June 14, 2014.

9. Tribes in Himachal Pradesh fall under the Fifth Schedule of the Indian Constitution, and the Panchayat Act was extended to these areas in 1996. While it was meant to grant autonomy to tribal areas, it had many shortcomings, including those posed by the question of caste striations within tribe.

10. A discussion of this song in Chinaal *bhashe* (local language) by Mr. Lal Chand Dhissa appears in a quarterly publication Temerel, in Kullu Valley. In his discussion he challenges that Sobhnu was even Dalit and points out gaps in the romantic story of Sobhnu and the queen.

11. The sun is often used by Dalit communities as a resistive metaphor that rejects caste. The metaphor is often used as analogous to the sun being "untouchable," as indeed the *avarnas* were deemed in Hindu society.

12. Vikram is Kavita's ex-husband, her first love despite his violence in acquiring her love and in their life together as a married couple in Kullu.

13. See Image 2.1.

4   NARRATING LOVE

1. Kavita is a 35 year-old Dalit woman whom I have known for several years in Lahaul. I discuss her life history in depth in chapter three and chapter five.

2. Kullu is the district (and town) bordering the Lahaul valley within the state of Himachal Pradesh, India.

3. The Lahaul Valley, often referred to as a "snow desert," is situated at an average height of 10,500 feet above sea level in the northern Indian Himalayan ranges, bordering Tibet on one side, Ladakh on the other, and the rest of the state of Himachal Pradesh on the third.

4. The term Dalit refers to a politicized identity of members of the most oppressed castes in India, previously known as untouchables. Literally "Dalit" means "ground down" or "broken" in Marathi.

5. Last names are often markers of caste identity in India—Sharma refers to a privileged-caste last name, and Lohar is an oppressed caste/Dalit.

6. Keerthi is a tribal-Dalit woman whose story appears in chapter three.

7. The Jajmani system is an exploitative institution entrenched in rigid caste hierarchies, which maintains an unequal system of labor, skill, and service flow (ostensibly labeled as "exchange of service based on hereditary trade") between different caste groups in India.

8. Commanding Officer of the unit stationed in Stingri, Lahaul.

9. "Sat with" (translated from the Hindi word "baithna") is a euphemism for sexual intimacy/relationships commonly use across different parts of Himachal Pradesh.

10. Here she is referring to the Fifth Schedule of the Indian Constitution which grants several tribal communities autonomy with regard to governance and technically upholds customary law. Within the complex politics of tribal autonomy and state-defined parameters of *backwardness* (a term used by the state to mark tribal communities across the country as against the *progress* of non-tribal *savrana* caste communities in Peninsular India), the Lahauli community falls within the purview of the Fifth Schedule of the Indian Constitution. Like many tribes in peninsular India, tribal self-definition and autonomy here too are balanced precariously on this play of tradition and modernity.

11. The direct translation of the hindi comes to "is," i.e., "the main question remains whether the love *is*" ("sawaal yeh hai ji, ki pyaar hai?").

12. Mandi is a nearby district in lower Himachal Pradesh, known for a particularly conservative Hindu Brahmanical and nationalist fervor.

13. Hindu Marriage Act, 1955.

5   MAGIC TRICKS

1. The incident took place when I was in Lahaul for fieldwork in 2005. It was initially filed as a murder and changed to suicide in a matter of months while I was still in Lahaul that year. Subsequently, after I returned to the United States I found out that her family had filed an appeal claiming her death as suicide due to domestic violence (thus charging abetment to suicide against her husband, covered under the DV Act of India). However, a year later, in 2009, the appeal made by her parents was dismissed; the case had been "resolved" and the man in question was no longer implicated, had indeed remarried, and her death had been legally established as caused by an accident.

2. Acquiring the legal case file and conducting interviews with local people.

3. While the usage of the term *tribe* when referring to Adivasis (literally meaning "original dwellers") in most parts of India is a complicated and contested issue (Baviskar 2005), in this chapter, as in the rest of the book I have opted to use both tribe and Adivasi based on what my interlocutors opted for in interviews. For a detailed discussion see chapter one.

4. Here I extend Lata Mani's (1998) argument of "competing modernities" (colonial and indigenous) in the context of *sati*, to the relationship between state and tribal patriarchies in postcolonial India.

5. I am borrowing from Ania Loomba's (1993) discussion of how women are "the targets as well as the grounds of the debates over tradition."

6. I returned to the area to update materials through another round of fieldwork in 2011 for this book.

7. Changing it from murder to suicide hadn't been enough, because it left room for a domestic violence case against the man, especially when her family chose to file under the Domestic Violence Act of India, 2005, charging him for abetment to suicide.

8. While I never spoke to Bina in person after the fire and before her passing, when I refer to her narrative, I am talking about the events as narrated by several people in her family, various drafts of the case file, and other information pieced together by me from interviews with women and men in Lahaul.

9. These quotes are parts of larger conversations and interviews during my fieldwork in 2011.

10. Shamsher, who lives in Keylong, and works in the district administration office often provided me with access to documents, files, books, and other material about Lahaul. In my early years in the valley he and I spent a lot of time discussing local politics, issues, problems, weather, and such. Most of these initial conversations were in his office while I was usually waiting for a meeting with one of the senior administrative staff. During the winter of 2005–2006 when Bina had passed away, he was among the first few people I discussed the incident with. His initial response was of shock and confusion. He was among the two local men I spoke with who even acknowledged that it could be a result of violence, and thus a murder. In subsequent conversations he appeared unsure about the possibility of violence as such, and finally this quote is part of a conversation we had about Bina's death in the summer of 2011.

11. However, this distinction from the plains is simultaneously complicated by the structure of the tribe itself, which is ironically rooted (and officially embedded) in caste hierarchies. Not only is the tribe stratified by caste, sections of its population are officially registered as both Scheduled Tribe and Scheduled Caste as per Government of India categories of "backwardness." Further as I discuss elsewhere (Bhattacharya 2008) there is a long and complex history for Dalit concerns (within tribe) to be subsumed under the broader rubric of (tribe) Lahaul.

12. This argument is based heavily upon Bhabha's theorizations of identity in his discussion of postcolonial political nationalisms. However, I would like to clarify that rather than simply map colonial and anti-colonial conceptualizations of self and other onto tribe–state relationships, I am drawing on these constructs to frame the historically and culturally specific relationship between the Lahaulis and the state as negotiated and compromised by their heteropatriarchal imperatives.

13. The Manali–Leh highway runs right through the Lahaul valley leading into Kargil, on the Indo-Pak border. In this particular instance the perpetrator is a member of an auxiliary unit of the Indian army.

14. The region is snowed in for six months of the year, and the army has to work hand-in-hand with the local community to open up the roads, and make them motorable for the purpose of a smooth functioning of the Manali–Leh highway, the Indian

army's primary route for accessing/supplying men and materials to the Indo-Pak border.

15. First, it was he, the husband who was responsible (murder/violence); then it was her, Bina who was responsible (suicide); finally nobody is responsible.

16. Elsewhere, I have discussed memories of violence as women themselves have remembered them and juxtaposed them with official memories (Bhattacharya 2013).

6   REMEMBERING FOR LOVE

1. A culmination of those initial years of work led to the start of a larger women's collective, which eventually disbanded in favor of smaller *mahila mandals*, since traveling across different parts of the valley to conduct meetings and campaigns was increasingly difficult for the larger group.

2. Kavita continues her work through an NGO in the Kullu valley now.

3. While this chapter does not necessarily theorize love within the framework of affect, it is indeed inspired by love.

4. At one point she had contemplated telling her story through a news channel, so that people across the state, and even the nation would find out about the violence against Adivasi Dalit women.

5. I discuss this in greater length in chapter two.

6. The first chapter of this book opens with another part of the same interview.

7. My emphasis is on the process of recall that entails more than a linear telling of the story, which even the individual may engage in.

8. This is a classic example of "symbolic violence" (Bourdieu 2004).

9. In conversation with the head of the only family in the village that was willing to stand by Kavita's father, this issue of compromise emerged several times. It was especially raised to justify why this one family also decided to step back from the case, as it was considered dishonorable of her father to have "benefitted financially" from his daughter's rape.

10. I have discussed the inapplicability of the Scheduled Castes and Scheduled Tribes Prevention of Atrocities Act of 1989 (also known as PoA Act), at the intersection of caste and tribe in the first chapter.

11. In conversations with other villagers, if the issue of compromise in Kavita's case would come up, her father and she were often ridiculed for accepting money "in place of honor" thus confirming Mookherjee's (2006) point.

12. For Taussig (1991), to understand the meaning of the violence, the question "Why do people do these (violent) things?" is embedded in the everyday. Thus, he distinguishes between the "truth of being" and the "social being of truth" to illustrate that what is important is "not whether facts are real but what the politics of their interpretation and representation are" (p. xiii). Thus, the violence itself has to be dialectically engaged. Here, I draw upon Taussig's "social being of truth" to emphasize that the memory of violence is not only about the facts of the violence as real, the motivations of the aggressor in question, or the factual events of the violence.

13. The backlash against Dalit communities for daring to speak against caste violence openly has a long history in India. For a detailed discussion of this trajectory, in situating one such backlash—the Khairlanji atrocity, see *The Persistence of Caste: The Khairlanji Murders and India's Hidden Apartheid* by Anand Teltumbde (2010).

14. Saptapadi is a mountain range visible from different parts of the Lahaul valley.

15. Ambedkar, in discussing untouchability and the violence of caste, used the language of "Broken Men" when referring to Adivasis and Dalits. Additionally, the word Dalit literally also means "crushed." Therefore, I situate Kavita's metaphor within a Dalit positionality as one where she actively chose to articulate her personal grief within a collective suffering. This is especially relevant given her overall articulation of resistance—as to what the violence *means* in her life.

16. As mentioned previously, and in the Introduction, Kavita has moved out of Lahaul and now lives in the Kullu valley, which offers her greater anonymity.

17. This is a poem written by someone who was a central presence in my life during my years in Lahaul, and also supported Kavita during the time she needed to get away from her violent partner. It is titled "Just Tonight" and has been published elsewhere by me.

18. Third world and women of color feminists across disciplines have cautioned against the tendency to seek borderlessness and move beyond issues of identity as though they were separate. I follow from such debates within and beyond the discipline of anthropology discussed by Lila Abu-Lughod (1990, 1991, 1993), Faye Harrison (1997), and Soyini Madison (2005, 2007), among others.

19. For me, the grounding of the project in terms of love and solidarity is clear, while I work through the "how-to" questions that she and others have raised. Chela Sandoval (2000) discusses the meaning of love as it appears in the works of third world writers who theorize social change. For them, love is "a hermeneutic, a set of practices and procedures . . . towards a differential mode of consciousness and its accompanying technologies of method and social movement" (p. 140). In my own work, I follow from an understanding of love that guides modes and practices of community, self, and solidarity in research—not only for me, but for several of my interlocutors, including Kavita.

EPILOGUE

1. In the prologue to the book I tell the story of Achi Yangmo's directive to me, to stop all the "phu phu phu" and instead work toward the completion of this book.

APPENDIX I: GENEALOGY OF PREVIOUS WORK

1. I refer to this particular form of violence as "customary violence" to indicate a current practice and not to refer to the historical location of the custom or the customary laws of the tribe. It is my hope to debunk casteist, reductionist and discriminatory positions taken by the government and often the media who view these violent acts as examples of "uncivilized" behavior among the tribal communities in India. At the same

time I am careful in not supporting a revival of essentialist, patriarchal behaviors in the name of "tradition" within the Lahula tribe.

2. Throughout I use the terms "longstanding," "traditional," and "current times." While there are no fixed chronological boundaries that I follow, I use these words to refer to large chunks of time. By "traditional" I refer to the practice as it existed before the Hindu Marriage Act of 1955. By "current" and "recent" I refer to the shape this practice had taken according to the women when I first visited the valley in July 1999. The women used these terms loosely to talk about the avatar of marriage by abduction that has been in practice since the 1970s up until my first fieldwork in 2005–2006.

3. In 2013, following the nation-wide protests after the rape and murder of Jyoti Singh Pandey, the rape law was amended into the sexual assault law at a pace unprecedented in the history of feminist legal reform in India.

GLOSSARY

Achi: Older sister
Amchis: Traditional medical practitioners
Angootha Chhap: Illiterate
Antariyan: Intestines
Ati Shudra: Untouchable
Avarna: Untouchable
Baanj: Sterile
Bahujan: Majority
Baithku: Seat
Balatkaar: Rape
Baniyas: Trader caste
Bethku(s): Seat
Chhang: Rice brew, stronger than beer
Chhi chhi: Expression of shame
Chholo: Gambling game
Cholu: Traditional clothing, usually worn by women
Chomo: Nun
Dhaba: Small roadside food joint, usually found on highways
Dharam: Religion, also used to refer to duty
Gompa: Monastery
Hisaab: Calculation
Izzat: Honor
Jajmani system: An exploitative institution entrenched in rigid caste hierarchies, which maintains an unequal system of labor, skill, and service flow between caste groups in India.
Jati-pratha: Caste system
Jawan: Foot soldier in the army
JDS (Janajatiya Dalit Sangh): The JDS is a grassroots 'Adivasi-Dalit' organization in Lahaul and Kullu, in Himachal, with a focus on gaining constitutional recognition of/for this constituency.

Ji: Honorific suffix often used at the end of a name to refer to an older, or highly respected person.
Jule: Greeting such as "hello"
Kinnauri: From Kinnaur
Kuji biyah: Marriage by abduction
Kuth: Traditional crop of the region
Kya fayda: What is the use?
Lamas: Monks
Maan-samman: Honor and respect
Mahila mandal: Women's group
Manch: Stage, used also to refer to a group
Mangni biyah: Marriage by engagement, arranged by families of the bride and groom
Mar-peet: Intimate partner violence
Men-tsee-khang: Tibetan medicine clinic
Miya-biwi: Husband-wife
Munshi: Book keeper
Nakhra: Making excuses
Namkeen chai: Salt tea
Neechi jaati: Lower caste
Ngya: Token seeking consent for marriage by abduction
Nono: Prince
Paharis: Mountain communities
Panchayat: System of local governance
PoA Act: Prevention of Atrocities Act
Prem kahani: Love story
Pucca: Concrete
Pyar: Love
Pyar ke commandos: Love Commandos (organization)
Raja Ghepan: Local deity
Rajputs: Warrior Caste
Reeti: Practices/customs
Samant: Ruling class
Sangathan: Organization
Sarkar: Government
Savarna: Caste-privileged
Satta: Government

Shaivaites: Those belonging to a religious sect which worships Shiva
Shiva: Hindu deity
Tandoor: Clay oven
Thangkas: Paintings
Thukpa: Noodle soup
TOP: Top, but colloquially used to refer to the Rohtang pass
Tsheshu: Harvest festival
Varnas: Caste
Wazir: Minister designated by the British
Zabardasti biyah: Marriage by force

REFERENCES

Abu-Lughod, L. (1986). *Veiled sentiment: Honor and poetry in a Bedouin society.* Berkeley: University of California Press.

Abu-Lughod, L. (1990). "Can there be a feminist ethnography?" *Women & Performance: A Journal of Feminist Theory* 5(1), 7–27.

Abu-Lughod, L. (1991). "Writing against culture," pp. 137–62, in Richard G. Fox (Ed.), *Recapturing Anthropology: Working in the Present.* Santa Fe: SAR Press.

Abu-Lughod, L. (1993). *Writing women's worlds: Bedouin stories.* Berkeley: University of California Press.

Agarwal, P. (1995). "Surat, Savarkar and Draupadi: Legitimising rape as a political eeapon," pp. 29–57, in Tanika Sarkar and Urvashi Butalia (Eds.), *Women and right wing movements: Indian experiences.* London and New Jersey: Zed Books.

Aggarwal, R. (2000). "'Point of departure': Feminist locations and the politics of travel in India." *Feminist Studies* 26(3), 535–64.

Aggarwal, R. (2004). *Beyond lines of control: Performance and politics on the disputed borders of Ladakh, India.* Durham: Duke University Press.

Aggarwal, R., and Bhan, M. (2009). "Disarming violence: Development, democracy, and security on the borders of India." *The Journal of Asian Studies* 68(2), 519–542.

Agnes, F., Chandra, S. and Basu, M. (eds.) (2004). *Women and law in India—An omnibus.* New Delhi: Oxford University Press.

Alexander, M. J. (2005). *Pedagogies of crossing: Meditations on feminism, sexual politics, memory, and the sacred.* Durham: Duke University Press.

Alexander, M. Jacqui, and Mohanty, Chandra Talpade (eds). (1997). *Feminist genealogies, colonial legacies, democratic futures.* Routledge: London and New York.

Ambedkar, B. R. (1916). *Castes in India: Their mechanism, genesis, and development.* BAWS Vol.1, Department of Education, Government of Maharashtra.

Ambedkar, B. R. (1936). "The annihilation of caste," in Ambedkar, B. R. (1990). *Annihilation of caste: An undelivered speech.* New Delhi: Arnold Publishers.

Ambedkar, B. R. (1943). *Ranade, Gandhi & Jinnah.* Delhi: Gautam Book Center.

Ambedkar, B. R. (1989 [1932]). "Gandhi and his fast," in Vasant Moon compiled, *Dr. Babasaheb Ambedkar: Writing and Speeches* (Vol 5.). New Delhi: Dr. Ambedkar Foundation.

Ambedkar, B. R. (1990). *B.R. Ambedkar: Writings and speeches,* edited by Vasanth Moon. New Delhi: Dr. Ambedkar Foundation.

Amit, V. (ed.) (2000) *Constructing the field.* London: Routledge.

Anderson, B. R. (1991). *Imagined communities: Reflections on the origin and spread of nationalism.* New York: Verso.

Anzaldúa, Gloria (1999). *Borderlands/La Frontera: The new Mestiza*. San Francisco: Aunt Lute Books.

Appadurai, A. (1996). *Modernity at large*. Minneapolis: University of Minnesota Press.

Appadurai, A. (1995). "The production of locality," pp. 204–225 in E. Fardon (Ed.), *Counterwork*. London: Routledge.

Asad, Talal (ed.) (1973). *Anthropology and the colonial encounter*. London: Ithaca Press.

Atkinson, Paul et al. (2001). "Editorial Introduction," pp. 1–7 in P. Atkinson, Amanda Coffey, Sara Delamont, John Lofland, and Lyn Lofland (Eds.), *Handbook of Ethnography*, 2/e. London: Sage.

Bama (1994). *Sangati*. New Delhi: Oxford University Press.

Bama (2005). *Sangati*. Trans. From Tamil by Lakshmi Holmstrom. New Delhi: Oxford University Press.

Barros, C. A. (1998). *Autobiography: Narratives of transformation*. Ann Arbor: University of Michigan Press.

Basu, Srimati (2006). "Playing off courts: The negotiation of divorce and violence in plural legal settings in Kolkata." *Journal of Legal Pluralism and Unofficial Law* 52, 41–75.

Basu, Srimati (2012). "Judges of normality: Mediating marriage in the family courts of Kolkata, India." *Signs* 37(2), 469–492.

Baviskar, Amita (2005). "Adivasi encounters with Hindu nationalism in MP." *Economic and Political Weekly* 40(48), 5105–5113.

Baviskar, A. (2006). "The politics of being 'indigenous,'" pp. 33–50 in Karlsson, B. G. and Subba, T. B. (Eds.), *Indigeneity in India*. London: Kegan Paul.

Baxi, Pratiksha. 2010. "Justice is a secret: *Compromise* in rape trials." *Contributions to Indian Sociology* 44(3), 207–33.

Baxi, Pratiksha. 2012. "We must resist the cunning of judicial reform." http://kafila .org/2012/12/29/we-must-resist-the-cunning-of-judicial-reform-pratiksha-baxi. Accessed February 26, 2013.

Behar, R. (2003). "Feminist ethnography as (experimental) genre." *Anthropology News* 44(9), 40.

Behar, R. and Gordon, D. (eds.) (1995). *Women writing culture*. Berkeley: University of California Press.

Behar, R. (1993). *Translated woman: Crossing the border with Esperanza's story*. Boston: Beacon Press.

Behar, Ruth (1996). *The vulnerable observer: Anthropology that breaks your heart*. Boston: Beacon Press.

Berlant, L. (2011). "A properly political concept of love: Three approaches in ten pages." *Cultural Anthropology*, 26(4), 683–691.

Berlant, L. (2012). *Desire/love*. Brooklyn, NY: Punctum books.

Bhabha, H. K. (ed.). (1990). *Nation and narration*. New York: Routledge.

Bhabha, Homi K. (1994). *The location of culture*. London: Routledge.

Bhattacharya, Himika (2008). "'Is my honor not honor?': Women's narratives of marriage practice and violence in Lahaul, India." Ph.D. dissertation. Institute of Communications Research, University of Illinois at Urbana-Champaign.

Bhattacharya, Himika (2013). "Remembering violence: Field memories from Lahaul, India." *Feminist Formations* 25(3), 98–122.

Bora, Papori (2010). "Between the human, the citizen and the tribal." *International Feminist Journal of Politics* 12(3), 341–360.

Bourdieu, Pierre (2004). "Gender and symbolic violence," pp. 339–342, in Scheper-Hughes, Nancy and Bougois, Philippe (Eds.), *Violence in war and peace: An anthology*. Malden: Blackwell Publishing.

Butalia, U. (2000). *The other side of silence*. Durham: Duke University Press.

Carrillo Rowe, Aimee (2008). *Power lines: On the subject of feminist alliances*. Durham: Duke University Press.

Census of India (2011). *Himachal Pradesh District Census Handbook: Lahaul & Spiti*. Retrieved from http://www.censusindia.gov.in/2011census/dchb/0203_PART_B _DCHB_LAHUL%20&%20SPITI.pdf.

Chakravarti, U. (2003) *Gendering caste through a feminist lens*. Mumbai: Popular Prakashan.

Chatterjee, P. (2001). *A time for tea: Women, labor, and post/colonial politics on an Indian plantation*. Durham: Duke University Press.

Chawla, D. (2014). *Home, uprooted: Oral histories of India's partition*. New York: Fordham University Press.

Chaudhuri, S. (2013). *Witches, tea plantations, and lives of migrant laborers in India: Tempest in a teapot*. Maryland: Lexington Books.

Chowdhury, E. H. (2011). *Transnationalism reversed: Women organizing against gendered violence in Bangladesh*. Albany: SUNY Press.

Christians, C. (2005). "Ethics and politics in qualitative research," pp. 139–164 in Norman K. Denzin and Yvonna S. Lincoln (Eds.), *Handbook of qualitative research*, 3/e. Thousand Oaks: Sage.

Clair, R.P. (1998). *Organizing silence: A world of possibilities*. Albany, New York: State University of New York Press.

Clifford, J. (1997). "Spatial practices: Fieldwork, travel, and the disciplining of anthropology," pp. 185–222, in A. Gupta, and J. Ferguson (Eds.), *Anthropological locations*. Berkeley: University of California Press.

Clifford, J., and Marcus, G. E. (Eds.). (1986). *Writing culture: The poetics and politics of ethnography*. Berkeley: University of California Press.

Comaroff, J. L. (1992). *Ethnography and the historical imagination*. Boulder: Westview.

Conquergood, D. (1991). "Rethinking ethnography: Towards a critical cultural politics." *Communication Monographs* 58(2), 179–194.

Crenshaw, Kimberlé (1991). "Mapping the margins: Intersectionality, identity politics, and violence against women of color." *Stanford Law Review* 43, 1241–1299.

Cukor, G., and Fleming, V. (Directors). (1939). *Gone with the wind*. [Motion Picture]. United States: Warner Bros.

Cvetkovich, Ann (2003). *An archive of feelings: Trauma, sexuality, and lesbian public cultures*. Durham: Duke University Press.

Das, V. (1995). *Critical events: An anthropological perspective of contemporary India*. Delhi: Oxford University Press.

Das, Veena (2000). "The act of witnessing: Violence, poisonous knowledge, and subjectivity," pp. 205–225, in Veena Das, Arthur Kleinman, Mamphela Ramphele, and Pamela Reynolds (Eds.), *Violence and subjectivity*. Berkeley: University of California Press.

Davis, Angela (2005). *Beyond the frame: Women of color and visual representations*. Edited by Neferti X. M. Tadiar. New York: Palgrave Macmillian.

Davis, Heather (2016). "Love," pp. 245–252, in Kelly Fritsch, Clare O'Connor and A.K. Thompson (Eds.), *Keywords for radicals: The contested vocabulary of late-capitalist struggle*. Edinburgh: AK Press.

Denzin, N.K. (2002). *Interpretive interactionism* (Second Edition, Series: Applied Social Research Methods Series, Volume 16). London: Sage.

Denzin, N.K. (2005). "Emancipatory discourses, and the ethics and politics of interpretation," pp. 933–958 in N. K. Denzin and Y.S. Lincoln (Eds.), *Handbook of qualitative research*, 3/e. Thousand Oaks, CA: Sage.

Denzin, N.K. (2003). *Performance ethnography: Critical pedagogy and the politics of culture*. Thousand Oaks, CA: Sage.

Denzin, N.K. (2008). *Symbolic interactionism and cultural studies: The politics of interpretation*. John Wiley & Sons.

Dhissa, L.C. (2011) *Samvidhan ke samajik anyay*. Kullu: Janajatiya Dalit Sangh.

Dominguez, V.R. (2000). "For a politics of love and rescue." *Cultural Anthropology* 15(3), 361–393.

Dorje, C. (2011). Personal communication, May 20.

Felman, Shoshana (1992). *Testimony: Crises of witnessing in literature, psychoanalysis, and history*. New York and London: Routledge.

Fetterley, Judith (1978). *The resisting reader: A feminist approach to American fiction*. Bloomington: Indiana University Press.

Foucault, M. (1980). *Power/knowledge: Selected interviews and other writings*. New York: Pantheon Books.

Foucault, Michel (1977). *Discipline and punish: The birth of the prison*. New York: Pantheon Books.

Foucault, M. (1978). *The history of sexuality*. New York: Pantheon Books.

Fregoso, R. L. (2003). *MeXicana encounters: The making of social identities on the borderlands*. Berkeley: University of California Press.

Ganguly, D. (2008). *Caste and Dalit lifeworlds: Postcolonial perspectives*. New Delhi, India: Orient Blackswan.

Geiger, N. G. (1986). "Women's life histories method and content." *Signs* 11(21), 334–351.

Giddens, A. (1990). *The consequences of modernity*. Stanford: Stanford University Press.

Gill, Manohar Singh (2010). *Himalayan wonderland: Travels in Lahaul and Spiti*. New Delhi: Penguin.

Ginsburg, F. and Rapp, R. (Eds.) (1995). *Conceiving the New World Order: The global politics of reproduction*. Berkeley: University of California.

Grewal, I., and Kaplan, C. (1994). "Introduction: Transnational feminist practices and questions of postmodernity," pp. 1–33 in I. Grewal, and C. Kaplan (Eds.), *Scattered hegemonies*. Minneapolis: University of Minnesota Press.

Grossberg, L., Nelson, C., and Treichler, P. A. (Eds.). (1992). *Cultural studies*. New York: Routledge.

Gupta, S. (2014). *The Himalayan face-off: Chinese assertion and the Indian riposte*. India: Hachette Digital.

Guru, Gopal (2007). "Twentieth century discourse on social justice: A view from quarantine India," pp. 10—221, in Sabyasachi Bhattacharya (Ed.), *Development of modern Indian thought and the social sciences*. New Delhi: Oxford University Press.

Guru, Gopal, and Sarukkai, Sundar (2012). *The cracked mirror: An Indian debate on experience and theory*. New Delhi: Oxford University Press.

Guttman, N. (2000). *Public health communication interventions: Values and ethical dilemmas*. Thousand Oaks, CA: Sage.

Hall, S. (1993). "Culture, community, nation." *Cultural Studies*, 7(3), 349–363.

Handrahan, L. (2004). "Hunting for women: Bride kidnapping in Kyrgyzstan." *International Feminist Journal of Politics* 6, 207–233.

Handrahan, L. (2002). *Gendering ethnicity: Implications for democracy assistance*. New York: Routledge.

Harcourt, A. Frederick Pollock (1871). *The Himalayan districts of Kooloo, Lahoul, and Spiti*. London: Allen & Co.

Harrison, Faye V., ed. (1997). *Decolonizing anthropology: Moving further toward an anthropology for liberation*, 2nd. ed. Arlington, VA: American Anthropological Association.

Havlin, Natalie (2015). "To live humanity under the skin: Revolutionary love and third world feminism in 1970s Chicana feminism." *Women's Studies Quarterly* 43(3 & 4), Fall/Winter, 78–97.

Hegde, R. (1998). "A view from elsewhere: Locating difference and the politics of representation from a transnational feminist perspective." *Communication Theory* 8(3), 271–297.

Hill, Anita (2011). *Speaking truth to power*. New York: Random House.

Hirsch, Marianne, and Smith, Valerie (2002). "Feminism and cultural memory: An introduction." *Signs* 28(1): 1–19.

hooks, b. (1989). "Choosing the margin as space of radical openness." *Framework* 36, 15.

Hurston, Zora Neale (1928). "How it feels to be colored me." *World Tomorrow*, 11 (May), 215–216.

Irudayam, Aloysius, Mangubhai, Jayashree P., and Lee, Joel G. 2011. *Dalit women speak out: Caste, class and gender violence in India*. New Delhi: Zuban.

Jaswal, S. S. (2005). *Reservation policy and the law: Myth and reality of constitutional safeguards to scheduled castes*. New Delhi: Deep & Deep Publications.

Johnson, E. P. (2003). *Appropriating blackness: Performance and the politics of authenticity*. Durham: Duke University Press.

Johnson, E. P. (2011a). "Gays and gospel: A queer history of sacred music," pp. 109–125, in Jill Austin and Jennifer Briers (Eds.), *Out in Chicago: LGBT history at the crossroads*. Chicago: Chicago History Museum.

Johnson, E. P. (2011b). *Sweet tea: Black gay men of the South*. Chapel Hill: University of North Carolina Press.

Jordan, J. (1974). "On Richard Wright and Zora Neale Hurston: Notes toward a balancing of love and hatred." *Black World*, 23(10), 4–8.

Jordan, J. (1978). "Where is the Love?" Address presented at Black Writers' Conference, Washington DC, Available on pp. 174–176, in Gloria Anzaldúa (Ed.), *Making face, making soul* (1990). San Francisco, CA: Aunt Lute Foundation Books.

Kamble, Baby (1986). *Jina Amucha*. Pune: Rachna Prakashan. Translated from Marathi by Maya Pandit (2008) *The Prisons We Broke*. New Delhi: Orient Blackswan.

Kamble, Shantabai (1990). Majya Jalmachi Chittarkatha. 2nd ed. Pune: Sugava Prakashan.

Kannabiran, Kalpana (ed.) (2014). *Women and law: Critical feminist perspectives*. New Delhi: Sage.

Kannabiran, Kalpana (2011). "Compromise in rape cases: Whither constitutional morality?" *Kafila* (blog), March 23. http://kafila.org/2011/03/23/compromise -in-rape-cases-whither-constitutional-morality-kalpana-kannabiran. Accessed January 4, 2013.

Kannabiran, Kalpana (2015a). "The complexities of the genderscape in India." Seminar 672. Available at http://india-seminar.com/2015/672/672_kalpana_kannabiran .htm. Accessed January 4, 2013.

Kannabiran, Kalpana (2015b). "Storytelling in the time of hate." *Economic and Political Weekly* 50(20), 76–83.

Kannabiran, Kalpana, and Kannabiran, Vasantha (2002). *De-erotizing assaults: Essays on modesty, honour and power*. Calcutta: Stree.

Kapur, Ratna, and Cossman, Brenda (1995). "Communalising gender, engendering community: Women, legal discourse and the saffron agenda," pp. 82–120 in Tanika Sarkar and Urvashi Butalia (Eds.), *Women and right wing movements: Indian experiences*. London and New Jersey: Zed Books.

Kaviraj, S. (2013). "Why is the mirror cracked?" *Comparative Studies of South Asia, Africa and the Middle East* 33(3), 380–391.

Kleinman, Arthur, Das, Veena, and Lock, Margaret (eds.) (1996). "Introduction," *Social Suffering*, edited by Arthur Kleinman, Veena Das, and Margaret Lock, special issue, *Daedelus* 125(1): xi–xx.

Kleinman, A., Das, V., and Lock, M. M. (Eds.) (1997). *Social suffering*. Berkeley: University of California Press.

Kleinman, A. (1995). *Writing at the margin: Discourse between anthropology and medicine*. Berkeley: University of California Press.

Kleinman, A. (1988). *The illness narratives: Suffering, healing and the human condition*. New York: Basic Books.

Kurup, Apoorv (2008). "Tribal law in India: How decentralized administration is extinguishing tribal rights and why autonomous tribal governments are better." *Indigenous Law Journal* 7(1): 87–126.

Landes, R. (1947). *The city of women*. New York: Macmillan.

Langer, Lawrence (1996). "The alarmed vision: Social suffering and Holocaust atrocity," *Social Suffering*, edited by Arthur Kleinman, Veena Das, and Margaret Lock, special issue, *Daedelus* 125(1), 47–65.

Lassiter, Luke. (2005). *The Chicago guide to collaborative ethnography*. Chicago: University of Chicago Press.

Lincoln, Y. S. (2005). "Revolutions in qualitative research: From just experience to experiencing justice." *Journal of Thought* 40(4), 25–40.

Lom, P. (Director). (2004). *Ala Kachuu* [Motion Picture].

Loomba, Ania (1993). "Dead women tell no tales: Issues of female subjectivity, subaltern agency and tradition in colonial and post-colonial writings on widow immolation in India." *History Workshop* 36, 209–227.

Lorde, Audre (1982). *Zami: A new spelling of my name*. Watertown, Mass.: Persephone Press.

Lutz, C., and Abu-Lughod, L. (eds.). (1990). *Language and the politics of emotion*. New York: Cambridge University Press.

Madison, D. Soyini (1993). "That was my occupation": Oral narrative, performance, and Black feminist thought, *TPQ* 3, July 13, 213–232.

Madison, D. Soyini (2006). "The dialogic performative in critical ethnography." *Text and Performance Quarterly* 26(4), October, 320–324.

Madison, D. Soyini (2005). *Critical ethnography: Method, ethics, and performance*. Thousand Oaks, Calif: Sage Publications. Second edn. 2011.

Madison, D. Soyini (2007). "Dangerous ethnography and utopian performatives," keynote presented at the Fourth International Congress of Qualitative Inquiry, May 2–5, University of Illinois, Champaign-Urbana.

Madison, D. Soyini (1998). "Performances, personal narratives, and the politics of possibility," pp. 276–286 in Sheron J. Dailey (Ed.), *The future of performance studies: Visions and revisions*. Annandale, VA: National Communication Association.

Madison, D. Soyini (2011). "The labor of reflexivity." *Cultural Studies? Critical Methodologies* 11(2), 129–138.

Mahato, P. P. (2000). *Sanskritization vs Nirbakization (A Study of Cultural Silence and Ethnic Memocide in Jharkhand)*. Calcutta: Sujan Publications.

Mani, Lata (1998). *Contentious traditions*. Berkeley: University of California Press.

Marcus, Sharon (1992). "Fighting bodies, fighting words: A theory and politics of rape prevention," pp. 385–403, in Judith Butler and Joan Scott (Eds.), *Feminists Theorize the Political*. New York: Routledge.

Massey, D. (1994). *Space, place and gender*. Minneapolis: University of Minnesota Press.

McLaren, A. E. (2001). "Marriage by abduction in twentieth century China." *Modern Asian Studies* 35(4), 953–984.

Menon, N. (2000). "Embodying the self: Feminism, sexual violence and the law," pp. 66–105 in Partha Chatterjee and Pradeep Jeganathan (Eds.), *Community, gender and violence: Subaltern studies XI*. Delhi: Permanent Black.

Menon, R. and Bhasin, K. (1998). *Borders and boundaries: Women in India's partition*. New Brunswick: Rutgers University Press.

Middleton, T. (2013). "States of difference: Refiguring ethnicity and its 'crisis' at India's borders." *Political Geography* 35, 14–24.

Mignolo, Walter D. (2000). *Local histories/global designs: Coloniality, subaltern knowledges, and border thinking*. Princeton and Oxford: Princeton University Press.

Mignolo, Walter D. (2011). *The darker side of western modernity: Global futures, decolonial options.* Durham and London: Duke University Press.

Mignolo, W. (2012). *Local histories/global designs: Coloniality, subaltern knowledges, and border thinking.* Second edition. Princeton: Princeton University Press.

Minh-ha, Trinh T. (1989). *Woman, native, other.* Bloomington and Indianapolis: Indiana University Press.

Mohanty, C. T. (2003). *Feminism without borders: Decolonizing theory, practicing solidarity.* Durham: Duke University Press.

Mohanty, Chandra Talpade, Ann Russo, and Lourdes Torres, eds. (1991). *Third world women and the politics of feminism.* Bloomington: Indiana University Press.

Mookherjee, Nayanika (2006). "'Remembering to forget': Public secrecy and memory of sexual violence in the Bangladesh War of 1971." *Journal of the Royal Anthropological Institute* 12(2), 433–450.

Moraga, Cherrie, and Gloria Anzaldúa (eds.) (1981). *This bridge called my back: Writings by radical women of color.* New York: Kitchen Table.

Muñoz, J. E. (2009). *Cruising utopia: The then and there of queer futurity.* New York: NYU Press.

Mutua, Kagendo, and Swadener, Beth Blue (eds.) (2004). *Decolonizing research in cross-cultural contexts: Critical personal narratives.* Albany: SUNY Press.

Nagar, Richa (2006). "Local and global," pp. 211–217, in Stuart Aitken and Gill Valentine (eds.), *Approaches to Human Geography.* Thousand Oaks, Calif.: Sage.

Nagar, R. (2014). *Muddying the waters: Coauthoring feminisms across scholarship and activism.* Urbana, IL: University of Illinois Press.

Nagar, Richa, and Geiger, Susan (2007). "Reflexivity and positionality in feminist fieldwork revisited," pp. 267–278, in Adam Tickell, Eric Sheppard, Jamie Peck, and Trevor J. Barnes (eds.), *Politics and practice in economic geography.* Thousand Oaks, CA: Sage.

Naples, N. and Desai, M. (Eds.) (2002). *Women's activism and globalization: Linking local struggles and transnational politics.* New York: Routledge.

Narayan, K. (2015). "Collaborative ethnography and a grandfather's stories." *Postcolonial Studies* 18(2), 234–236.

Narayan, K. (2004). "'Honor is honor, after all': Silence and speech in the life stories of women in Kangra, North-West India," pp. 227–251 in D. Arnold and S. Blackburn (Eds.), *Telling lives in India: Biography.* Bloomington: Indiana University Press.

Narayan, K. (1997). *Mondays on the dark side of the moon.* New York: Oxford University Press.

PM, Lata (2015). "Silenced by Manu and 'mainstream' feminism: Dalit-Bahujan women and their history." *Savari,* May. Available at http://www.dalitweb.org/?p=2805. Accessed June 10, 2015.

Paik, Shailaja (2009). "Amchya Jalmachi Chittarkatha (The bioscope of our lives): Who is my ally?" *Economic and Political Weekly,* October 3, 44(40), 39–47.

Paik, S. (2014). *Dalit women's education in modern India: Double discrimination* (Vol. 6). New York: Routledge.

Pawar, Urmila (2008). *The weave of my life: A Dalit woman's memoirs*, trans. Maya Pandit from Marathi. Kolkata: Stree.

Pawar, Urmila, and Moon, Meenakshi (2008). *We also made history: Women in the Ambedkarite movement*. New Delhi: Zubaan.

Prashad, Vijay (2000). *Untouchable freedom: A social history of a Dalit community*. New York: Oxford University Press.

PWDVA (2005). http://chdslsa.gov.in/right_menu/act/pdf/domviolence.pdf.

Rao, Anupama (2009). *The caste question: Dalits and the politics of modern India*. Berkeley and Los Angeles: University of California Press.

Rapp, R. (1993). "Accounting for amniocentesis," pp. 55–76, in S. Lindenbaum and M. Lock (Eds.), *Knowledge, power, and practice: The anthropology of medicine in everyday life*. Berkeley: University of California Press.

Rawat, R. S., and Satyanarayana, K. (2016). *Dalit Studies*. Duke University Press. Durham, NC

Rege, S. (1998). "Dalit women talk differently: A critique of 'difference' and towards a Dalit feminist stand point position." *Economic and Political Weekly* 33(44), October 31, pp. WS39–WS46.

Rege, S. (2006). *Writing caste, writing gender: reading Dalit women's testimonios*. Zubaan.

Rege, S. (2013). *Against the madness of Manu: B. R. Ambedkar's writings on Brahmanical patriarchy*. New Delhi: Navayana.

Rose, T. (2004). *Longing to tell: Black women talk about sexuality and intimacy*. New York: Macmillan.

Rycroft, Daniel J., and Dasgupta, Sangeeta (eds.) (2011). *The politics of belonging in India: Becoming Adivasi*. New York: Routledge.

Saikia, Yasmin (2004). "Beyond the archive of silence: Narratives of violence of the 1971 liberation war of Bangladesh." *History Workshop Journal* 58(1), 275–287.

Sandhu, K. (2007, February). "Testing times for devout Scheduled caste youth stripped, tortured for entering temple in Kinnaur village." Retrieved from http://www.tribuneindia.com/2007/20070207/himplus1.htm. Accessed June 20, 2015.

Sandoval, Chela (2000). *Methodology of the oppressed*. Minneapolis: University of Minnesota Press.

Sangtin Writers, and Nagar, Richa (2006). *Playing with fire: Feminist thought and activism through seven lives in India*. Minneapolis: University of Minnesota Press.

Sarkar, T. (2011). "Rebellion as modern self-fashioning," pp. 65–81 in Daniel J. Rycroft and Sangeeta Dasgupta (Eds.), *The politics of belonging in India: Becoming Adivasi*. Routledge: London and New York.

Scott, J. C. (1990). *Domination and the arts of resistance: Hidden transcripts*. New Haven and London: Yale University Press.

Seawright, G. (2014). "Settler traditions of place: Making explicit the epistemological legacy of white supremacy and settler colonialism for place-based education." *Educational Studies* 50(6), 554–572.

Sen, Debarati (2012). "Illusive justice: The gendered labour politics of subnationalism in Darjeeling tea plantations," in Srila Roy (Ed.), *New South Asian feminisms: Paradoxes and possibilities*. London: Zed Books.

Shah, Alpa (2010). *In the shadows of the state: Indigenous politics, environmentalism, and insurgency in Jharkhand, India.* Durham: Duke University Press.

Skaria, A. (1997). "Shades of wildness tribe, caste, and gender in western India." *Journal of Asian Studies,* 56(3), 726–745.

Smith, L. T. (1999). *Decolonizing methodologies: Research and Indigenous peoples.* London: Zed Books.

Smith, S. H. (2013). "'In the past, we ate from one plate': Memory and the border in Leh, Ladakh." *Political Geography* 35, 47–59.

Spivak, G. (1988). "Can the subaltern speak?" pp. 271–313 in Cary Nelson and Larry Grossberg (Eds.), *Marxism and the interpretation of culture.* Chicago: University of Illinois Press.

Stacey, J. (1988). "Can there be a feminist ethnography?" *Women's Studies International Forum* 11(1), 21–27.

Sunder Rajan, R. (1993). *Real and imagined women: Gender, culture and postcolonialism.* New York: Routledge.

Swarr, A. L., and Nagar, Richa (eds.) 2010. *Critical transnational feminist praxis.* Albany: SUNY Press.

Taussig, Michael (1991). *Shamanism, colonialism, and the wild man: A study in terror and healing.* Chicago: University of Chicago Press.

Taussig, Michael T. (1999). *Defacement: Public secrecy and the labor of the negative.* Stanford: Stanford University Press.

Teltumbde, Anand (2010). *The persistence of caste: The Khairlanji murders and India's hidden apartheid.* London, New York: Zed Books.

Theidon, Kimberly (2007). "Gender in transition: Common sense, women, and war." *Journal of Human Rights* 6(4), 453–478.

Theodossopoulos, D. (2014). On de-pathologizing resistance. *History and Anthropology* 25(4), 415–430.

Thompson, A.K. (2014). "Waging war on Valentine's Day." *Truthout.* February 14. http://truth-out.org/opinion/item/21795-waging-war-on-valentines-day. Accessed June 20, 2014.

Tobdan (1993). *The people of the upper valley: The Stodpas of Lahul in Himalayas.* Delhi: Book India Pub. Co.

Tobdan (1984). *History and religions of Lahul.* Oriental Publishers: New Delhi.

Treichler, P. (1999). *How to have theory in an epidemic: Cultural chronicles of AIDS.* Durham: Duke University Press.

Treichler, P., et al. (1998). *The visible woman: Imaging technologies, gender and science.* New York: New York University Press.

Van Beek, M. (2000). "Beyond identity fetishism: 'Communal' conflict in Ladakh and the limits of autonomy." *Cultural Anthropology,* 15(4), 525–569.

Varshney, A. (1993). "Contested meanings: India's national identity, Hindu nationalism and the politics of anxiety." *Daedulus* 122(3), 227–261.

Viswanathan, R. (2012). "The textbook case of exclusion." *The Indian Express,* July. http://www.indianexpress.com/news/a-textbook-case-of-exclusion/973711/0. Accessed January 10, 2014.

Visweswaran, K. (1994). *Fictions of feminist ethnography*. Minneapolis: University of Minnesota Press.

Visweswaran, K. (1988). "Defining feminist ethnography." *Inscriptions* 3(4), 27–47.

Visweswaran, K. (1997). "Histories of feminist ethnography." *Annual Review of Anthropology* 26, 591–621.

Xalxo, Madhuri (2012a). "Delhi protests and the caste Hindu paradigm: Of sacred and paraded bodies." *Savari*, December 27. Available at http://www.dalitweb.org/?p=1388. Accessed January 10, 2014.

Xalxo, Madhuri (2012b). "Of struggles, setbacks & awe-inspiring achievements," *Savari*, February 24. Available at http://www.dalitweb.org/?p=42. Accessed January 10, 2014.

Xaxa, V. (1999a). "Tribes as indigenous people of India." *Economic and Political Weekly* 34(51), December 18, 3589–3595.

Xaxa, V. (1999b). "Transformation of tribes in India: Terms of discourse." *Economic and Political Weekly*, 34(51), 1519–1524.

Xaxa, V. (2001). "Protective discrimination: Why scheduled tribes lag behind scheduled castes." *Economic and Political Weekly*, 36(29), 2765–2772.

Xaxa, V. (2005). "Politics of language, religion and identity: Tribes in India." *Economic and Political Weekly* 40(13), March 26, 1363–1370.

Xaxa, V. (2008). *State, society, and tribes: Issues in post-colonial India*. New Delhi: Pearson Education India.

INDEX

Adivasi, 8, 9, 14; community, 8, 11, 14–15, 34, 43, 47, 134, 173n10; discrimination against, 46; disenfranchisement of, 34, 46; gendered violence against, 48; Hinduization of, 15; indigenous, 14, 31, 101; meaning of, 173n10; "Nirbakization," 46; Orang, Laxmi, 46; racial Other, 123. *See also* Dalit-Adivasi

Adivasi-Dalit. *See* Dalit-Adivasi

Aggarwal, Ravina, 42, 137, 145

Alexander, Jacqui, 12, 126, 139, 143

Ambedkar, B. R., 8, 11–12, 24, 29, 35, 84; on caste as system of domination, 83, 132; *Castes in India* (1916), 45; conversion to Buddhism, 66, 176n24; critique of caste as race, 45; Dalit emancipatory movement, 13, 14, 27; discussion of love, 84; inter-caste marriage, 64, 66, 74, 76; intersectional critique of Brahminism, 24; Poona Pact (1932), 177n6; untouchability, issue of, 84; vision of modernity, 45

Ambedkarite-Phule movement, 13

anti-rape campaigns, 13

ati shudra. *See* "untouchables"

Atrocities Act of India. *See* Prevention of Atrocities (PoA) Act of 1989

authenticity, notions of, 115

avarnas, 51, 177n11

baanj (sterile), 70, 73

backwardness, state-defined parameters of, 115, 178n9

Baxi, Pratiksha, 133

Beda community, 47

Bhaga river, Stod Valley, 21

Bina's narrative on violence, 107–108, 119

black feminism, 85

#Blacklivesmatter movement, 84–85

Black Panther movement, 12

bonded labor, 83

Bora, Papori, 26

Border Area Development Programmes, 33

Bourdieu, Pierre, 133

Brahmanical: caste hierarchies, structures of, 127; feminism, 13; patriarchal modes of power, 142; patriarchy, 18, 28, 45, 51

bride price, 161, 163

Buddhism, 23, 28–29, 31, 45, 66, 114, 163, 176n24; Ambedkar and, 66, 176n24; and caste, 45; dual existence of Hindu/Buddhist, 42; merging with Hinduism, 31; and tribe, 28

caste: Brahmanical patriarchy and, 18, 28, 45, 47, 51; caste-privileged position/writing, ethics of, 5; Civil Rights Act of 1955, 41, 47, 175n14; classification systems of, 11; ethnic identity of, 41; hierarchical relationship between, 42; last name, 47; as material "lifeworld," 15; politics of, 41–49; purity, regulations of, 41, 47, 127; rape as atrocity, 134; reform (Gandhi), 45; relationship between, 15; sociality of, 43; society, 45; structural violence, 139; as system of domination, 83, 131, 132, 139; varna system, 15; violence and oppression, 48, 52, 101, 125, 127, 134, 142. *See also* Dalit-Adivasi; Prevention of Atrocities (PoA) Act of 1989

caste–tribe politics, 10, 134; collective, 149–156, 161

caste violence, 11, 48, 52, 139; discrimination, 47, 67, 83–84; Indian Penal Code (IPC) against, 48; protection for Dalits against, 47–48

caste violence domination, 83, 132; gendered violence to uphold, 131; through rape, 139

patriarchal violence, 104; processes of, 10, 24; Sati system and, 119; sexual abuse, 49, 69; shame and dishonor associated with, 13; suicide, 55, 57–60, 62, 103, 106, 108–110, 117; "tribal" women, 103; "victim–agent" framework of, 13; violence against women (VAW), 3, 103. *See also* rape; sexual violence

wazir (minister of the British), 16, 87, 95, 175n13
women's empowerment, 3

Xaxa, Virginius, 14, 26, 174n11

Yangchen, Abeley, 85–89
Yangmo, Achi, 4, 6–7, 15–16, 156
Yangzin, Achi, 20, 38, 159

ABOUT THE AUTHOR

HIMIKA BHATTACHARYA is a researcher and educator, currently Associate Professor of Women's and Gender Studies and South Asian Studies at Syracuse University. Her research and teaching interests include transnational, U.S. women of color and Dalit feminisms; caste, race, and gender; violence, love, and resistance; and qualitative research methods. Some of her writings on gender and caste violence, ethnography, and civil rights movements in India appear in *Meridians*; *Qualitative Inquiry*; *Feminist Formations*; *The Handbook of Emergent Methods*; *The Encyclopedia of Qualitative Research Methods*; and *Kafila*.